THE LOST PRINCE

THE LOST PRINCE

A Search for Pat Conroy

MICHAEL MEWSHAW

Counterpoint
Berkeley, California

Library of Congress Cataloging-in-Publication Data
Names: Mewshaw, Michael, 1943– author.
Title: The lost prince : a search for Pat Conroy / Michael Mewshaw.
Description: First hardcover edition. | Berkeley, California : Counterpoint, 2018.
Identifiers: LCCN 2018024660 | ISBN 9781640091498
Subjects: LCSH: Conroy, Pat—Friends and associates. | Mewshaw, Michael, 1943– —Friends and associates. | Authors, American—20th century—Biography.
Classification: LCC PS3553.O5 Z74 2018 | DDC 813/.54 [B] —dc23
LC record available at https://lccn.loc.gov/2018024660

Jacket design by Nicole Caputo
Book design by Wah-Ming Chang

COUNTERPOINT
2560 Ninth Street, Suite 318
Berkeley, CA 94710
www.counterpointpress.com

Printed in the United States of America
Distributed by Publishers Group West

10 9 8 7 6 5 4 3 2 1

For Emerson Wallace Mewshaw,
my first grandson

Your lacerations tell the losing game
You play against a sickness past your cure.
How will the hands be strong? How will the heart endure?

ROBERT LOWELL, "Mr. Edwards and the Spider"

THE LOST PRINCE

PROLOGUE

P at Conroy was a manic talker and tireless narrator of stories, some much too tall to be true, some so searingly true they left scars on his listeners, just as they had on him. More than a gifted soliloquist, he invested as much energy in listening as he did in speaking, and the telephone was for him a piece of equipment every bit as crucial as a breathing apparatus for a deep-sea diver. A roster of friends received calls from Pat around the clock and stayed on the line with him for hours. He referred to his fellow phone junkies as his "go-to guys," as if he were still a college point guard feeding teammates the basketball on a fast break.

During the 1980s when we both lived in Rome, Italy, and in the '90s after we returned to the States, we maintained constant contact. Our wives, Linda and Lenore, became close friends, and our kids were classmates at school. The Conroy and Mewshaw families traveled together in Italy, Austria, Germany, France, and England and exchanged stateside visits in Virginia, Florida, New

York, California, Georgia, and South Carolina. It seemed inevitable that Pat and Lenore's daughter Susannah would invite Linda and me to be her godparents.

Whether eating dinner at each other's homes or spending hours at a Roman trattoria, Pat and I seldom stopped talking—or as our wives viewed it, trading intersecting monologues. It was uncanny how much we had in common—a boyhood love of books and basketball, harsh Irish Catholic upbringings as military brats, abusive alcoholic parents, a deep amazement that we had survived to write about early turmoil and our attempts to overcome it. Pat in particular produced work that was the prose equivalent of lacerating confessional poetry, the kind in which a courageous artist unbandages his wounds in public and through some precious alchemy brings healing to others. Yet for all he disclosed about himself and his vulnerabilities, there's much that he never acknowledged, perhaps never allowed himself to know.

I expected us to be best friends forever. But then Pat's second marriage fell apart, and as he once wrote: "Each divorce is the death of a small civilization," and there's always collateral damage. He went stone silent on me. For almost six years there were no calls, no letters, no contact of any type. It was only through a literary agent we shared for a short time that Pat and I got back in touch by email and tried to reconcile.

During that period, I was cobbling together a collection of reminiscences about older, famous writers I had known who had influenced me as a young aspiring author. Titled *Do I Owe You Something?* the manuscript contained chapters on William Styron, James Jones, Robert Penn Warren, Graham Greene, Anthony Burgess, Paul Bowles, and Gore Vidal among others. In mid-June 2001, Pat wrote me an email in his distinctive hunt-and-peck style:

dear michael. i asked Carolyn krupp to send me a copy of your memoir and i just finished it. the book is perfectly wonderful, mike, and i fell in love with your writing once again. i used to own your entire collection, mike, but i left all your books at lenores believing that you had chosen her at the tailend of that awful marriage. i think you know who collected and read those books with great appreciation and care. but they remain in lenores house where i felt they belonged until i read your memoir and fell in love with them all over again. . . your book is a cautionary tale and lets me know why i have avoided writers like the plague for most of my life and why i ended up living on an island at the end of an american highway. the book is great, mike, but . . . i have an idea. i suggest that you write a full chapter on me and you and what happened. this is not sheer egomania because i know it would cause much pain to both of us. but here is what that story has that none of your others have. you and i got to know and love each other like none of those other writers, mike, and we were intimate parts of each others lives and our families knew each other and as i have told you before, mike, i was the guy that loved you most and you were the guy i referred to as my best friend and i said it to people as close to me as cliff graubart and doug marlette. but that chapter would have an emotional power that i think would help the book, mike. and to prove to you how much i like the book, i offer to write an introduction . . .

Touched by his generosity and reminders of our friendship, I took heart from Pat's enthusiasm. Louisiana State University Press agreed to bring out the book in 2003 and was interested in Pat's doing an introduction, but was adamantly against including a separate chapter about him. They believed this would violate the book's theme. *Do I Owe You Something?*, they pointed out, was a coming-of-age story about a novelist and his mentors. Conroy was my contemporary and former friend, not a literary influence. Then, too, if I added a section about him, it would raise suspicions that this was payback for his introduction and perhaps a bribe to bring him back into my life.

When I explained this to Pat, he was disappointed but replied, "I'm going through my own personal nightmare and can't wait for this long edit [of his memoir *My Losing Season*] to be over. Nan [Talese] doesn't know the difference between a basketball and a Buick LeSabre and I'm having to do most of this myself." Still, he took the time to send LSU Press a blurb, calling *Do I Owe You Something?* "the best book about the American expatriate experience since the publication of Ernest Hemingway's *A Moveable Feast*."

For years, Pat's suggestion that I write about "me and you and what happened" stuck in my mind. The story deserved to be told. I agreed with him about that. But I hesitated to tear open old wounds or to divulge anything that might undermine Pat's image as an icon of suffering and survival. It caused me no small torment as I vacillated between the impulse to protect Pat and the urge to understand the events that had estranged us. I also wanted to recall what had first brought us together. I wanted to remember the years in Rome and the man he used to be—not yet famous but on the brink and already revealing tiny fissures that would result in the damage ahead.

Once at an American Booksellers Association convention, Pat described his mother on her deathbed, whittled down to a skeletal eighty pounds. He promised that after she died, he would write about her: "And because you taught me how to be a writer, I can lift you off that bed and I can set you singing, I can set you dancing. And I can make you beautiful again for the entire world."

In the same spirit, now that Pat's dead, I have decided to do as he urged and write about us as honestly as I can. I can't promise that what I write will make everything Pat said and did appear to be beautiful, or that I can raise him from the dead and set him singing and dancing and talking again. But I can fulfill one of the few favors he ever asked of me and tell the story he wanted told. Whatever else it shows, I mean it to declare as I never did when he was alive that I loved Pat every bit as much as he loved me.

1 No Italian ever asked why I uprooted my family—a wife and two sons, one five years old, the other an infant—and relocated to Rome. As locals viewed it the city lacked nothing that made for a sweet life. The skyline hadn't changed in centuries, and viewed from a rooftop terrace, the landscape resembled a vast lesson from an architectural textbook, every dome, campanile, and famous ruin a monument to long history and deep culture.

Moreover, Italy was cheap in those days, the food first-class, the wine a revelation compared to the gallons of Gallo Hearty Burgundy I had chugged at faculty parties. For a novelist who aspired to support himself with his writing, Rome in the early '80s was a perfect berth.

Americans, however, did question why we chose to live in Italy. A whiff of suspicion attached itself to anybody who turned his back on the land of the free and home of the brave. Because I had resigned a tenured position at the University of Texas, people of a practical disposition regarded me as deranged while conspiracy theorists thought I must be running from something. Those were Italy's "years of lead," an era of urban terrorism when the Red Brigades were rampant. That was part of my reason for settling in Rome—to write a novel about the kidnapping and assassination of the Italian premier Aldo Moro.

Through the American Academy, I rented a humid, pumpkin-colored cottage that bore an ominous skull and crossbones on the facade and a sign that said *Pericolo di Morte*—Danger of Death. Constructed atop an electrical transformer, the place was as cramped as a ship's cabin, and Linda and I slept in shifts, like sailors on duty for four hours, then flaking out for four. In the morning, after my son Sean caught the bus to kindergarten, I strapped his brother, Marco, into a backpack and hiked around the Doria Pamphilj park in the batik-patterned shade of umbrella pines. Later, I tottered back to Pericolo di Morte, woke Linda, transferred Marco to her, and tumbled into bed myself.

Progress on the novel was delayed not just by parenting but by a calvary of colds, flus, and viruses that Sean carried home from school and passed on to his brother. A perfect little incubator of diseases, Marco spread them on to Linda and she to me. For a time it appeared we might have to medevac to the States. But then a grant from the Guggenheim Foundation allowed us to upgrade our accommodations and hire better doctors.

We moved outside the Aurelian Wall to a three-bedroom apartment, furnished with plush purple couches that looked as if they had been salvaged from an antique railroad car. It cost $140 a month, minimal rent for a minimalist residence that appealed to our conviction that we had pared our lives down to the essentials. Free of distractions, with the family in restored health and our finances solvent, I looked forward to a long stretch of calm and quiet—little knowing that a cyclone was about to sweep through our lives.

One hot morning, more like mid-summer than September, our upstairs neighbor flung a carpet over her balcony railing and began beating the dust out of it with a broom. It sounded like she was pounding a snare drum. Because of the racket, I barely heard the phone ring and didn't catch the caller's first name. His last name was Conroy and he said he was a writer, recently arrived in Italy. He explained that Jonathan Yardley, the book reviewer at *The Washington Post*, had suggested he contact me.

"I was hoping," Conroy went on, "you might help me get a handle on this city. It's a pretty confusing place for a Georgia boy." He had a Southern accent, a faint one that was less countrified than the slow cadence of his sentences.

"*Stop-Time* is one of my favorite books," I told him.

He giggled. "I'm the other guy—*Pat*."

"Jesus, I'm sorry. The lady upstairs is beating her carpet."

"No problem. I'll pretend to be Frank Conroy if that'll make a difference. I'm fucking desperate, man. I need a friend."

It wasn't uncommon for newcomers to crack up in Rome, unhinged by the amiable mayhem, the blaring traffic, and the habit locals had of speeding the wrong way up one-way streets. Visitors often called me for the name of a good doctor or a trustworthy lawyer. Some craved a patient listener in lieu of a psychiatrist. Pat was the first and only one to admit he yearned for a friend.

He spoke in great gusts of language, salted with self-deprecating humor, his diction Faulknerian one moment and locker-room the next. As he rattled on, I recalled the little I knew about Pat Conroy. He had written *The Great Santini*, a novel I hadn't read, which had been made into a movie I hadn't seen. By way of apology I told him Rome lacked a respectable English-language bookstore and seldom showed American films. Then, too, busy with my books and the kids, I hadn't kept current with the U.S. literary scene.

"I've got three kids myself and one on the way," Pat said. "All of them bitching they'd rather be back in Atlanta rooting for the Georgia Bulldogs. I swear to Christ I'd rather have my dick cut off than spawn another baby."

By now I was chuckling along with Conroy. It was astounding how many slapstick laughs he could milk out of his misadventures.

"Look, Mike," he said, "I'm sweating my balls off in a phone booth beside a snack bar toilet. No place or time for beating around the bush. You and your family have to promise to come to my house for lunch this Sunday. I'll fix whatever food you like. I'll lay on second and third helpings. What the hell, I'll pay you money. I'll give you a blowjob. But hey, don't get the wrong idea. It's not just because I'm lonely that I'd like to meet you. I'm your greatest fan. You write like a prince."

I didn't ask what he had read of mine. Most writers regarded compliments as little more than air kisses; they seldom touched solid flesh. But I agreed that we'd join him for Sunday lunch.

EXPATS WHO COULD AFFORD IT or who lucked into rent-controlled apartments preferred to live in the *centro storico*, an atmospheric nest of narrow alleys and splendid piazzas. In those gilded precincts, with Gore Vidal, Alberto Moravia, Italo Calvino, and various movie stars for neighbors, one could indulge in the delusion that *la dolce vita* had never ended and that Hollywood-on-the-Tiber still purled along between polished marble banks.

Temporary residents on sabbatical tended to huddle on the Gianicolo Hill, within walking distance of the American Academy. Historically the Academy had always attracted distinguished classicists, architects, artists, and composers to its McKim, Mead & White palazzo to conduct independent research. But in the '80s it hosted an impressive group of authors, including Nobel Prize winners Joseph Brodsky and Nadine Gordimer, and American grandees Mary McCarthy and Francine du Plessix Gray. Regardless of one's own modest station in the Great Chain of Being, it was easy to feel like the scion of a wealthy family when one had access to the Academy's lectures, concerts, exhibitions, and, especially for me, its tennis court.

Yet somehow Pat Conroy had marooned himself out on the Via Cassia, in the nouveau riche gated community of Olgiata. This presented a mystery—how the hell did he wind up there?—and a problem for Linda and me. We didn't own a car and couldn't afford a taxi, which, on Sunday, would tack on supplemental charges and cost a fortune. The bus trip to Olgiata involved several transfers and would eat up hours. So I asked Pat if he minded that we brought along friends, an American couple who had a car and two kids.

"Bring anybody. Bring everybody," Pat said.

Steve and Joan Geller lived in a luminous, sprawling apartment at a legendary address, Palazzo Cenci, the ancestral home of Beatrice Cenci, a sixteenth-century aristocrat who had been executed for murdering her sexually abusive father. To Steve, a devotee of crystal power and occult practices, it seemed a thrilling piece of synchronicity that he and I had met when he was hired to write the screenplay for *Life for Death*, a true crime book I had written about child abuse and parricide. That the book contained elements of memoir, centering on two boys I had known since adolescence, added to Steve's conviction that karma connected us. Our link remained intact even after one of the boys filed a libel suit that killed the movie as surely as his brother had murdered their parents.

Now that Pat Conroy had entered the equation, Steve marveled again that some cosmic force seemed to control events. He had seen the film of *The Great Santini*, which in synopsis sounded similar to the Cenci family tragedy and to *Life for Death*. Conroy had been an abused child who harbored murderous rage toward his father, just like Beatrice, just like the central character in my book.

Geller, an Academy Award nominee for his script of Kurt Vonnegut's *Slaughterhouse-Five*, had graduated from the Yale School of Drama. In addition to his screenplay credits, he had produced a number of novels, one of which had been made into the movie *Pretty Poison* starring Anthony Perkins and Tuesday Weld.

He also held the distinction of being the last café writer in Rome. Weather permitting, he worked outdoors in front of the Pantheon. Starting in the a.m. at Bar di Rienzo, he followed the arc of the sun and switched across the piazza to Bar Rotonda for the afternoon. Unlike a traditional café writer, he didn't scribble in a notebook. He pecked at a battery-powered Brother ER44 portable typewriter, whose hum appeared to mesmerize his Maltese dog, Brio, poised on a wicker chair opposite him. Gore Vidal once taunted Steve, "You're taking dictation from your dog. You're ghosting *The Tales of Fluffy*."

The Gellers' car, a slinky Citroën DS saloon, had a pneumatic suspension system, which lifted the chassis when the gears were engaged, then let it sag when the engine died. It was a bit like riding on a water bed—a water bed crammed that Sunday with four adults and four kids ranging in age from infancy to adolescence, everybody competing for space with the barking Brio. Joan Geller, like Steve, was tiny, and she was a yoga teacher who could coil herself into a corner. Their two daughters, Hillary and Polly, had babysat our boys before, but today they couldn't stop Sean and Marco from squirming and squawking.

Undaunted, Steve drove with the aplomb of a New York cabbie, and as we whizzed past Renaissance fountains, the two of us speculated about the Conroys and what had possessed them to pitch their tent out in the boondocks. In that pre-Internet era we couldn't just Google Pat and read his Wikipedia entry. I had ordered his books and resigned myself to weeks of waiting while the somnolent Italian postal system slow-boated them from the States. None of us had a clue what he looked like or what had drawn him to Italy.

At Olgiata's front gate, an officious guard collected our IDs and compared our names to those on the visitors list. Three years after Aldo Moro's assassination, most security measures in Rome were a mere charade, but this guy took his job seriously and stuck his mug into Steve's window. "I could have you arrested for carrying too many passengers," he said.

"*Tante grazie.* Thanks for not doing that."

Steve accelerated into Olgiata, past horse stables, tennis courts, and a golf course bordered by massive villas. Private swimming pools glinted like faceted jade around the deeper green of fairways. With all the conveniences of an upscale American retirement community, Olgiata was popular with diplomats and corporate executives who feared having their kneecaps blown off by the Red Brigades.

Rather than raucous cobblestone street life, Olgiata featured a grid of smooth asphalt that rippled with heat mirages at each deserted intersection. There must have been an ordinance against hanging laundry outdoors, leaving trash cans at the curb, or speaking above a whisper. The neighborhood was dead as a doornail. While most of the architecture paid lip service to the Mediterranean vernacular—red tile roofs, terra-cotta-colored walls—the Conroys' house was a sturdy ensemble of concrete slabs and glinting windows. At this time of year I guessed it was hot as a sweat lodge. In winter it would be cold as an alpine ice cave.

"Jesus, what were they smoking when they rented this place?" Steve asked.

Pat Conroy advanced on us with the rolling, pigeon-toed gait and the meaty girth of an ex–football player, a linebacker ten years and thirty pounds past his prime. An inch shy of six feet tall, he wore a white polo shirt, rumpled khakis, and thick-soled jogging shoes. Everything about him—his shoulders, his head, his belly, his personality—was outsized. Everything, that is, except his hand, which was warm and small when I shook it.

He looked, as my grandmother would have put it, as Irish as Paddy's pig, with the same pale high coloring I inherited from my Hibernian forbearers. Prematurely grey hair was another genetic trait we shared, but at the age of thirty-five, he was going bald and had an unfortunate comb-over, later described in *Men's Journal* as lobster claws clinging to his scalp. With its small blue eyes, snip of a nose, and nearly lipless mouth, his face, at rest, seemed stripped to the basics, but when he smiled it couldn't have been more expansive and expressive.

His wife, Lenore, six months pregnant, wore a chic silver-grey maternity dress. Her hair was dark and hung straight to her shoulders, and her lustrous tan made it seem as if Pat had cowered in a root cellar while she spent the summer sunbathing. Although she had lived in Atlanta for a long time, she didn't have a hint of Pat's Southern accent, and where he favored flowery, declarative sentences, she spoke in sly, sassy asides. Much later, watching Uma Thurman in *Pulp Fiction*, I became convinced that Quentin Tarantino had originally had Lenore Conroy in mind for the role of Mia.

Pat introduced Megan, an eleven-year-old daughter from his first marriage. She had chosen to spend a year in Rome with him and was thoroughly at ease with Lenore's children, Greg and Emily, from her previous marriage. Greg had attended private school with Megan in Atlanta. Emily was a couple of years younger, a shy, self-conscious girl, with slight strabismus in her right eye. She recognized Sean as a schoolmate at St. Francis and beamed at him.

"These international schools are going to bankrupt us," Lenore said.

"Hell, I'm already flat broke," Pat said. "Lenore's ex, the famous brain surgeon Dr. Bonzo, is suing my fat ass for my last red cent." With that he served notice that this wouldn't be an afternoon of amiable chitchat.

We circled the house to a patio of white concrete slabs and green squares of grass. Although the checkerboard pattern had eye appeal, the alternating hard and soft surfaces twisted the ankles of the unwary. Spread on a picnic table was a selection of antipasti: prosciutto and *melone, mozzarella di bufala,* tomatoes and *basilico,* and fiascos of white wine on ice. For the main course, Pat had prepared pasta with shrimp sauce, combining, he said, a South Carolina Low Country recipe with local ingredients.

Thirteen of us squeezed in around the table. That black-magic number might have troubled Steve Geller, but he was as hungry and eager to eat as the rest of us. Seated on my lap, Marco, sixteen months old, ate from my plate, and while his manual dexterity left a lot to be desired, he had mastered one Italian gesture. Every time he swallowed a bite, I asked, "*È buono?*" and he jabbed his index finger at his plump cheek and rotated it like a true *trasteverino.*

While Pat poured the wine, Lenore explained how the family wound up in Olgiata. Through Pat's editor, Jonathan Galassi, they met an Italo-American music teacher in Rome, who introduced them to some impecunious nobles, one of whom had an aunt who owned a castle in La Storta with vast drafty rooms, flocks of sheep grazing on its grounds, and a staff of what Lenore described as "Micronesians inhabiting tiny spaces like those pull-out drawers on German tour buses. The trouble was the aunt was demented. She wanted to rent out the castle, but refused to move from her bedroom. We wisely decided against that weird arrangement."

"So we ended up with this weird arrangement," Pat interrupted. "It's like Stalag 17. Every time I go jogging, I get chased by guard dogs."

"I thought the kids would like it better than being in town," Lenore said. "And there's space for Pat to work. I had no idea how isolated we'd be and how bad the traffic is on Via Cassia. I'm liable to give birth in the backseat of the car."

"We're trying to break the lease and move. That'll be another fortune down the drain." Pat mentioned their monthly rent, a flabbergasting figure, more than Gore Vidal paid for his penthouse on Largo Argentina. Yet for all their complaints, the Conroys didn't really sound perturbed. Pat in particular delivered every lament as an elaborate joke, with him as the bumbling straight man.

"There's one iron law here," he said. "Nothing works quite as it should, nothing is quite as it appears to be, nothing is easy when with just a bit of effort it could be rendered impossible. Italians accept this. I can't."

Memory tends to turn the past sepia-toned. When I glance at photographs of that day we all appear so young and happy—thirty-somethings surrounded by beautiful children on a warm autumn day in Italy, enjoying an alfresco lunch. In his brown corduroy coat Steve looked like the college professor he would eventually become. Linda wore stylish velour slacks and a purple silk blouse, while I had on a safari jacket as if about to audition for *Animal Kingdom*.

And yet even back then, long before life had taught us its lessons, I sensed melancholy lurking beneath the surface layer of bonhomie. Like writers the world over, we griped about agents and editors, fickle producers and directors, paltry advances and late royalties, dread of the empty page and deeper dread of the empty bank account. The conversation kept veering back to the same themes: failure, crippling disappointment, and black-ass depression.

Surprisingly, even the Gellers, who seemed so rooted in Rome, admitted to clinging on precariously. They had counted on *Life for Death* being produced and Steve receiving full payment for his script. Now that the project was in turnaround, he had to fly to LA and hustle for work.

Pat heard out the details of the libel suit against me. After commiserating, he described how Lenore's ex-husband was dragging him through court.

"I don't have the dough to compete with a wealthy brain surgeon," Pat said. "Not with my book sales. I've been luckier with movie and paperback deals." Although Pat didn't mention it, the paperback rights to his most recent novel had sold for $695,000, a stupefying figure in those days. But he maintained, "I'm up to my ass in debt. I'm not just paying support for Megan, but for two other daughters my first wife has from a previous marriage. In December, after the new baby's born, I'll have more mouths to feed than a mamma robin. And now Alan Fucking Fleischer's bleeding me white."

I glanced at Alan Fucking Fleischer's kids, Greg and Emily. They appeared to regard Pat's excoriation of their father as no more than a Punch-and-Judy show, mean but funny. Conroy laughed and they followed his lead. We all did.

"Dr. Bonzo is hell-bent on punishing us," Pat said. "He started harassing Lenore for custody of the kids. One day he went too far and got up in my grill. I pushed him off Lenore's front porch and he landed in some shrubs. He wasn't really hurt, but he had me arrested for assault and battery. Rather than stay for round two, we decided to light out for the territories."

"So you're on the lam from the law," Steve said.

"More or less," Pat brightly agreed.

"We considered Paris," Lenore put in. "But we don't speak French."

"Do you speak Italian?" Linda asked.

"No, but we're learning."

"Good. Italians are more forgiving than the French."

"The question is whether we can forgive the Italians," Pat said. "The other day I caught the mailman picking mushrooms in our backyard."

"And you wonder why it takes a month to get a letter from the States," Steve joined in.

"We've also had this ongoing argument with the landlady," Lenore said. "The lawn furniture and TV were locked in a storage room, and we asked over and over—always politely—for the key."

"So a flunky shows up," Pat cut in, "and tells us, 'No *chiave.*'" Pat pronounced it *key-ave.* "I tell him, 'Here's the *key-ave,*' and I pointed to my foot and kicked the door down."

"Good luck at getting the damage deposit back," Lenore said.

"Nobody gets a deposit back," I said.

There might have been a transition. If so, it escaped me. Suddenly, Pat segued from one set of tribulations to another and began recounting anecdotes about his traumatic childhood, the urtext of all his books. With impeccable timing and perfectly pitched lines, he described his father, the template for the Great Santini, beating him and his siblings black and blue. Then he brought in his mother, Peggy, an alternate target of Santini's sadism, and told how she once tried to protect herself with a kitchen knife, only to have her husband knock her to the floor.

"Mom had seven children and suffered six miscarriages," Pat said. "Those were the lucky ones. The fortunate fetuses! The ones who got away. The rest of us had to go on living and take it on the chin."

I swapped Pat anecdote for anecdote, the two of us dancing a choreographed recital of family dysfunction. Neither my biological father nor my stepfather ever beat me, but the former had been a compulsive gambler who frittered away the mortgage money; the latter, a foul-tempered alcoholic who left a trail of wreckage in his wake. In our house, it was Mom who meted out the physical abuse, walloping her four kids with whatever lay close to hand—belts, sticks, hairbrushes, broom handles. Attempting to one-up Pat, I told about the time Mom served piping-hot bean soup for supper. When my older brother bent down and sniffed it, Mom clapped a hand to the back of his head and shoved his face into the bowl.

Conroy howled in glee and high-fived me across the table.

The afternoon ended as swifts flickered out of Olgiata's pine forest and dive-bombed the fairways. While we cleared the table and packed up the kids, Pat pulled on a red V-neck sweater against the evening chill. Then he showed Steve and me around the house, which had been designed by a yacht owner, with built-in furniture, highly lacquered floors, and sleek fittings. Up a broad curved staircase lay the master bedroom, which boasted a grey suede headboard almost as high as the ceiling and a matching suede bedspread. Just off the room, in a sitting area, Pat had his office.

There was a desk, but no typewriter, only a pad of yellow legal paper and a Montblanc pen. Like me, Pat wrote longhand. Unlike me, he listened to music as he worked and had imported a hi-fi phonograph from the States. Galley proofs of new novels by other writers littered the floor. Publishers were eager to get blurbs from Pat, and he confessed he was "a whore, completely promiscuous" with his praise.

Starved for reading material, I coveted those galleys. A fellow sufferer of lower back pains, I also coveted the ergonomic chair that he had shipped over to Italy. But what sparked the worst covetousness was a bronze trophy in the shape of a regulation-size basketball. It was inscribed *Pat Conroy, Most Valuable Player, the Citadel, 1967.* He had played for a Division I team and had starred.

Pat brushed off my compliments. "We were a weak team in a weak conference."

"To a benchwarmer at DeMatha High School, your career sounds big-time to me."

"You played for Morgan Wootten," he exclaimed.

"I did. I'm surprised you've heard of him."

"Come on, DeMatha's legendary and Wootten's a Hall of Fame coach. I went to Gonzaga High School when Dad was stationed at the Pentagon. I probably saw you play."

"Not unless there was a minute left in the game and DeMatha was ahead by thirty points."

"I'll leave you two jock-strappers to your reveries," Steve razzed us, and drifted back through the house.

"Next time we get together," Pat said, "let's skip the family bullshit and talk basketball." As if a deeper connection had been established—or else he just felt the need to clear the air—he confessed, "I lied. It wasn't Jonathan Yardley who suggested I call you. The mother of a girl at St. Francis School mentioned you were a writer and gave me your number. Hope you don't hate me. I really am desperate for a friend."

"Did this mother tell you I wrote like a prince?" I teased him.

"No, honest, I read your novel—I don't remember its title— about a Catholic priest in Texas recovering from a mental breakdown. Usually, I skip anything to do with Texas. Can't stand all the bragging about their favorite sports—football, fighting, and fucking. But I figured such a funny well-written novel had to be by an okay guy."

On the Via Cassia, battling the traffic back from a Sunday in the country, Joan Geller gave voice to what I was thinking. "We have to help the Conroys. Otherwise Olgiata will drive them out of their minds."

"Okay, Olgiata's awful," Linda said. "But what's this BS with Pat calling it a Mafia compound?"

"Poetic license," Steve suggested.

2 Like most foreigners in Rome, Linda and I didn't give a fig about visas or resident permits. We didn't consider ourselves illegal aliens, but rather the brother and sister of those millions of Italians who lived off the books and between the lines, never registering on census rolls or tax records. Without a bank account, we paid all our bills in cash and rented apartments from landlords who declined to provide written leases. The downside to this catch-as-catch-can existence was our vulnerability to arbitrary eviction. In the course of a decade and a half we were forced to move ten times.

Families with corporate or diplomatic connections shopped at the Embassy PX, depended on international courier services instead of the slowpoke Italian post office, and hired Sri Lankans and Filipinos as maids and baby minders. But Linda and I were obliged to practice petty economies and hiked across town to dispatch our mail from the Vatican PO. Every envelope bore a mosaic of stamps picturing saints and popes. We drank our cappuccinos standing up in cafés to beat the supplemental charge for sitting down at a table. With meals at home we served *vino sciolto* from open carafes and saved bottles with corks for special occasions.

Far from feeling deprived, I felt adrenalized and believed that

Italy fed me what Rome-based British novelist Muriel Spark referred to as "writer's meat." The city's unfathomable rituals infused it with the aura of a secret society accessible only to those who took the trouble to wise up to its ways. A great part of the pleasure of living there was learning the ropes and not getting tangled in them—or laughing at yourself when the red tape did trip you up.

Italians pursued their own lives with perfect indifference to "foreigners"—a term they applied to pretty much everyone except the immediate family. That was fine by me. Eventually I came to believe I occupied the same private spaces as they did, and my eyes slid in a slow ellipsis over the cityscape, eliminating the stock footage. The Colosseum, St. Peter's, the Campidoglio exerted little purchase on my imagination. But I was hyper-alert to chunks of marble veined with green moss like slabs of gorgonzola cheese and busts of famous men, their noses knocked off, their hands gloved in green lichen, their feet shod in dead leaves.

This was the Rome I introduced to Pat on walks through obscure bends and elbows of the city. He was eager to explore everything, be it a trattoria off the tourist path or the tiny jewel of a church, Santa Barbara, fittingly located on Largo de' Librari, Bookbinders Square. As we stared up at its powdery blue vault, we exclaimed almost simultaneously, "It looks like pool cue chalk."

He joined Joan Geller's yoga group and dressed for class in jogging shoes and a sweat suit, as if for football practice. The lone man among a dozen women, he made a lasting impression on Portuguese artist Celeste Maia, who remembered him lying stiff on his mat, eyes locked on the ceiling. But Joan soon had him doing the downward-facing dog and deep meditative breathing. He regretted that he often found himself striking poses behind elegant, egret-thin Francine du Plessix Gray, who never acknowledged his existence or spoke to him. I consoled him that perhaps Francine had attained a state of satori.

Pat set about studying Italian, and although he never acquired anything approaching fluency, he formed a friendship with his teacher, Edward Steinberg. A fellow Southerner from Montgomery, Alabama, Edward gravitated to Rome after graduating from Harvard. An attractive Finnish cellist spotted him in Il Delfino snack bar on Largo Argentina and immediately made up her mind to marry him. This was the sort of serendipitous story that the city supplied with spendthrift abundance. For a writer of Pat's omnivorousness, it was a goldmine. One night at a dinner party he encountered a one-armed woman who had had the limb torn off by a tiger at the Rome Zoo. Right away, Pat put a tiger into his novel in progress, *The Prince of Tides*.

From the start, the Conroys cut a swath through the expat community, not because Pat was famous—at that time his books were barely known in Italy—but because of his charm and ribald sense of humor. A combination of Mark Twain and Lenny Bruce, of Martin Luther King and Richard Pryor, his anecdotes about his bellicose father riveted his growing crowd of friends.

When Pat's books reached me from the States, I promptly devoured two of them, which went down as easily as buttered grits. *The Water Is Wide*, Conroy's nonfiction account of teaching black kids in a one-room schoolhouse on Daufuskie Island, had the same hallmarks as his fiction—lush descriptions of the South Carolina coast, a lovable first-person narrator, dialogue crackling with quips. The book's film version, entitled *Conrack*, starred Jon Voight, who vaguely resembled Conroy and gave an appealing impersonation of him on his best behavior. Later, Pat admitted that as a schoolteacher he had been "an impulsive, combative young man lacking any skills for compromise and diplomacy." But on the page and on the screen, he portrayed an American hero battling small-minded provincialism and injustice.

This theme, along with the same lovable first-person narrator, carried over to his first novel, *The Great Santini*. Now instead of confronting a racist school board, Ben Meechum, the Pat character, faced a ferocious father, a Marine Corps fighter pilot, who bullied his wife and kids like a drill sergeant running troops through the meat-grinder of Parris Island. As often as Ben fantasized about revenge, he craved love from the very person who tormented him.

The obvious and overwhelming identification between Pat and his central characters made it difficult for me to know what to say about his books, beyond expressing admiration for the energy of his prose and the lyrical evocation of place. The slightest reservation, I feared, would strike him as cruelly personal while even the highest praise might sound to him faint in view of what he seemed to have suffered.

THE CONROYS HAD BOUGHT A new BMW, to be delivered in Munich, Germany. Rather than fly north or catch an overnight train, Pat decided to drive a rental car over the Brenner Pass, pick up the Beamer, and break it in on a leisurely return trip through Italy. He invited me to tag along, riding shotgun. "We'll be like Hemingway and Fitzgerald tooling around France in an open car," he said. "Remember that chapter in *A Moveable Feast*? Remember F. Scott worrying about the size of his dick and begging Papa for reassurance? Me, I'm hung like a chipmunk, but I promise I won't show it to you."

Because we lacked legal status in Italy, Linda and I couldn't buy a car there. But foreign models, registered outside the country, usually deceived the *carabinieri*. So I strapped $3,000 into a money belt and joined Pat, hoping to find a used German car I could afford.

On a smoky, leaf-scented morning in late September, traffic tore past the hill towns of Orte and Orvieto, two Etruscan gems hazy in sunlight. Pat didn't give them a glance. A cautious driver, he clamped both hands on the steering wheel and wouldn't let tailgating Italians goose him into violating the speed limit. Alfa Romeos and Lancias hurtled past us, blaring their horns. Several motorists waggled their fingers in the *cornuto* salute. The *autostrada* could be an X-rated experience. Still Pat wouldn't be rushed.

Yet while he kept a light foot on the gas, he pressed the pedal to the metal with his talking. Mile after mile, hour after hour, words spilled out of him. "I'm nothing like Dad," he said. "I could never be a pilot. I've got bad eyesight. Plus speed scares me. Wouldn't you know it, I'm the son of a famous fighter pilot and I'm afraid of flying."

I assured him this was something else we shared in common. "I avoid airplanes whenever possible. And I get seasick every time I set foot on a boat. One summer in college I signed on to sail a skipjack from the Chesapeake Bay down to the Virgin Islands. We hit a gale off Cape Hatteras and I thought I'd die of the dry heaves."

Laughing, Pat told me he had worked aboard shrimp boats and developed steady sea legs. But drinking often left him queasy and he described himself as a veteran vomiter. "You ever reach the islands?" he asked.

"We barely made it to South Carolina. I jumped ship in Georgetown."

"That's just up the coast from Beaufort, the setting of *The Great Santini*." Pat viewed this as another link between us. "Both of us saddled with lawsuits and legal bills," he listed another. "Both of us aging basketball stars from the DC Catholic League."

"I was no star."

"What was the problem? You suffer white man's disease?"

"No, I could jump."

"Could you dunk?"

"That's something I was desperate to do—dunk during the pre-game drills. The problem was I couldn't palm a fully inflated basketball. So I deflated one enough to get my hand around it, then I took a good running start and jammed that sucker down."

"Great."

"Not so great. The ball splatted on the floor. Didn't bounce an inch. I might as well have dunked a beanbag."

"Who's the best player you ever guarded?" he asked.

"Fred Hetzel."

"Bullshit!" Hetzel had been an All-American at Davidson and later played for the LA Lakers. "He must have been six nine," Pat said. "You had no business guarding him."

"This was in a summer league game, DeMatha versus Landon High School. I held him to eighteen points and scored fourteen myself. What about you?"

"I guarded Pete Maravich when he played at LSU. He carved me up like a turkey and scattered my bones on the court."

It didn't escape me that I brought up Fred Hetzel and the absolute zenith of my career, while Pat, who was a much better player, chose to disparage himself.

"You mentioned your father was an alcoholic?" he said.

"My stepfather," I corrected him.

"Dad was a terrible drunk. He laid on the worst beatings when he got liquored up at the Bachelor's Officer's Quarters."

"My stepfather tended bar at the BOQ," I said. "Which was like Willie Sutton working as a bank teller. He poured himself a drink for every one he served."

We were circling Florence, the Duomo visible in the distance across fields flecked with cypress trees. Pat had his eyes fixed on the road and his mind on our mutual experiences. "Were you an altar boy?"

"Of course. And you?"

He answered by reciting the Confiteor. "I remember all the Latin responses. But I forget the last time I went to Mass."

"I go every Sunday."

"You're not serious."

"Yes, I am."

"Me, I still hate all the mean nuns who taught me and all the mean Catholic girls who wouldn't date me."

"I didn't have much luck with Catholic girls myself. I married a Methodist."

"Lenore's Jewish," he said. "She comes with a lot of baggage. Her parents, the Gurewitzes, are Communists. I mean real card-carrying reds. But . . . well, she's beautiful. The first beautiful woman who ever loved me."

I agreed that she was beautiful. Pat observed that Linda was beautiful too. Again, I agreed, and with that truth established, we followed the cutoff toward Bologna. "About your mother," he mused, "you mentioned she slapped you around."

"Not just me. She belted her husband and the other kids too."

"What's the worst thing she ever did to you?"

"I don't know. I guess bang my head against a wall."

"You're shitting me." He swiveled his eyes from the road for an instant. "My brother swears his first memory is of Dad holding me by the throat and banging my head against the wall."

"Smarts, doesn't it?" The rhythm of our talk reminded me of teammates setting each other up, executing a pick-and-roll or the give-and-go. "Sometimes Mom grabbed my brother and me by the hair," I told him, "and cracked our skulls together. She didn't discriminate on the basis of age or size or sex. I saw her slug my sister at the age of twenty-one and bloody her lip."

"Jesus, she sounds worse than Dad."

"I bet the Great Santini had a harder punch."

Pat didn't treat this as a joke. "Okay, he was a monster—about six three and 220 in his prime. But there's something, I don't know, just horrible about getting hit by your mother."

As the bond between us tightened, I told Pat how painful it had been when Mom asked me to protect her against my stepfather, Tommy Dunn. "He never hit me, but sometimes he got loaded and belted her. When I was older, I put a stop to that. But Mom would still hit me when she got a wild hair and I couldn't fight back. That was the worst."

Pat described his mother, Peggy, as non-violent, yet deeply duplicitous and given to genteel airs. "She never wanted anyone to know she came from a dirt-poor family of Alabama crackers. At bedtime, she used to read us *Gone With the Wind* and change the names of the characters to the names of her children. She saw herself as Scarlett O'Hara. She was petrified somebody would discover Dad wasn't Rhett Butler. His knocking her around was something she hid as long as she could.

"She loved language, the more highfalutin the better," he continued. "She did everything she could to encourage me to become a novelist. But then when *The Great Santini* came out, she accused me of dragging the family name through the mud. Her redneck relatives and Dad's shanty–Irish Chicago brood picketed bookstores, protesting that I wrote a pack of lies. Later when she divorced Dad, she changed her tune. She wanted me to testify against him. When I refused, she submitted *The Great Santini* to the judge as evidence of Dad's cruelty."

I didn't just sympathize with Pat; I identified and filled him in on Mom's rabid response to my book, *Life for Death*. She cut off all contact, accusing me of disclosing intimate details, such as the fact that she had divorced my father thirty-five years ago. Memoir-schmemoir—she wouldn't concede that I had a proprietary right to my life's story. Only now, two years later, were we tentatively back in touch. "She's obsessed with secrecy," I told Pat. "It's a family tradition. Her mother, my grandmother, changed her name and lopped ten years off her age when she emigrated from Ireland. It's like we're all in the Witness Protection Program."

"Ah, the old sod," Pat shrieked with laughter. "What a polluted gene pool we swam out of."

On the flat plains of the Po Valley we had a lunch of *panini* and coffee at a Pavese Autogrill. Amid the clatter of plates and cutlery and the hiss of the espresso machine, our talk never ceased. I had given Pat a copy of *Life for Death*, and he said, "When I read the part where the kid, Wayne Dresbach, loads the rifle and shoots his parents, I swear to Christ I stood up and cheered. Those people had it coming. I can't count how many times I fantasized about killing Dad."

"Glad you didn't or we'd be having this conversation through bulletproof glass at a maximum security prison."

"Your book makes your mom sound like a saint. Maybe she'd have gotten me sprung just like she did Wayne Dresbach."

"My mother has her saintly side," I granted. "Then there's the other side. *Life for Death* is an example of artistic selection."

"Tell me about it. I'm a master at selective memory."

IN THE CAR AGAIN, HEADED north, Pat said, "I never met anybody I have so much in common with. The only difference I guess is you're not a military brat."

"Actually, I kind of am. My stepfather was in the navy, then went on working for them after World War II. I virtually grew up at the Naval Receiving Station in DC. Learned to swim in the base pool. Practiced basketball in the gym. My first job was at the PX warehouse. Whenever I got sick, navy medics treated me."

Pat hooted. "Medics, my ass. Pecker checkers."

"Okay, they fell short of being real doctors. I caught polio as a kid, and they misdiagnosed it. Same thing happened when I broke my arm, then again when I developed osteomyelitis."

"Anything more complicated than the clap, they're in over their heads."

"I'm not complaining. Polio kept me out of the draft. How'd you beat it?"

"The *Reader's Digest* version: I was the only man in my class at the Citadel who turned down a military commission. I became a hippie war protester and taught high school in Beaufort and got married. Going back to your stepfather, what did he do for the navy?"

"He ran the laundry and dry-cleaning plant that covered all the military bases in the DC area. When your father was at the Pentagon, my stepfather probably washed your family's underwear and socks."

"Goddamn, connections don't come much more personal than that."

I told Pat that Walter Reed Hospital was one of Tommy Dunn's accounts and from adolescence until I left home, I wore what he pilfered from the laundry's lost and found. When sailors and marines shipped out or, in the case of Walter Reed, when patients died, I inherited their wardrobes. The DeMatha yearbook shows me in strangers' coats, shirts, and trousers, some too tight, some flapping loose. "Then at the University of Maryland, before military cast-offs came into fashion, I already dressed in dead men's clothing. At least they were clean," I said.

"Ah, our golden youth." Pat sighed. "Aren't you glad that shit is behind us? Dad would have killed me if he caught me wearing military surplus after I dodged the draft. But to save money, Peggy sewed a sport coat for my high school senior prom. It fit me like Quasimodo's cape."

THE *AUTOSTRADA* STARTED TO TILT beneath us. I felt the upward incline and heard the engine strain as we ascended the Alps. Everything got steeper—the pitch of slate roofs in villages, the gothic bell towers of churches in Trento and Bolzano, and the mountainous spires sparkling with glacial ice. At the Brenner Pass, long-haul trucks stalled at the frontier, like Hannibal's army of el-ephants linked trunk to tail.

As Pat and I had our passports stamped and changed lire into Austrian shillings, an invisible waterfall gurgled over a cloud-shrouded cliff and reappeared as vapor puffs at the bottom of a canyon. Smaller vapor puffs formed at our mouths while we rem-inisced about college. This was one subject on which we figured to have little in common. No matter how unpleasant it had been for me as a penniless commuter at the University of Maryland, my plight couldn't compare to the savage hazing Pat had endured as a new cadet—a "knob"—at the Citadel.

"Knobs were lower than whale shit," he said. "Between study-ing and marching and basketball practice, I didn't do anything except polish my shoes and stand punishment details. I don't re-member having a date until my sophomore year. Then I fell head over fucking heels in love for the first time. But I was a little slow on the uptake," he added. "My girlfriend was screwing another guy and got pregnant before I got to first base."

If he expected me to laugh—if he counted on cauterizing a wound by making himself the butt of a joke—he was talking to the wrong man. "What did you do?" I asked.

"I told her I loved her and swore I'd stand by her. I must have been stealing my lines from a country and western song. I wore a path between the barracks and her house. We talked about getting married but never did anything more than kiss."

I had no trouble guessing where the narrative led next. With abortion illegal in the United States back then, everybody's choices had been circumscribed. His girlfriend planned to put her baby up for adoption, Pat told me. But she went into premature labor and gave birth to a stillborn child.

"Were you with her?" I asked.

"No. I never saw the baby. I never saw much of the girl again."

There was a lot I might have said. I could have quoted the friend who consoled me with the rough wisdom, "Well, there's one bullet you dodged." I might have clapped him on the shoulder and welcomed him to the club. Instead I asked, "Did you ever write about this?"

"Yeah, in my second novel, *The Lords of Discipline*."

"Maybe I should sue you for plagiarism. Your story is right out of my second novel, *Waking Slow*. The same thing happened to me."

We sped into the mountains, toward a tunnel. Above its yawning mouth an old rockslide had spread through a pine forest like frantic fingers digging for a grip. "When my girlfriend, Adrienne, got pregnant by another guy, we moved to California and lived in Los Angeles for six months," I told Pat. "I offered to marry her and raise the baby as mine. She had other ideas. After the adoption we went back to Maryland and—"

"She said, 'Adios, motherfucker.'"

"No, she'd never say anything like that. Adrienne had been very properly brought up."

"And properly fucked."

"I was an idiot. I had read too many novels. I believed in love. She believed in a future that didn't include me."

"This is starting to creep me out," Pat said as we entered the tunnel. "All this stuff in common—I thought that kind of cosmic synchronicity was just something Steve Geller invented in his screenplays."

WE STOPPED FOR THE NIGHT in Innsbruck, and after a stroll around the old town, we ate in a Rathskeller where murals of rosy-cheeked milkmaids smiled at us from the walls and a band in the back room played Viennese schmalz. Although Pat's appetite for food and drink was Falstaffian, he fed himself in a fastidious fashion, with small bites, after each of which he patted his mouth with a napkin. Then he swigged from his beer stein and blotted his mouth again. He caught me staring and shoved his hands out of sight.

"I know, I know," he said. "My fingernails are filthy. I forget to clean and clip them. That's something my mother never taught me." He spoke as if the only lessons that stuck were those imparted by Peggy Conroy, and whatever she hadn't drummed into him as a child, he had no hope of mastering as an adult.

"Can I ask you a personal question?" I said.

"They're the kind I like."

"Do you ever wonder why your college girlfriend ditched you?"

"No need to wonder. She showed up at a bookstore and had me sign a novel for her. I figured if she had the balls to do that, I had the right to ask why she dumped me. She said after the shame of getting knocked up and the pain of losing the baby, she couldn't bear to be around me. She said if we had stayed together, I'd have been a constant reminder of nothing but bad news."

"I assumed my girlfriend bugged out because I didn't do a better job of taking care of her in California," I said. "Maybe I need to rethink things."

WE REGISTERED AT A SPOTLESSLY clean hotel whose rooms called to mind monastery cells. Stretched out on one of the hard single beds, I was eager for sleep. But Pat insisted on updating his diary, a buckram notebook as big as an accountant's ledger. When he finished writing, he went into the bathroom to shower, leaving the ledger open on the night table. A Freudian might speculate that he was inviting me to take a peek. At least that's how I justified invading his privacy.

"Mewshaw is the first writer I've ever met who at one time in his life could dunk a basketball," Pat had scribbled, failing to note that I had deflated the ball and told the story as a joke on myself.

He repeated another anecdote I had told, this one about a boy on the DeMatha football team who was notorious for being afraid of physical contact. When this reputed chicken-shit started dating a teammate's girlfriend, the aggrieved party challenged him to a fight. The "non-hitter" showed up carrying an axe handle. The other guy snarled, "You don't have the nerve—" which were the last words he uttered before the axe handle cracked his skull. Pat invented dialogue, as well as the boys' height and weight, which I hadn't mentioned.

It's not uncommon for a novelist to keep notes on the day's events, to record striking lines of dialogue or rough out a scene, then later reframe this raw material for his fiction. But Pat frequently skipped the interim stage and moved straight from experience or observation to fictionalized details in his diary. He ended that day's entries by remarking on "the human need to tell stories, the exact stories that shape you, and made you *you*." Yet as I would learn, regardless of whether Pat was writing a novel or a memoir, his stories were seldom "exact." He always shaped them for his own purposes.

IN MUNICH, WE CRASHED WITH a German woman named Uta who had attended high school in the States with Linda. Now divorced, she lived on a sylvan lake outside the city, and as lovely as the setting was, she conceded she suffered from loneliness. She welcomed us into her A-frame house and into her confidence. In Pat, a complete stranger, she discovered a kindred spirit and empathetic listener who elaborated on the turmoil of his own divorce. He said he had been in and out of therapy, in and out of clinical depression, on and off the brink of suicide for years.

Touched by his candor, Uta unburdened herself. She was now involved with a married man who kept promising, and failing, to leave his wife.

"Get rid of that asshole," Pat advised her. "Find a different guy."

"But I'm getting older. If I wait too long, I'm afraid I won't be able to have children."

"I've got half a dozen. Believe me, you can live without them."

The next day, at the BMW distributorship, Bavarian efficiency suffered a serious glitch; the sales papers had been misplaced. It took five hours to locate and process them, prompting Pat to joke, "Everyplace is becoming like Italy."

In what remained of the afternoon, we made the rounds of

used car lots, searching for something I could afford. Pat did his best to be patient, but his heart wasn't in it and I didn't blame him. Few experiences in life are as dispiriting as dealing with used car salesmen who sound the same no matter what language they speak. At three places in a row a grinning German guided me behind the wheel of a clunker that failed to start. Shaken, I decided I wasn't in the market after all.

That evening, at Uta's urging, we ate at a lakeside restaurant hung with hunting trophies, whose matted fur and bristling horns curdled my appetite. While Pat ordered stag meat, I stuck to sausage and a salad that to my disgust was seasoned with shredded eel. Pat scraped the slimy excrescences onto his plate and pronounced them "delicious." He judged me as suffering from "a timid palate, a legacy of your lower-middle-class upbringing."

"Don't bullshit me," I fought back. "I realize your father was an officer. But I bet your family didn't dine on bear meat or sheep eyeballs from the PX."

"No, I grew up eating the same shit you did. Now I want to taste everything."

This ardent quest defined the way Pat went headlong at everything in life. He even read the newspaper as if devouring it. To watch him consume the *International Herald Tribune* was like looking at a starving man cleaning his plate. Page by page, he didn't skip a morsel, not even the world weather report or fashion tips from Paris.

The following day, at his instigation, we dropped by Oktoberfest where, surrounded by drunken college kids, fat waitresses in dirndls, and oompah-pah bandsmen in lederhosen and knee-length stockings, he declared, "Dad brags that he majored in gooks. He's proud of bombing Japan, Korea, and Vietnam. But I bet he'd sacrifice his left testicle for a chance to drop the big one here."

•

AUTUMN VANISHED OVERNIGHT, ROUTED BY wind and rain full of icy intimations of the winter ahead. Pat and I beat a retreat across the Alps to Italy where summer lingered, and the land fell away in green folds, smelling of plowed fields and harvested grapes. Amid palm trees, flame-shaped cypresses flickered. "As we have candles to light the darkness of night," D. H. Lawrence had written, "so the cypresses are candles to keep darkness alive in full sunlight."

The Beamer had a radio. I suggested that Pat remove it, at least while he lived in Italy, where thieves targeted cars with radios. A news story, perhaps apocryphal, claimed twenty-two German dentists, all Mercedes owners, had driven to Milan for a conference and returned home minus their automobiles. Pat noted this in his journal—not that he took out the radio. He was simply a compulsive recorder of odd vignettes.

I exhorted him to step on the gas and get us back to Rome before dark. But he kept to his resolute pace and continued talking. Language, some salty and scabrous, some as baroque as a Borromini sculpture, poured out of him. He had no appetite for small talk or banal exchanges of information. He craved bold, heartfelt conversation in which everything was on the table and nothing was taboo. He may no longer have been a practicing Catholic, but he appeared to have retained an abiding faith in the sacrament of confession.

He told me that after college he returned to Beaufort and taught high school. He rented a cottage on a huge estate, and nearby lived Barbara Bolling. They struck up a friendship which flowered into love. In his free time he wrote and self-published *The Boo*, a book about Thomas Nugent Courvoisie, the assistant commandant at the Citadel. After Barbara and he married in 1969, Pat switched to teaching on Daufuskie Island, which entailed a three-hour daily commute by boat.

"When the school board fired me," Pat said, "they claimed I didn't follow the state curriculum. The real reason I got canned—I'm quoting here—'You're too cozy with the niggers.' Plus, I wouldn't use corporal punishment on the kids. So there I was in my mid-twenties, unemployed and with a wife and two children and one on the way."

"Hold on a minute," I said. "You'd just got married."

"Guess I forgot to mention Barbara was pregnant when we met and she already had a two-year-old daughter." He chuckled. "To plant a cherry on top of the sundae, she was a widow. Her husband was killed in combat in Vietnam. Her family was military, just like mine, and they were none too pleased with her marrying a draft-dodging peacenik who couldn't even hold on to a job teaching black kids.

"They made noises about going to court and getting custody of the kids," he continued, "on the grounds that I was an unfit father. I was furious." In fact, he sounded positively giddy about the recollection. "So I—you'll love this—so I sallied forth like a white knight and adopted Jessica and Melissa. I adored them and nobody was about to take them away from us. Then we had Megan."

I sat there dead silent, stifling what I wanted to say: How had he gotten trapped in such a sticky web so soon after his affair with the pregnant college girl ended?

"When they made *The Water Is Wide* into a movie," he resumed, "that gave us the money to move to Atlanta and for Barbara to enroll in law school at Emory. But I was in an awful state. I was writing *The Great Santini*, dredging up a whole raft of family shit, and that strained the marriage. Barbara said she promised to stay with me for richer or poorer, not for crazy."

When he wrote, Pat said he required isolation and quiet, not the exuberant company of three little girls. His first novel bled from him line by line, and he had to hole up out of town to get any work done. Barbara blamed him for withdrawing from the family, and Pat didn't deny it. Becoming a published author made him more difficult to live with and at the same time more attractive to other women. He was drinking heavily and running around, all the while wracked by guilt. Then in 1975 he swallowed a fistful of sleeping pills.

"They didn't work," he said. "I was the sort of fuck-up who couldn't even manage to kill himself. Instead of me dying, Barbara and I got a divorce. Which in a lot of ways felt worse than dying."

As we crossed Tuscany into Umbria, the timbre of Pat's voice altered. There was no mistaking the shift in tone; his self-mocking metamorphosed into high-minded sentiments. "Each divorce is the death of a small civilization," he said. "Two people declare war on each other, and their screams and tears and days of withdrawal infect their entire world with the bacilli of their pain."

When he told his daughters that Barbara and he were splitting up, the girls gazed at the floor and refused to look at either parent. "I felt like Judas Iscariot as he fingered his thirty pieces of silver," Pat said. "I was ashamed of being a man. By the time I started dating again, I searched for women who would make me be more like a woman."

I assumed what he said was in italics and he would soon return to his wisecracking self. But then the rhythm of his sentences persuaded me he was repeating something he had written in earnest. Later I learned he was quoting from "Anatomy of a Divorce," an article he had published in *Atlanta Magazine*. I didn't doubt that his emotions, even as he plagiarized himself, were genuine. Still I wondered whether anything in his life had eluded his writing.

As his voice swung back to its default setting of self-deprecating humor, he said, "After Barbara got the law degree I paid for, she wrote up our divorce agreement. I felt so guilty I signed whatever she set in front of me. Child support for Megan, and the other girls' expenses up through college."

"Wait a minute. Don't the dependents of soldiers killed in combat get financial benefits?"

"Beats me."

"Come on, man. You can't have grown up in a military family and not know about VA benefits."

He shrugged. "I don't care about money."

"Spoken like a guy in the market to buy the Brooklyn Bridge."

I nagged him until he acknowledged that Barbara and her first two daughters did receive VA benefits. But these didn't cover all the expenses of private schools, and when the girls went to college there would be bills for room and board and so forth. Within a matter of minutes, Pat massaged the story in one direction, then gave it an altogether different spin. After suggesting Barbara had somehow tricked him, had played on his naïveté, he ended up admitting that her drafting their settlement made the divorce cheaper.

In the whirlpool of rush hour traffic on the Raccordo Anulare, Rome's ring-road, Pat brought up Lenore, another woman with two kids and one on the way. "When I met her," he said, "it relieved me to learn her ex-husband was a brain surgeon. I figured that meant there would be no trouble about his paying child support." He found this tremendously funny. "You'd think I would have learned something about women and marriage by now, but you'd be wrong. I fell for another damsel in distress, hook, line, and sinker."

After the seething length of Via Aurelia and the great grinding stone of cars at Porta San Pancrazio, we entered the calmer streets of Monteverde. At our building on Via Carini, I invited Pat up for a drink and breathed easier when he begged off. I liked him and hoped we'd be friends. But he wore me out and he worried me. He slid from his new Beamer and kissed me on both cheeks as he had learned to do after his two months in Italy. He was a big guy and strong. But he'd have to be lucky too, I thought, if he hoped to hold up under all the weight he had haphazardly taken on his shoulders.

3 Having returned from Germany without a used car, I improvised. Alfred Moir, an art historian from UC Santa Barbara, spent several months a year at the American Academy and, during his absences, he left behind his VW Derby. Rather than have it rust into disrepair, he agreed to let Linda and me drive it. In exchange, we kept the car insured and serviced, and we delivered it to Alfred freshly washed and full of gas whenever he flew into town.

As time passed and Alfred aged, however, he took fewer trips to Italy and eventually forgot about the VW Derby. Because its tax-free tourist plates were long out of date, the *carabinieri* occasionally questioned us at roadblocks during terror alerts. But they never arrested us, and we ended up driving the Derby for a decade. Only for death, as Italian wisdom has it, is there no solution.

Three days a week, I played tennis on the American Academy's court, which was bordered by an umbrella pine at one end and by a green waterfall of ivy at the other. Along the western sideline grew a grape arbor, and during long rallies I sometimes lost track of the score and simply admired the arabesque shadows encroaching on the red clay.

I invited Pat Conroy to play and he arrived in a bulky sweat suit, resembling the roly-poly Michelin Man. Although out of shape and soon pink in the face, he had lost none of the nimbleness that had made him a star point guard. For his size he possessed surprising quickness, nifty footwork, and fine hand-eye coordination.

Between sets as we cooled off under the grape arbor, we chewed the fat about basketball more often than we did about backhands and forehands. He was still passionate about hoops, and reminisced nostalgically about practicing in stifling gyms in summer and on icy outdoor courts in winter. After hours of dribbling, he said, the skin on his hands cracked like alligator hide, and because he always dived for loose balls, the scars on his knees never healed. A tireless student of the game, he described how he had broken the jump shot down into its component parts, honing his wrist-snap and follow-through.

Sean and I sometimes shot around on a court near our apartment, and I asked Pat to help teach my son the rudiments of the sport. But he said, "I've retired." Then he added, as he often did when talk turned to life's passage, "It's a short season."

It didn't occur to me until later that he may have been protecting me against the fact that he was far better at basketball and didn't care to show me up in front of my son. He preferred that we play tennis, where I won easily. It was an example of his incessant envy preemption. Starting with his family of origin, people had been jealous of him. Now he did his utmost to avoid that ugly emotion, encouraging everybody to believe they were better than him so he could feel okay about himself.

In November, he let it drop that he had an enlarged heart. My reaction echoed that of Joan Geller, who exclaimed, "Of course everybody knows Pat Conroy has a big heart." I didn't take him seriously until he announced that he was flying back to Atlanta to consult a cardiologist. "Be nice to me. Li'l Abner's on his last legs." Naturally he played his predicament for laughs.

With Pat away, we saw Lenore alone at St. Francis School functions. It amused her that Emily had learned the sign of the cross and was praying to Jesus. After an ob-gyn appointment at Salvator Mundi Hospital around the corner from our apartment on Via Carini, she stopped by for a visit. Due to give birth any day, she displayed no great concern about being on her own. The few complaints she voiced were all so lighthearted, even serious troubles sounded like mere inconveniences.

Lenore had a wonderful laugh and a wicked sense of humor. Pat liked to portray her as a ditzy material girl, accustomed to the luxuries a doctor's wife could afford. But as a single mother between marriages, she had worked a variety of jobs and was now a stay-at-home mom in a country where she fearlessly negotiated in a new language with rapacious garage mechanics and the gangs of repairmen required to keep the house in Olgiata functioning. To watch her at the wheel of the BMW, threading the needle's eye in Roman streets, was to realize how competent she was to protect herself. She pithily summed up her marriage to Alan Fleischer with a pair of anecdotes, both of which featured her wreaking revenge at the wheel of a car.

Alan had cheated on her, Lenore said, but swore he was "processing out of that relationship" and wanted to rebuild their marriage. He suggested they celebrate their reunion with a dinner at home. But as Lenore drove back after shopping for the meal with baby Emily strapped into a car seat beside her, she noticed Alan's car parked in his lover's driveway.

"I pulled in behind him, sneaked into the house through a side door, and found them upstairs in bed. I started breaking things as I went back downstairs. Then I drove into Alan's car and hit his girlfriend's car and ran over the mailbox. All this with poor little Emily witnessing the utter insanity."

Lenore leaned over her big pregnant belly, rocking back and forth, laughing in merriment. "Naturally after that I needed therapy, and Alan showed up for a session. We were hoping to figure out a way of *not* getting a divorce. The therapist thought divorce was the worst thing you could do to your children. But I asked the doctor if he'd recommend his own daughter stay in a relationship with a guy like Alan, who got his girlfriend pregnant and made her have an abortion. When the doctor couldn't answer, I left, and Alan followed me to the parking lot, taunting me. He stood so I couldn't move my car. I revved the engine and asked him to step aside. He propped his foot on the bumper and dared me."

"Dared you to do what?" Linda asked.

"Go ahead and hit him. I told him to get out of the way, then I just stepped on the gas."

"You what?" Linda gasped.

"I accelerated and he crashed over the hood."

"You could have killed him."

"At the moment I didn't care. But there wasn't enough space to build up speed, so it only knocked him down."

"What happened then?" Linda wanted to know.

"I called an ambulance, and they called the cops." Lenore collected herself and spoke with feline delight. "He was hurt, but not critically. He told the police he didn't want to press charges. He was on crutches for weeks. He had to pee through a catheter. Still, he sent me flowers."

"Wait a minute," I said. "Didn't Pat write an article about this?"

"Yes. He heard about it before we even met. The gossip was all over Atlanta. Pat thought it showed how insane a marriage break-up can be."

"What a brave guy," I said, "marrying you, knowing what you're capable of."

"I doubt I'd ever do it again. I got it out of my system."

"I'm going to put this in a novel someday."

"As long as you describe me as thin."

It came to me that Lenore's appeal to Pat was like his love for Rome—both were exotic, seductive, and dangerous.

WINTER HOWLED INTO TOWN ON a *tramontana* wind out of the Alps, and by early December, Christmas stalls cropped up in Piazza Navona, selling hard candy, soft figs, and tacky figurines for Nativity scenes. In Campo de' Fiori, fish vendors hawked eels for the traditional Christmas Eve dinner, while florists hustled poinsettias and what appeared to be holly. On closer inspection, the holly was fake. Sprigs of prickly leaves and blood-red berries from different bushes were painstakingly attached by narrow-gauge wire. Some viewed this as evidence of Italian deviousness. I regarded it as entrepreneurial ingenuity.

Shortly after Pat returned from the States, Lenore went into labor on December 7, the eve of the Feast of the Immaculate Conception. Despite the blitz of holiday traffic on the Via Cassia, Pat transported her to Salvator Mundi with no mishaps, and Linda and I stayed in all day, awaiting word. Occasionally Linda peeked out the bedroom window of our apartment, as if she believed that, like the Vatican announcing a new Pope with a plume of smoke, the hospital would send up a signal as soon as Baby Conroy was born.

At dusk, the intercom rang, and a voice, distorted by street noise, crackled, "It's Pat."

"Boy or girl?" Linda shouted.

"Girl."

We buzzed him in and raced to the elevator to congratulate him. Wind or cold or grit had reddened his cheeks, and tears trickled from Pat's eyes. He smelled strongly of whiskey. Once we were in the apartment, he broke into sobs.

"Is Lenore all right?" Linda asked.

He nodded and flopped into a chair.

"And the baby?"

"The baby's fine. She's beautiful. Do you have something to drink?"

I fetched a bottle of Scotch and poured him a double shot. He drained the glass in a gulp. In a plaid flannel shirt and flat wool cap, he might have been a rough-and-ready lumberjack. Lifting the cap and patting his comb-over into place, he had a look about him of abject defeat.

"This is the worst, the most humiliating, day of my life." He gestured for me to top up his glass. "Lenore had to have a cesarean."

"But you said she and the baby are okay."

"They're fine and dandy. I was, too, until I learned why Lenore couldn't give birth vaginally. She has herpes, and they were afraid she'd infect the baby. That's the delightful news the doctor told me in front of a bunch of nurses and nuns," Pat said. "Lenore has already infected me with herpes. That's another bit of news the doctor announced. Now no other woman will ever want to have sex with me."

I didn't think to ask why he was telling us this. I didn't ask how no one had noticed the herpes until now. I didn't ask why Pat was worried no other women would have sex with him. My response was to put myself in his place and pity him. After his fractious history with women, how could he not feel furious and betrayed?

"If you could have seen how those nuns looked at me," he said, "when they heard I have a venereal disease."

"Don't call it that," Linda said.

"Whatever you call it, it's incurable."

"But you can control it. The important thing is the baby's okay. Tell us about her. What did she weigh? Who does she look like?"

Slowly, with fewer and fewer outbursts of fury from Pat, Linda coaxed him into discussing names for the baby and how long Lenore would have to stay in the hospital. Had he told the other kids? But when she asked whether they'd move now to an apartment in the *centro storico*, Pat snapped, "I'd be happy in a place like yours. But Lenore feels entitled to a penthouse with a view of the Forum and the Colosseum."

"I'm with Lenore," Linda said. "She's going to be spending a lot of time indoors. Why not in a nice place?"

We invited him to eat dinner with us before returning to the hospital for visiting hours. He had me pour him more whiskey and ignored our apologies about the menu—frozen fish sticks, *bastoncini di pesce*, as Sean called them. Both boys loved this batter-fried dish, and Pat pronounced it not half-bad. After a bite, he cued Marco, "*È buono*," and jabbed a finger at his cheek.

"By this time next year, your daughter will be fluent in Italian sign language," I said.

"Yeah, if Lenore and I are still together."

In silence, he finished his fish sticks and a cup of coffee, plopped his flat cap on his comb-over, and departed. Normally even when I didn't know what to say, I said something. That night, once Linda and I were alone, I said nothing, and neither did she.

I feared Pat would leave Lenore. Or that he'd berate her so mercilessly, she'd leave him. On December 17 he called in an agitated state and I steeled myself against the worst. But political events had pushed his personal woes to the periphery. In their most audacious escapade since the assassination of Aldo Moro, the Red Brigades had kidnapped U.S. Brigadier General James L. Dozier in Verona.

"Right away I thought of your novel," Pat said. "It'll put the Red Brigades back on the front page and make it easier for you to find a publisher in the States. When'll the manuscript be ready?"

Year of the Gun needed revisions, I told him. To refer to it as a work-in-progress was to dignify a mercurial process that had recently persuaded me to transform a central character, an adrenaline-addicted combat photographer, from a man into a woman.

"Great idea," he said. "Just let me know when I should recommend it to Houghton Mifflin."

"How's your work coming?" I asked.

"Let's not talk about that."

"Okay, let's talk about the baby."

"She's a little princess. Thank God she got Lenore's looks. Let's hope she doesn't have my scrambled brain."

"What's her name?"

"Susannah Ansley Conroy. Lenore's and my first date started with drinks at a friend's apartment in Ansley Park." This sentimental allusion to their past encouraged me to believe he and Lenore had a future. Still, when he invited us to Olgiata for Christmas dinner, I hesitated. "You sure you're up to having a houseful of guests?"

"There won't be a crowd. The big kids have gone back to Atlanta for the holidays. More peace and quiet for the rest of us."

ELEANOR CLARK'S *ROME AND A VILLA* declared that for Italians to go out into the streets is to go home. On most holidays, they flood the piazzas and stream through the city's complex venous system of *vicoli* as whole families—tottering infants as well as doddering old folks—indulge in the pleasure of circulating in patterns that were probably hardwired in them at birth. But on Christmas the streets of Rome resemble a home abandoned. Behind iron grates, shop windows show their wares through prison bars, and the tables and chairs outside of cafés are chained together like coffles of slaves.

Through this extraordinary emptiness, our borrowed VW Derby advanced along the Lungotevere, past the Ponte Milvio, and onto Via Cassia, where brutal apartment blocks alternated with a few graceful private villas that had survived the bulldozers of real estate developers. Beside me Linda held Marco on her lap while Sean bounced around in back, unrestrained by a seatbelt. These days we'd be arrested and charged with child endangerment. Back then we considered ourselves doting parents.

Strung with faerie lights and wreaths, Olgiata looked like an almost appealing place to live. The Conroys' kitchen was warmed by a blaze in the fireplace, and the smell of woodsmoke added to the seasonal atmosphere. Susannah lay content in her bassinet, while Pat worked with Lenore in what seemed to be harmony. Although I felt it had been wrong for Lenore to hide her herpes from him, I was glad that they appeared to have patched things up.

"You're lucky to have a husband who cooks," Linda told Lenore.

"The problem is he makes a mess. He dirties every pot and pan and I have to clean up after him."

"That'll be Mike's job," Linda said. "He's a terrific dishwasher."

"A real man cooks." Pat strapped on an apron as if it were chest armor. "Not like Cliff here, who's too sexually insecure." This was how he introduced Cliff Graubart, a longtime friend from Atlanta, a bookstore owner, who had flown in for the holidays.

"I'm fixing an avocado mousse that was a big hit at our wedding reception," Pat said. "I decided tonight was the perfect occasion to repeat the recipe. But because I know just two numbers in Italian—one and twelve—I wound up with a dozen avocados. Everybody better come back for second helpings."

"They're good for the heart," Linda said.

I had completely forgotten Pat's coronary problem. When I asked what he had learned in Atlanta, Cliff piped up, "Look at this man, and tell me how a little thing like heart trouble could bother him. He absorbs sickness, lets it sink into his blubber until it smothers to death."

Two more guests arrived, a young married couple, Garrett Epps and Spencie Love, who were studying Italian at the University for Foreigners in Perugia. Garrett had published his first novel, *The Shad Treatment*, and was finishing his next, while Spencie wrote *One Blood: The Death and Resurrection of Charles R. Drew*. Linda asked what it was like for two authors to live in close quarters. Spencie laughed. "We have separate typewriters. I'd rather share a toothbrush than a typewriter."

Garrett Epps's uncle, George Garrett, had been my creative writing professor at the University of Virginia. It turned out we also had a mutual friend, James Fallows. Garrett and Jim had worked on the *Crimson* together at Harvard. Then after a couple of years at Oxford as a Rhodes scholar, Fallows moved to Austin, and he and I regularly played tennis together, both of us dogged baseline retrievers exhausting each other in the Texas heat. When Jimmy Carter hired Jim as his head speechwriter, we briefly entertained the fantasy of continuing our competition on the White House court. In that instance, common sense triumphed.

As Pat and Lenore served up platters of turkey and dressing, I mentioned the misadventure Fallows had suffered when Carter's press secretary, Jody Powell, arranged a match between the twenty-eight-year-old speechwriter and the fifty-four-year-old president. I could have predicted the result. Jim shellacked the Leader of the Free World, but rather than win praise for his performance he got his ass chewed out for embarrassing the commander in chief.

Pat, who loved tales of the mighty brought low, crowed with delight.

"Remember the article Jim wrote for *Atlantic Monthly*," Epps asked, "after he resigned from the White House? He characterized Carter as a micro-manager who controlled everything, right down to who played on the tennis court and when."

"What's Fallows doing now?" Linda asked.

"He went back to journalism."

"The old revolving door," Pat said. "Hemingway blasted literary critics as a bottle of tapeworms. The same holds true for Washington reporters. I hate that inside baseball bullshit."

"You mean inside the Beltway," Garrett said.

"I mean all those Ivy Leaguers trapezing from one top job to the next, never touching the sawdust and elephant dung on the ground."

"Jim's a good writer," I said. "You'd like him, Pat. He did a terrific piece, 'Daddy, What Did You Do During the Class War?' It's about his dodging the draft, then realizing that's a privilege available exclusively to rich white kids."

"Jim's new book, *National Defense*," Garrett said, "advocates re-instituting the draft."

Without preamble, Pat erupted in paroxysms of rage. "Now that his lily-white ass is safe, he's ready to send other boys into battle. These guys who claim they regret not going to war piss me off."

"That's not what Jim wrote," I put in.

"Eight members of my class died in Vietnam," Pat roared.

Then silence descended upon the table. Susannah lay wide

awake but quiet in her baby carrier. Marco quit wriggling and sat motionless as a Buddha on Linda's lap. For Pat, it appeared that Vietnam, like his childhood, was a war that would never end.

Lenore raised her wineglass. "Well, merry merry, everybody."

4 Starting research for my next book, *Short Circuit*, I set out on the 1982 men's pro tennis tour with many misconceptions, none more quickly apparent than my delusion that because I loved traveling as much as I loved tennis, the project would prove to be doubly pleasurable. In the following months, I took trains, planes, buses, and a long-haul ferry. But these led less to places than to a pervasive state of unease.

In Genoa, at the first tournament, the top players received under-the-table appearance fees and demanded and got preferential treatment. Players routinely tanked matches, split the prize money, and orchestrated the action during sets to make them more exciting and to fill TV time slots. You didn't need to be Woodward or Bernstein to unearth these improprieties. Players, reporters, even umpires and tour administrators openly discussed who had no incentive to win, who intended to tank and catch an early flight out of town.

My first reaction was that I had fascinating information that no tennis journalist had previously revealed. My second thought was that I didn't dare publish it and risk the legal consequences. The libel suit prompted by *Life for Death* had, after two years of misery, just been settled. That learning experience cost me

$70,000—and I had no stomach, and no money, for another losing battle. I wrote my editor and compared myself to a miner who discovers uranium while digging for gold. Both are valuable minerals, but uranium is radioactive and dangerous. Unless the publisher indemnified me, I swore I would delete from *Short Circuit* all controversial material and deliver the lyrical hymn to tennis I had originally proposed.

My editor encouraged me to go for the uranium, not the gold; the publisher promised to pick up the legal bills. Still leery, I discussed things with Pat and he blurted, "Put everything in the book. Don't leave anything out."

That was his approach in to all spheres of life. Cram in everything—food, alcohol, knowledge, opinions, quotes. Whether fighting Alan Fleischer in court or grappling with family turmoil, he went all in.

Yet at the same time he expressed concern for my safety and insisted on driving me to the Foro Italico to collect my press credentials for that spring's Italian Open. He feared I'd be attacked by a player or tournament official for asking too many awkward questions.

In one of those *commedia dell'arte* extravaganzas commonplace in Italy, the Red Brigades terrorists who had murdered Aldo Moro were standing trial in a gymnasium adjacent to the tennis courts. It was as if John Hinckley, President Reagan's would-be assassin, presented his case to a jury at Flushing Meadows during the U.S. Open. Seeing squads of soldiers armed with automatic weapons patrolling near the main stadium, Pat murmured, "I guess I overreacted to the danger you're in."

"Who? You? Overreact?" I razzed him. "I've been meaning to tell you it's time to lighten up and change your tactics. Just go limp and let your problems solve themselves."

"It's not my nature to go limp," he argued.

"Make it your nature."

Pat parked the car and sagged behind the wheel. "It's more than Lenore and Alan Fleischer breaking my balls. It's my mother. She has leukemia. At least that's what she claims."

"She wouldn't lie about that."

"She's done it before. Years ago, after she divorced Dad, she said she had terminal cancer and started traveling overnight with a priest. Supposedly he was her spiritual counselor."

"He must have helped." I tried to get a laugh out of him. "She's still alive."

"She says she's in remission now and means to fly to Rome as soon as we're in our new place. She doesn't want to die before seeing Susannah. I suspect she secretly plans to baptize her. Assuming you haven't already done that."

AT THE END OF MARCH, the Conroys moved to Via dei Foraggi, in the shadow of the Forum and Palatine. Their apartment, like most of those rented by rich foreigners, boasted a lineage of celebrity tenants. Omar Sharif had preceded the Conroys, and Pat felt less than welcome there. When he washed the Beamer in a fountain on his street, a *carabiniere* fined him for desecrating a classical ruin. From then on he polished the car in his private courtyard, which had its own fountain and a wisteria vine that webbed the second-story windows with branches as thick as Pat's bicep.

In a corner of the *cortile*, a staircase led to a large living room and an ornately decorated dining room. The building belonged to a couple of Yugoslavian brothers who also owned an antique shop, and they had furnished the apartment from their vast inventory of bibelots in what Pat referred to as "fag gothic style." The pièce de résistance was a painting of St. Sebastian with his torso pierced by arrows. Pat maintained this was a portrait of him and offered to buy it. But the brothers refused to sell.

Up on the third level, a sitting room and terrace gave onto half a dozen of the city's signature landmarks. When I first gazed at that view, I realized that ruins in the *centro storico* looked newer than recent construction on the Gianicolo. Two-thousand-year-old monuments were kept in good repair for tourists, while buildings like the one Linda and I occupied sank into shabby dilapidation after a few decades.

Pat proclaimed that he had the perfect place to write. With the three older kids away at school all day and the baby in a crib on the bottom floor, he enjoyed as much silence and isolation as he could reasonably ask for. But the total absence of distractions was driving him mad. "People say they envy me living here. They say Italy must be an inspiration. But I'm completely blocked."

Now with his mother due to visit, he had another excuse not to write. He loved her, but the intensity of that love contained the seeds of what sounded like a disease.

"I owe her everything," he said. "The trouble is she expects to be paid back with interest, and nothing I do is ever enough."

"Maybe it'd help to write about her as honestly as you have about your father."

"I've thought of that. I'm just not sure how honest I could be, especially since she has cancer. It'd kill her to hear what I really think."

"Which is what?" I asked.

"She's a liar and a manipulator. She has as much to do with fucking up my life as Dad does. Still, she made me a writer."

This was a declaration Pat would repeat for the rest of his life. Once, at the American Booksellers Association convention, he reduced the audience to tears by proclaiming, "It is the power of her voice that moves me to write. My mother taught me what we all look for as writers. It is the moment when language and passion and the beauty of writing all come together."

But that day in Rome, staring at the astonishing view that failed to inspire him, he spoke to me about his loneliness as a child, and the tribulations of transferring every year to a new military base. When he complained, his mother demanded that he suck it up and suppress his hurt feelings. Even as a little boy he was supposed to sacrifice for the country, like a good Marine. He recounted Peggy Conroy's penchant for building him up, then knocking him down and withholding love unless she got what she wanted. Above all he recalled her failure to protect him from his ruthless father.

ON MY WALK HOME FROM the Conroys', I passed the ancient pillars that erupt from the sidewalk in front of a row of Jewish restaurants. The damp ghetto air smelled of *carciofi alla giudia* and olive oil. As I swung behind Palazzo Cenci and the Gellers' apartment, the drizzle became rain and I hurried toward Piazza Sonnino, where I could catch a bus up to the Gianicolo. Nothing seemed sadder at the moment than a city, made for sunlight, moldering in wet weather.

On Ponte Garibaldi, I paused and peered down at the Tiber where it foamed over the Isola Tiberina as if over the prow of a ship. In the frothing water below the weir, stray soccer balls and plastic bottles plunged, disappeared under the river, then rose again. They looked as trapped and hopeless as Pat had sounded. I wished I could cheer him up. I wished I could cheer myself up.

Then by some improbable magic, it transpired that the random bottles and balls in the whirlpool cohered for several seconds into a shape, a kind of kinetic art installation. If you were patient and lucky, Rome often provided such lovely fleeting consolations.

PEGGY CONROY'S TRIP TO ITALY commenced with a similar miracle. Groggy after an overnight flight, she set her purse down in the arrivals area and hugged Pat and didn't remember the handbag until they were in the car on the parking lot. With little hope of recovering her cash, credit cards, and passport, Pat raced back to the terminal, and to his astonishment found another passenger, an Italian lady, protecting the purse. Not satisfied with thanking her, he bought the woman a bouquet of roses at a flower stall.

By the time I showed up at Via dei Foraggi that evening, his mother still marveled at her good luck. But in Peggy Conroy's ebullient presence Pat seemed more subdued than I had ever seen him. His tendency to tease and needle vanished, and the timbre of his voice dropped into a softer register. It was as if he feared that any loud sound, any abrupt movement, would shatter Peggy.

He had composed a list of sites he planned to show her. He had crossed off the catacombs. As he explained to me, he had no intention of taking her underground to the shelves of skulls and skeletons, catalogued like a grotesque library.

Pale and fragile as a porcelain doll, Peggy had lost her hair during chemotherapy and wore a champagne-colored wig in a perky, slightly bouffant fashion. Because of her slow Southern drawl, her fatigue, complicated by jetlag and medications, seemed fathomless. She had been a great beauty in her day, and still carried herself like a grande dame, not the dirt-poor daughter of rednecks.

Just as Pat showed his mother none of the ambivalence he bore her, she demonstrated none of the passive-aggressiveness he had warned me about. Because her son had prepped her in advance, she knew precisely the right questions to ask about my books, and about Linda and the boys. She performed a credible impersonation of the mother in *The Great Santini*—Blythe Danner as a battered wife trapped between a monstrous husband and a passel of moiling kids, yet still poised and well-groomed. To watch Pat and Peggy together was to witness a ballet, full of ritual bows and pirouettes, all as false as her wig. I feared that one of them might trip, collapsing the charade. But they remained sure-footed during her visit, each playing a deeply rehearsed role. Behind her back, he referred to her as "Queen Lear." What she called him, I never knew.

AFTER FIVE TENNIS TOURNAMENTS I felt I had competed in hundreds of matches, not merely watched them. At the Italian Open, I was feverish and on antibiotics, but I had to fly to Paris for the French Open. There I soldiered on for a few rounds, then landed in the American Hospital, laid low by a virulent intestinal virus. Convinced I had been poisoned, Pat volunteered to come to Paris and serve as my bodyguard. I assured him I just needed rest and would soon rejoin the circuit, which had begun to seem like a snake consuming its own tail and me along with it.

Crossing the English Channel, I joined Linda and the boys in London for Wimbledon. We leased a flat in Knightsbridge, a posh neighborhood surprisingly full of low-rent crannies formerly occupied by servants. Ours lay at the bottom of a basement behind Harrods, and it offered everything a short-term tenant might require except windows. One morning an explosion shook the submarine gloom as if we had been hit by a depth charge. Two massive IRA bombs, packed with nails and bolts, had slaughtered four soldiers of the Blues and Royals at Hyde Park and seven bandsmen of the Royal Green Jackets at Regent's Park.

That evening during dinner, Mom phoned from Maryland. I thought she was worried the IRA bombs had hit us. As was her habit whenever there was terrible news to deliver, she asked, "Are you sitting down?"

"No."

"Maybe you'd better."

I stayed standing.

"Tommy has cancer," she said. "The bad kind."

Is there a good kind, I wondered, and sat down.

"He was trimming a tree in the yard," she went on, "and felt a sharp pain between his shoulder blades. The doctors checked him and found a tumor. It's already spread."

"How long do they give him?"

"Not long."

"Is he there? Is he sober? Can I talk to him?"

"Of course he's sober," she scolded me. "He's been on the wagon almost a year."

"I didn't know that."

"How could you—over there in Europe."

"Please let me speak to Dad."

When she handed over the receiver, he was halfway through a sentence, "—and I swear to Christ I'll fight this thing and beat it."

"Of course you will." To my own ears the words sounded hollow of hope.

"You bet your ass I won't throw in the towel."

I broke into tears. I tried to stifle my sobs, in part not to upset Tommy, in part because it seemed hypocritical to cry now when I had so often wished him dead. I told him that he was a lion-hearted fighter, when in fact I had never seen him fight anyone except Mom, the pair of them drunk and brawling in the living room.

Mom came back on the line. "I have my hands full here, Mike. He can barely walk and I don't have the strength to carry him."

I asked if she had contacted Karen and my brothers. She snapped, "They have jobs. They can't help me."

I promised I'd fly home rather than to the next tournament. Linda and the boys would stay with her parents in Pittsburgh.

Providentially Pat Conroy passed through London before we left. He was escorting his three teenage daughters—Jessica, Melissa, and Megan—on what he facetiously referred to as The Grand Tour. While the girls were as effervescent as the carbonated drinks they carried with them everywhere, Pat confessed to being frazzled. Before they caught the boat train from Paris, he had had to fight off a pickpocket at the Gare du Nord, and during the tussle the pocket of his khaki pants had been ripped. He wore the torn trousers like a badge of honor. Now, in addition to a needle and thread, he said, he needed—he was absolutely famished for—grown-up conversation.

While in England he planned to visit the set of *The Lords of Discipline*, currently being shot as a feature film at a British boarding school. "The fucking Citadel refused them permission to make the movie on campus. They claimed my novel slandered the college and cast it into disrepute—as if the shithole didn't deserve its reputation for racism and cruelty."

When he heard my stepfather was dying, Pat stayed in London several extra days, and while Linda and the kids went to Madame Tussauds wax museum, he and I walked in Hyde Park, to the site of the IRA bombing, still surrounded by crime scene tape. Pat asked about my earliest memories of Tommy Dunn.

"I remember him in his navy uniform," I said. "He bragged that he had been the boxing champ, lightweight division, of his unit. He laced gloves as big as pillows on my brother Pat and me and taught us to spar."

"Wait a minute. You've got a brother named Pat? You never told me that."

"Yeah, he's two years older. We were close as kids. But we didn't have a lot in common once we grew up. He's the type of guy, in high school he built a television out of a Heathkit. He joined the air force and became a computer expert."

"I'll be damned. Another Pat in your life. A pity you're not close to him."

"I love him. But he's tough to talk to. He doesn't show his feelings, and I'm never sure he understands when I tell him how I feel. He's not open like you."

"I'm the most falsely open person you'll ever meet," Pat said. "How old were you when Tommy got together with your mother?"

"About three. We lived in Anacostia, and he was based nearby at the Naval Receiving Station. He brought us steaks wrapped in butcher paper from the PX. A big treat back when meat was rationed."

"Where was your real father?"

"In the army. Mom sent him a Dear John letter."

"I used to pray my parents would get divorced," Pat said. "When, that is, I wasn't praying Dad's plane would crash. They didn't split up until it was too late to do me any good. But hell, from what I know from my own divorce, it doesn't make anybody happy. Was Tommy a mean drunk, like Dad? Or a funny one, like me."

"Basically he's good-natured. He'll have a few drinks and start singing. Have a few more and start dancing. But then he'll have one too many, and everything goes to hell."

"Oh, I know about going to hell," Pat said as we pushed on to Regent's Park, where the seven Royal Green Jackets had died. "I've been there myself. It scares me I'll end up like Dad—a drunken wife- and child-beater. You say Tommy never hit you. Were you ever tempted to hit him?"

"All the time. Actually I did slug him when I was little. He was giving me a bath and . . . I don't know why, I just balled up my fist and punched him."

"Jesus, if I did that, Dad would have torn me a brand-new asshole."

"I was a kid. Tommy probably thought I was joking."

"That wouldn't have mattered to Dad. He loved any excuse to punch my lights out."

"That's where Tommy was different. By the time I was in my teens, I was taller than him and weighed more. One night when he and Mom were slapping each other around, I pushed him and he fell down. He wasn't hurt, just insulted. 'I don't deserve that,' he said, 'I used to change your dirty diapers.'"

"Jesus," Pat repeated.

I told him that Tommy sometimes drove home drunk after tending bar at the BOQ and passed out at the wheel of his car, slumped against the horn. My brother and I had to go and shake him from his stupor before the neighbors complained.

I opened up to Pat as I had to no one else in my life except Linda. It was such a relief I rattled on and on, describing the night before I left to meet my pregnant girlfriend in Los Angeles. As I was packing, Tommy blundered into my bedroom to wish me goodbye and good luck. He had the shakes and steadied his head against my chest. He believed there were bugs on his arms and legs, crawling on his skin and inside him.

"What did you do?" Pat asked.

"I held him. His sweat smelled like Scotch whiskey, his hair like cigarette smoke. Then I walked him into the family room and eased him down in front of the television. There was a pre-season NFL game on TV, and he lost track of me and I tiptoed out of the room."

I never adequately thanked Pat for hanging around London and letting me talk. It wouldn't be the last time he appeared at precisely the right moment and proved that I could count on him. Later he wrote that most men of our generation were "lock-jawed . . . [and] lacked a specific language to communicate in the deepest places those hardest of things." Instead, they tended to trade insults and obscenities. But that wasn't our way. Pat and I never lacked the words to communicate.

BY THE TIME I REACHED my parents' house, my stepfather had endured several bouts of chemotherapy and been released from the hospital. Doctors said there was nothing more they could do. The tumor had metastasized to his brain. His speech was slurred and he shambled around as he did during drunken benders.

Mom asked me to help edit the obituary she had prepared for *The Washington Post*. I feared Tommy could hear us from where he lay in the bedroom. Perhaps at that point he was beyond caring and it didn't matter that she spoke as if he were already dead. Still, I was relieved when she sent me out to fetch fast food for dinner. She insisted that when Tommy retired she retired too and never cooked again. For years they ate nothing except carry-out from Arby's, McDonald's, and Pizza Hut. I brought home greasy bags of burgers and fried chicken, but Tommy couldn't force anything down.

Much as he protested that he'd rather die at home, he was hospitalized again, and that's where we said goodbye. As he wavered between drowsy consciousness and drugged sleep, nurses tended the wires that attached him to monitors. Periodically Tommy murmured names I didn't recognize. He had had a first wife and family in Cincinnati, Ohio, and maybe he was calling out to them.

When I asked in a whisper whether there was anything I could do for him, he told me to switch on the TV. As fate would have it, a pre-season NFL game was in progress, just as there had been eighteen years earlier, the night he shook with the DTs. Before I left him for the last time, I pressed my lips to his papery dry forehead and mumbled that I loved him. To my astonishment he replied, "I love you too. I'm not your father, but I always considered you my son."

I HAD BEEN BACK IN Rome a week when Mom phoned with news of his death. She said it made no sense to return for the funeral. In any event, I couldn't have afforded another transatlantic flight. But she pleaded with me to have a Mass said for Tommy. She figured that a church near the Vatican would offer greater remission for his sins.

The pastor at Santa Susanna, who had baptized Marco, agreed to dedicate the 10:10 a.m. Mass on September 27, 1982, to the repose of my stepfather's soul. The church was nearly empty. Linda, Sean, Marco, and I had the front pew to ourselves. This was what came of having nothing but non-believers for friends, I thought. I felt like apologizing to the priest. But then, to my everlasting gratitude, Pat and Lenore, along with Megan, Greg, Emily, and baby Susannah, slid into the pew beside us, and together members of the Mewshaw, Conroy, and Fleischer families launched Tommy Dunn into eternity.

5 Linda and I moved that fall from the apartment on Via Carini to one on Via Maurizio Quadrio, three blocks away. The new place, a fifth-floor *attico*, had two large terraces and plenty of space for Sean to play with his action figures and for Marco to pedal his Big Wheel across the red tiles. I watered the potted oleanders, dwarf palm, and orange tree each evening as the sky turned the color of an intoxicating negroni. The rooftop garden's largest urn contained an agave plant as lethal as a clutch of swords, and for fear the boys would impale themselves, I barricaded it behind wrought iron chairs.

On October 10, Palestinians attacked Rome's synagogue while worshippers emerged after services. Lobbing hand grenades and spraying machine gun fire, they killed a young toddler and wounded thirty-seven others. Susan Levenstein, an American physician who lived on Via del Tempio, witnessed the carnage and dialed the emergency number to report the attack. Then she rushed out and treated the injured until ambulances arrived. Impressed by Dr. Levenstein's courage and professional sangfroid, Pat named the psychiatrist in *The Prince of Tides* Susan Lowenstein.

On the same day as the synagogue attack, a bomb exploded outside the Syrian Embassy. It caused no casualties, and as far as

I observed, no great consternation. The U.S. Embassy issued no color-coded alerts, and there was no noticeable diminishment in the numbers of visitors in Rome who contacted us for tips about restaurants and black market currency exchanges.

AMONG THE NEWCOMERS WAS ANDY KARSCH, a former quarterback of the Brandeis University football team. He never expected this to impress anybody, but it had prompted an invitation from the Kennedy clan to compete in their touch football games. In turn, this led Ted Kennedy to make Andy the Issues and Media Director of his 1980 U.S. presidential campaign. When Kennedy lost the Democratic nomination, Karsch returned to his first love, filmmaking. A friend gave Karsch our number, and he explained that he was in town to produce an independent feature, *Stars Over the City*, based on a script he co-wrote. He begged for help with everything from laundry to his love life. The latter he hardly needed. He soon wound up with a woman married to a member of the black nobility.

I introduced him to Pat Conroy, and the two of them eventually joined forces with Barbra Streisand to put together a film of *The Prince of Tides* that won them Academy Award nominations. Meanwhile Andy introduced the Conroys to Susanna Styron, the daughter of William Styron, the bestselling author of *The Confessions of Nat Turner* and *Sophie's Choice*. As the script supervisor on Andy's film, Susanna lived in a group apartment with the rest of the production team. But when the lease expired before the movie wrapped, she had to scramble for temporary accommodations and bestowed herself upon Pat and Lenore and their four kids in the flat on Via dei Foraggi. In those days, that's how things rolled in Rome; one thing seamlessly connected with another.

When Susanna's parents checked into the Hassler Hotel, the

Conroys invited them over for drinks. To ensure that he had the right liquor on hand, Pat asked Susanna what her father liked. "Scotch," she said. "And lots of it."

The next night Linda and I gave a dinner party for the Styrons, Conroys, and Gellers. It was 1982, the pinnacle of William Styron's career. The movie of *Sophie's Choice* had premiered earlier that year and raised his public profile, which had been high with bookish people since the publication of his first novel, *Lie Down in Darkness*, in 1951. Norman Mailer, seldom generous to his contemporaries, had written ". . . one felt a kind of awe about Styron. He gave promise of becoming a great writer, great not like Hemingway nor even like Faulkner whom he resembled a bit, but perhaps like Hawthorne. And there were minor echoes of Fitzgerald and Malcolm Lowry."

A Southerner from Newport News, Virginia, now displaced to rural Roxbury, Connecticut, Styron was the kind of writer Pat Conroy longed to be and would in many respects become, even down to the demons the two men battled. But there was no thought of demons that night as Bill arrived at our apartment in a pink-and-white-striped shirt open at his fleshy, sunburned neck. His wife, Rose, wore an outfit by the Italian designer Krizia. Deeply tanned and attractive, she was outgoing, unlike her husband, who held back a bit in shyness or instinctive reserve.

Despite his reputation for aloofness, Styron had been a warm supporter of mine since we met in the mid-1960s, when I was a graduate student at the University of Virginia. He had warned me straight off that he loathed academics, and it didn't help that I intended to do my PhD dissertation on him. But he forgave me when he learned that I also wrote fiction.

He promised to read the manuscript of my first novel as soon as he finished the final revisions on *The Confessions of Nat Turner*.

Not only did he read this manifestly unpublishable manuscript, he drafted a four-page letter identifying its few merits and its myriad flaws. While he recommended that I shelve the book, he added, "The important thing to me is that you are a writer, with all the fine potential that that simple word implies. Just as important is the fact that you are still very young (24), and have so much opportunity to do the big thing in the fullness of time . . . I would not have gone on at such length about your work if I did not have faith in what will come to you in the future."

Even back then when I was ignorant of so much, I recognized I had experienced a miraculous rite of passage. I clung to his encouragement, and whenever I reread Styron's letter I recalled not just the morale boost it gave me, but what it revealed about him—his kindness, his collegiality, his willingness to assume an obligation to a neophyte for no better motive than that we both, though vastly different in talent, temperament, and accomplishment, were committed to writing.

If all Bill had ever done for me was write an encouraging letter, I'd be deeply in his debt. But he also nominated me for a Fulbright fellowship to France where, while visiting Paris, he treated me to lunch at La Coupole and taught me how to winkle garlic-drenched snails out of their shells. He introduced me to James Jones, who in turn introduced me to Carlos Fuentes, and all that combined to introduce me to a larger world than I had ever imagined.

Later, when I taught at the University of Texas, he had read to the student body from an early draft of *Sophie's Choice* and he brought Willie Morris along for the ride. Linda and I held a reception at our house in the Hill Country, and I doubt the guest list has ever been equaled in Austin for its literary star power and sheer diversity. Molly Ivins, Ronnie Dugger, William Broyles, James Fallows, William Wittliff, Bud Shrake, David Wevill, and Zulfikar

Ghose were all there struggling to be heard over the nasal twang of country and western singer Jerry Jeff Walker, who regaled us with countless choruses of "Up Against the Wall Redneck Mother"— until finally Styron shouted for him to shut up.

THOUGH NOT AS RAUCOUS AS the party in Texas, the dinner in Rome had its moments. As he hammered back refills of Scotch, Bill said that he used to be a bourbon drinker, but a doctor had persuaded him that Scotch had fewer calories and was healthier. I doubted that anything, even Holy Water, was healthy when consumed in such quantities. But as he topped up his glass with Johnnie Walker Black, Styron swore that he was a teetotaler compared to Gore Vidal. "The guy's killing himself with alcohol."

He and Rose had visited Vidal in Ravello at his sumptuous villa, La Rondinaia. For the Styrons it was a sentimental journey. In the '50s they had settled as newlyweds on the Amalfi Coast while Bill completed *Set This House on Fire*. "No young novelist could afford to live there now," Styron said. "The upkeep on Gore's place must be a fortune. But of course fags don't have kids to support and send to college."

Steve Geller was eager to discuss the script of *Sophie's Choice* and what he judged to be Sydney Pollack's slick and predictable direction. But Pat changed the subject to the Marines. Styron, who had served two tours of duty in the Corps, had no qualms about stepping out of the spotlight, and Pat seized it, segueing from tales about the Great Santini to accounts of his hilarious humiliations as a young writer. After self-publishing his first book, *The Boo*, and paying the printer with funds he borrowed from a local bank, he found an agent, Julian Bach, for his second book, *The Water Is Wide*. When Bach called with the happy news that Houghton Mifflin wanted to publish it, Conroy was nervous about the financial arrangements. "How much?" he asked.

"Seventy-five hundred dollars," Bach told him.

"My stomach dropped," Pat said. "I really wanted to be published by a famous Boston house. But I couldn't afford to pay that much, and I didn't believe any bank in South Carolina would lend me the money. Julian had to explain that Houghton Mifflin meant to pay *me*."

The table exploded in peals of laughter. Heartened, Pat pushed on and spoke about James Dickey, whose creative writing course he had audited at the University of South Carolina. A celebrated poet and author of the bestselling novel *Deliverance*, Dickey, as Pat characterized him, was a towering egotist, a nasty drunk, and a notorious womanizer. "He was the living embodiment of everything I didn't want to become—a classroom pasha with a harem of worshipful grad students. I swore to myself—"

"Mike, tell them about the time Dickey came to UVA," Linda interrupted.

"Let Pat finish," I said. "Anyway, it's your story. You should tell it."

"No, you," she insisted.

"Stop teasing us and tell it," Bill Styron demanded.

"This was before we were married," I explained. "Dickey tooled into Charlottesville in an XKE Jag convertible and gave a reading to about a thousand cheering students. But in the middle of 'The Sheep Child' he paused to register his disappointment at the paltriness of the crowd. He paused again during 'Cherry Log Road' and sang out in praise of himself, 'Goddamn, I forgot how good this poem is. It deserves to be heard by everybody at the University, not just a handful.'

"Afterward a group of faculty and grad students gathered at the

Colonnade Club to be introduced to the great man. Dickey didn't pay me a damn bit of attention. With a highball glass in his hand and a leer on his face, he leaned cozy close to Linda, and said in a voice loud enough to be audible to everybody in the room, 'Honey, why don't me and you go back to my motel.'

"Linda, God love her, tried to paraphrase that famous line from Paul Newman. Whenever anyone suggested he was unfaithful to Joanne Woodward, Newman supposedly said, 'Why would I go out for hamburger when I have steak at home?' But Linda gave her putdown a sweeter spin. 'Why would I go out for a Hershey bar when I have *mousse au chocolat* at home?'

"In a perfect demonstration of why you play word games with poets at your peril, Dickey shot back, 'At least a Hershey bar's hard and has nuts.'"

Pat choked so hard with laughter, Lenore had to administer the Heimlich maneuver. That ended the party, and as Bill and I waited on the terrace, peering down at Via Maurizio Quadrio for the taxi that would sweep him and Rose back to the Hassler, he said, "I haven't been up this late or laughed this hard since I was a sophomore in college."

SEVERAL YEARS LATER I WAS on the tennis court at the American Academy when Francine du Plessix Gray leaned out of the window of her studio. "Did you hear about Bill Styron?" she shouted. "He had a mental breakdown. Doctors don't expect him to recover."

Although he survived that first onslaught of clinical depression, he suffered a number of relapses and was never the same writer again. He did, however, produce *Darkness Visible*, a brief memoir about his descent into madness. Each sentence as finely

wrought as hammered silver, the book was candid about his obses-
sion with suicide. The theme of self-destruction had been a constant in his work. Now it became apparent how pervasive it was in
his personal life.

Yet *Darkness Visible* skated over an issue that struck me as
central to Styron's career and to his illness. Like many American
authors—Faulkner, Hemingway, Fitzgerald, Sinclair Lewis, Stein-
beck, Eugene O'Neill, Tennessee Williams, and Gore Vidal—
Bill was, by any reasonable definition, an alcoholic. Whether
he drank because he was depressed or was depressed because he
drank amounted to a distinction without a difference. The sad
truth was that liquor accelerated his professional and emotional
deterioration—a fact which his memoir didn't acknowledge. In
the last twenty-seven years of his life he never published another
novel. But he left behind a mash-up of manuscript pages for *The
Way of the Warrior*, a futile effort to create a convincing portrait of
an intelligent, deeply cultured Marine Corps officer.

After Bill's death in 2006, his youngest child, Alexandra,
published an article in *The New Yorker* that later became a full-
length book, *Reading My Father*. The memoir depicts Bill as
cruelly indifferent, when not downright despicable. Before his
crack-up in 1985, she writes, he was already a "petty despot," a
man of "cloven-footed madness" who terrorized his children and
tormented his wife. Although he didn't physically assault them,
like the Great Santini, he verbally upbraided them, and erupted
into rages that frightened the whole family. At Christmas one
year he dragged all the gift-wrapping paper onto the front lawn
and set it ablaze, bellowing, "Who *are* you people?"

His studio behind the main house in Roxbury was strictly
off-limits to the kids. He worked late and often woke past noon,
badly hungover and belligerent. Rose took refuge in writing po-

etry and traveling. With his wife gone, Styron sometimes moved his mistress, whoever she happened to be at the moment, into his home with the kids. Alexandra relates an incident when as a baby she fell down the basement stairs and lay there bleeding because her sisters and brother were too scared to wake their father from his sacrosanct nap.

In the loftier echelons of bourgeois bohemia, authors have always been granted privileges. For a male novelist of Styron's stature, a certain amount of philandering was predictable. Yet even by the most permissive standard, he went overboard. He once propositioned Kaylie Jones, thirty-five years his junior and the daughter of Bill's deceased friend, James Jones.

"My father would turn over in his grave," Kaylie told him.

"Let him turn," Bill said.

When I interviewed Alexandra Styron about her memoir, she said she had forgiven her father and had no interest in judging him. The process of writing had proved cathartic. When I spoke to her mother, however, Rose laughed and declined to say whether the book had brought her closure.

This called to mind that long-ago dinner party in Rome with the Styrons, the Gellers, and the Conroys. I have recorded what the writers at the table said. I can't remember much of what the women contributed, perhaps because they mostly stayed silent. They listened, they smiled, they laughed as the men performed and preened. Even Linda had deferred to me when it came to telling what was, after all, her story about James Dickey.

I wonder whether Pat Conroy ever reflected on that evening. He yearned to become a literary figure like William Styron, and he did so, it occurs to me, in ways he never would have imagined.

6 Writers constantly pitched up in Rome, some on their way to Africa or the Middle East, others for an extended stay. I was always on the lookout for ones who might be good company, and better yet, tennis partners. Mark Helprin was no tennis player, but he arrived in the autumn of 1982 as the Prix de Rome winner at the American Academy, the esteemed author of two collections of short stories, most of which had appeared in *The New Yorker*, and a critically acclaimed first novel, *Refiner's Fire*. He seemed poised to become seriously famous and rich. The rights to his new novel, *Winter's Tale*, had sold at auction to Harcourt Brace Jovanovich for a quarter of a million dollars, then a remarkable sum for serious literature.

At the Academy where ego gridlock exerted a perennial grip, it wasn't rare for a fellow to stand out by refusing to fit in. But Mark Helprin was in a category all his own. Disparaging the place as "a shallow think tank," he kept a calculated distance from that year's crop of university professors, painters, composers, and architects. A political and social maverick, Helprin was an outspoken conservative and supporter of Israel. He claimed to have served in the Israeli Army and Air Force, and for good measure, in the British Merchant Marines. Because he was only thirty-five and had done a stint at Harvard graduate school, then Oxford, it was a puzzle how he had crammed so much writing, serious study, and military service into such a short period. During the '96 U.S. presidential campaign, he would go on to draft speeches for Republican candidate Robert Dole and editorials for *The Wall Street Journal*. Later still, he was made a member of the Council on Foreign Relations.

While this might suggest a policy wonk in a pinstriped suit, Mark favored North Face outdoor wear and climbing boots with cleated soles. Physically he resembled the rightwing commentator George Will—a resemblance enhanced by Mark's neatly parted hair. But in personality he wasn't the buttoned-down type. He showed off his mountaineering skill by clambering over the American Academy's tall iron gate rather than strolling through it. At the Christmas pageant for children, he played the Wicked Witch of the North and rappelled off the roof to stalk Santa, in the person of architect James Sterling, with Poet Laureate Mark Strand in the guise of Mrs. Claus.

Apart from this theatrical foray, Helprin and his wife, Lisa, a lovely Jackie Kennedy lookalike, mostly sequestered themselves in the writer's studio, a cottage barnacled to the Aurelian Wall. There, they cooked meals on a hibachi, and Mark corrected the galleys of *Winter's Tale* and did pull-ups on an overhead beam. He told me he detested parties, the smell of coffee, the taste of liquor, and the vileness of literary logrolling. When I suggested introducing him to Gore Vidal, he gave an emphatic no. He loathed Vidal's position on Israel and his sexual politics.

Still, we got along amicably, and I viewed him as a superb comic character, a bit like Evelyn Waugh whose curmudgeonliness contrasted with his regal writing style. I regarded Helprin's work, at its best, as beautifully fine-grained, and at worst as overstuffed as a

Thanksgiving goose. *Winter's Tale* followed the furrow first plowed by South American magical realists; its New York City setting was full of flying horses and a bridge built of light beams. What he made of my writing he never divulged, which was fine by me.

Along with the Conroys, we ate out with the Helprins at La Tana de Noantri in Trastevere, a trattoria around the corner from the Pasquino, the city's lone English-language movie theater. La Tana was a cheap treat which, we didn't learn until much later, the Conroys hated. Yet they loyally remained silent, mindful of our budget.

Pat and Mark had the same agent, Julian Bach, and the evening began with lit biz chat. But then the Gellers joined us, and something about eight people jammed around a table for six changed the dynamic. Steve Geller had recently started writing a satirical column, Disaster Agent, for *National Lampoon* that skewered the film industry and publishing pretensions. Now, as if trial-ballooning material for future columns, he unspooled hilarious vignettes, which Pat tried to top. Then I tried to top them both.

"You think that's bad?" all the stories started. "You think you came out of that book contract or that movie deal with egg on your face and shit on your shoes? Well, listen to this one."

But Mark Helprin didn't catch our drift. After Pat portrayed himself as Li'l Abner lost in a world of his betters and Steve Geller described walking down Hollywood Boulevard beside Daryl Hannah looking like a hairy spider in danger of being stepped on by a stiletto heel, Helprin boasted about his exploits during the Six-Day War. Self-deprecation wasn't Mark's mode.

"Wait a second," Pat said. "Weren't you still at Harvard in 1967?"

"The war lasted from June fifth to June the tenth. Harvard was on summer break. I hopped the first available flight."

"Were commercial airlines flying to Israel?" Steve asked.

"I flew to Cyprus, then caught a ferry to Haifa."

"So by the time you got there, it must have been . . . what? A four- or five-day war?" Pat teased him.

Mark sprang to his feet in a karate stance. To demonstrate his military expertise, he executed several close-quarter combat moves he had mastered in the Israeli Army. "The same principle applies whether it's a man with a knife or a vicious dog that attacks you. Take the first strike on the fleshy part of your arm. Then once the blade or the dog's teeth are firmly embedded in your muscle, rip out his throat with your free hand."

"Goddamn, Mark," Pat exclaimed, "I wish I had known this back when Dad was walloping me."

"Sit down, Mark," Lisa begged her husband. "Your pizza's getting cold."

THE DAY I FRETTED TO Pat about my mother flying to Rome for the Christmas holidays, he recommended, "Take it on the fleshy part of your arm. I survived Peggy's visit. You'll survive this."

I wasn't convinced. Mom hadn't seen us since Sean's birth in Texas eight years ago. She had never met Marco. That was her choice, but somehow she had shifted the guilt onto me. True, I felt sorry for her. Was that the same as loving her? After telling me by telephone about her visit, she posed what struck me as a trick question. "Did I ever beat you when you were a little boy?"

"Why do you ask?"

"Something your sister said set me wondering."

"What did Karen say?"

"She said I used to slap the shit out of you and her."

Was she coming to Rome to apologize? "Karen's right," I told her.

"Strange," Mom said. "I don't have any memory of that."

•

SHE LANDED AT FIUMICINO ON a dank December morn-
ing, worn to a nub by the overnight flight. Although her marriage
had always teetered on the brink of mayhem and murder, she and
Tommy had been completely co-dependent. Now she was alone for
the first time in her life.

Dressed in lace-up shoes and a quilted beige parka that she
might have bought at a charity shop, she resembled those women
with cardboard suitcases and dazed expressions who traveled by
bus from Poland, intent on receiving Pope John Paul's blessing before they died. Her hair was dyed in a frowsy Eastern European
fashion, shiny black as patent leather.

As I stepped forward to kiss her, she drew back. "What are you
doing to your hair?" she demanded.

"Nothing."

"Well, then, do something. White as it is, you look like an old
man. People'll think I'm a hundred."

The VW Derby, by now dented and rusty, offended her almost
as much as my hair. "Is this jalopy safe?" When we stalled in traffic
on the bleak ring road around Rome, she muttered, "I might as
well be at the Baltimore airport."

To defend the city, I detoured onto the Aurelia Antica, a
scenic route past beautiful villas swagged with geraniums and
bougainvillea.

"What do you call those trees?" she asked.

"Umbrella pines."

"You're kidding," she said scornfully.

"Call them whatever you like." It shamed me to sound so hostile. Mom looked like a broken doll, no longer the monster who
had bitch-slapped me from childhood into adulthood. Softening, I

pointed to the Villa Doria Pamphili park, where Sean and Marco played.

"It's pretty," she agreed. "But I don't know where I am. I look at this place and I look at you and I can't figure out who you are."

In the succeeding days I did my best to prove who I am. Pat did his best too, putting on a full-court press of Southern charm. At dinner on Via dei Foraggi, he showered her with affection and praised me as a fellow novelist and friend. "I love your boy's behind"—he pronounced it *bee*-hind.

"You sound like a homo," Mom said.

"I probably am one. But I promise not to lay a finger on your son. I just want you to know he's a special guy."

"Of course he is. I raised him the same way I raised all my kids."

"I bet you raised them by hand." Pat made a slapping motion.

"What if I did? It's none of your business."

Unaccustomed to anyone he couldn't win over, Pat was an impeccable host, steering Mom to the most comfortable chair in the warmest corner and topping her glass up with wine. It amused him that she behaved just as I had described her. Unlike his mother, who gloved her talons in velvet for my benefit, Mom kept her claws out.

ON THE DRIVE HOME THAT night, Mom squeezed into the backseat with Sean and Marco. Rust had pocked small holes in the rear floorboard, and while the boys tranced in on the road zipping past beneath them, she said, "That baby Susannah is a living doll. Too bad she'll grow up to look like her father. What does Lenore see in him?"

I struggled to stay calm. At least to sound calm. "You mean

other than the fact that he's smart and generous and funny and a famous writer?"

"He's a big bullshit artist, if you ask me."

Before I could bark, Nobody's asking you, Linda spoke up. "He had a terrible childhood."

"That's what everybody says."

"So you've read what he went through with his father?" Linda asked.

"Not a word. It's just everybody these days claims they had it awful as a kid. You wait—Sean and Marc will grow up and complain about riding around in this rattletrap."

WE GOT MOM TOGETHER WITH the Helprins, the Gellers, and Harry Antrim, a professor from my grad school days at UVA, who was honeymooning with Mary Volcansek, a political science professor whose specialty was Italian law. Mom cheerfully predicted marital disaster for all three couples. What she made of my marriage she revealed obliquely by sympathizing with Linda. "I bet you had a nice break while he was off watching tennis."

As for her estimation of my parenting, I anticipated that she'd find me too lenient. Instead, she admonished me for being too strict on the boys. When Marc knocked over a candle and set fire to the tablecloth, and Sean spilled a bowl of *bucatini all'amatriciana* on the carpet, she wouldn't hear of my punishing them.

In theory, the heat in our apartment functioned eight hours a day—four in the morning, four at night. In reality, the radiators remained cold around the clock. Mom kept her quilted parka on indoors, wisecracking, "This is like camping out." Yet she volunteered to sleep on a glassed-in porch that had previously been a greenhouse. "If it was good enough to keep plants alive, I guess I'll survive," she said, as though we had sentenced her to the bed she chose for herself.

One morning, Sean left a note, printed in block letters and spelled out phonetically, informing us he was sick of scrambled eggs for breakfast and was running away from home. Convinced he had to be somewhere in the apartment, Linda and I didn't panic. We prowled around, cajoling him to quit hiding. When coaxing didn't work, I bellowed as I imagine the Great Santini would have. That proved futile, and Linda started sobbing, which upset Marco, who started crying too. Tears misted Mom's eyes. "I knew it. I just knew from the way you treated the boys, something bad would happen."

"Nothing's happened," I protested. "I'll find him."

Linda cuddled Marco, comforting him and at the same time herself. Rigid with worry, Mom prayed the rosary. When the phone rang, I feared it was the police or a hospital. It was Pat wanting to play tennis. When I told him Sean was missing, he blurted, "I'm on my way."

I threw on a coat and reached the street just as Pat thundered up Via Maurizio Quadrio in his BMW. He bumped over the curb and parked on the sidewalk, *all'italiana*, and together we patrolled the neighborhood block by block. I dreaded Sean had been flattened by speeding traffic. Or had some predator enticed him into a car? Unlike Mom who had warned me early and often about sex maniacs, I had never lectured Sean about child molesters.

"I was always running away," Pat reassured me. "I never got far."

We checked at the American Academy, where the *portiere* swore he hadn't seen Sean. So we retraced our steps up Via Giacomo Medici, a lover's lane affectionately known as Jack'em Off

Medici. Through an arch in the Aurelian Wall, cars sluiced down to Via Dandolo. At the age of eight, Sean was forbidden to cross streets alone. Had he sprinted past this death trap to Villa Sciarra and its merry-go-round?

On a wintry day, the gravel paths were deserted, a fountain gurgled into a marble basin like a leaky bath tap, and the calliope was mute. Pat spotted Sean on a bench next to a boxwood hedge that topiary artists had sculpted into triangles. He appeared sheepishly relieved to be rescued—so happy that I hesitated, unsure whether to hug him or spank him. While I dithered, Pat slid in beside him, joking and jostling him, warning him never ever to worry us like this again.

Persuaded that her prayers had been answered, Mom claimed full credit and granted Pat Conroy no gratitude. But I did. "I'll pay you back," I promised.

"Don't say that." Pat and I were out on the terrace, freezing our butts off while Sean was inside fussed over by his mother and grandmother. "Whenever somebody promises to repay me, I'm afraid I'll lose a friend."

"Are we talking about repaying a favor or cash?"

"Either one. I have this sick habit of throwing money around. To me a tightwad is the lowest life-form."

People in Rome had already hit him up for thousands of dollars. A mutual friend here borrowed $20,000 for a down payment on an apartment. In the States Pat reckoned he was owed roughly $800,000, none of which he expected to get back.

"Jesus, don't put me in that category, Pat. I'd never ask for money."

"If you need it, go ahead and ask. Just don't make a big deal about repaying me. Consider it a gift."

"You're nuts not to collect what people owe you."

"That's what Lenore says. But how's that supposed to work?"

"Hire a lawyer if you have to."

"And what? Sue my relatives? Sue my friends? I regard it as bread cast upon the water."

THAT NIGHT WHILE LINDA READ the boys a bedtime story, I stayed in the living room with Mom as wind blew out of the north, blustery enough to shake the Persian blinds. Curled up in her parka, feet tucked under her rump, she had her face set in the distant, distracted expression she assumed when praying. I tried to picture myself in her place, an exercise I had vainly attempted since childhood. What made her the way she was? What accounted for her alternating currents of anger and exhilaration, her saintliness and satanic temper?

She had been diagnosed as manic-depressive—the term "bi-polar" hadn't then been invented—and prescribed lithium. When she couldn't tolerate that drug, doctors suggested different ones, and her life devolved into a quest for the precise elixir whose side effects wouldn't make her more abrasive. Meanwhile, she prayed for her special intentions, which included the salvation of John F. Kennedy, Elvis Presley, and John Lennon.

As if reading my thoughts, she broke the silence. "I'm praying your next book will be a bestseller."

"Just pray that it'll get published."

"No. Before I die, I want to see your name on the bestseller list."

"I'm not that sort of novelist." Not that I didn't yearn to be better known and better remunerated.

"How come a lard-ass like Pat Conroy is famous and you're not?" she asked.

"Pat's my friend. We're not in competition. Look how quick he was to help today."

"Doesn't it gall you that a guy with a big gut and funny hair sells better than you do?"

"It's not a beauty contest. We're different kinds of writers."

"Well, I'm praying you become his kind and write a bestseller."

To change the subject, I told her I had managed to buy tickets to midnight Mass at St. Peter's. That was the best place and time, I pointed out, to pray for whatever her heart desired.

STEVE GELLER, NOMINALLY JEWISH, HARBORED his own notions of the divinity and invoked "the gods of laughter," whom he believed gummed up the gears of life and doled out random rewards. Shortly before New Year's, with Mom still in afterglow from crossing paths with Pope John Paul II at St. Peter's, I allowed myself the luxury of praying we might make it through the holidays with no lasting damage. Linda and I hired a babysitter and took Mom to Trastevere to meet friends. Avoiding the spider trap of twisting alleys, I parked at the foot of Via Garibaldi, and we followed a staircase down to Via della Frusta—Street of the Whip.

In the '80s, muggers and purse-snatchers marauded through this *rione*. To be on the safe side, Linda and Mom strapped their purses on bandolier-style, and the three of us linked arms and marched toward the restaurant like a phalanx of centurions on guard against barbarians.

The meal proved to be pleasantly uneventful, and afterward, because our friends were unfamiliar with the neighborhood, they asked me to walk them to a cab stand. Linda and Mom stayed behind, finishing the last of the wine, waiting for my return.

But I got delayed by a piece of guerrilla street theater. Even at that late hour, bums and winos, backpackers and guitar pluckers surrounded the fountain in Piazza di Santa Maria. When a Fiat careened into the square, it swerved so close, it almost ran over their feet. Then it swung around for a second ambuscade, and several of the backpackers and guitar pluckers pulled guns. Maybe they were plainclothes cops. Maybe thugs. Whatever they were, they chased away the deranged driver, and by the time I reached the restaurant, eager to describe what I had witnessed, Mom and Linda had set out on their own.

Hurrying to catch them, I intended to read Linda the riot act. She knew better than to roam around at this hour. Discarded syringes crunched underfoot as I scrambled up the steps to the car. The two women sat inside with the doors locked, looking shell-shocked. The knees of Linda's slacks and the elbows of her coat had been torn and she was bleeding badly. Mom groaned, cradling one arm to her chest.

"A man jumped us on Via della Frusta," Linda said.

"I thought he was going to rape us," Mom added.

"He grabbed my purse," Linda said, "and tried to rip it off my shoulder. He dragged me and I kicked him in the crotch until he let go and ran away. There's one guy who'll never have children." She did her best to pass it off as a joke.

"Why didn't you wait in the restaurant?"

"Don't blame your wife," Mom growled. "She saved me from getting raped."

I sped to Nuovo Regina Margherita Hospital, which was anything except *nuovo*. Built a thousand years ago as a monastery, its only "new" section was an emergency room constructed in the '60s and already so stenciled with graffiti it resembled an Egyptian tomb inscribed with hieroglyphics.

In the ER, I rang the bell at the admissions desk until a yawning fellow in a lettuce-green smock stumbled out of a back room. With no urgency, he ambled along a hallway, switching on lights. Mewling cats frisked around our feet.

In the radiology department, a well-nourished body occupied the x-ray table. It might have been a corpse laid out on a morgue slab. But the gent in the green smock nudged the guy awake and informed him there was a patient who appeared to have a broken arm. While Linda stepped behind a screen and had her cuts and abrasions treated, the radiologist instructed Mom, "*Spogliati*," adding in accented English, "Off the clothes."

"I'm not stripping for him," Mom said.

"Just take off your parka and roll up your sleeve." I spoke calmly, hoping to keep her from flying off the handle.

The radiologist urged her to hold her arm motionless under the x-ray machine. He was picking up what he believed was a previous break. Had *la bella nonna* fractured her wrist before, he inquired through me?

"This guy's a quack," Mom said. "Get me out of this dump."

The radiologist suggested I bring Mom back tomorrow when she was less agitated. By now the other doctor had dressed Linda's raw elbows and knees. I requested the bill, but there was no charge. National health covered everything.

"It's free," Mom sniffed, "and that's what it's worth. Nothing!"

THE DURATION OF THE HOLIDAYS passed for her in what must have been a delirium of pain. Her wrist ballooned to the size of a purple eggplant. But she wouldn't hear of getting a second opinion from our family physician, Susan Levenstein. Linda contrived a sling out of a scarf, and Mom wore it like a ceremonial sash and sang the praises of her daughter-in-law, whom she continued to brag had saved her from sexual assault.

The moment Mom landed in Maryland, my sister Karen drove

her to a doctor, who determined that she had suffered a compound fracture. Fortunately, she didn't hold me personally responsible for her medical treatment at Regina Margherita. She wrote that she regarded the entire episode as a great adventure. Second only to Pope John Paul at midnight Mass, the mugging had been the high point of the trip.

ON A GREY JANUARY DAY, Pat and I met at his apartment for a postmortem. The view of the Forum from his office provided a fitting backdrop. I felt that Mom lay shattered at my feet like a frieze that had fallen from an immense height. As I fumbled to pick up the pieces, I told Pat, "I noticed so many things I hadn't noticed before. Things about Mom I see in myself. Things I doubt I can change. I thought all I had to do was leave America and I'd never be like my family.

"Did you notice Mom didn't travel with a camera?" I asked. "Everybody brings a camera to Italy. Not my mother. She's like the players on the tennis tour, totally uninterested in what's around her. Then it hit me: I never travel with a camera either."

"Your medium is words," Pat said. "Not pictures. You're nothing like your mother. But me, I'm terrified of turning into Dad— the kind of guy who carpet-bombs a country with napalm and never feels a twinge of conscience."

He pushed out of his chair and fetched his journal, a new one. Flipping to *1 Gennaio*, he invited me to read his resolutions for 1983:

Finish [*The Prince of Tides*] to my satisfaction.
Take copious notes for a non-fiction work—a collection of
    essays.

Finish that short, troublesome piece for *Destinations* [*Magazine*] and try to discover the root cause of why I cannot hammer out a simple journalistic piece.

Work hard on writing every single day. Let nothing get in your way. I will be 38 this year: remember that Thomas Wolfe died at 38.

Become a better and a content husband and father.

Do not neglect the spiritual side of life.

Exercise often. Try to become a competent, patient tennis player.

Study the techniques of fiction: Have more patience with experimentation.

Write from the heart, not the gut, not the head.

Become a better and more generous friend.

Deepen everything, concentrate. Keep this journal.

Learn to relax. To appreciate silence and solitude.

Try to use my disadvantages as a writer—make them strengths.

Do not be afraid to write everything down.

Believe in myself as a writer. Believe deeply.

I am young no longer. I am now writing the books I was meant to write. I'm not preparing for any future books. These are the ones I was born to write. Make them wonderful.

After four books, three of them made into successful movies, Pat still struggled to believe in himself, still struggled to become a better son, father, husband, and friend. He sounded like nothing so much as the altar boy he used to be. Yet obscenity came to his mind as quickly as Latin responses. "Compared to your mother," he told me, "the Great Santini's a pussy."

By the time I met Pat's father, Don Conroy had retired from the Marine Corps and was greatly reduced by age and ailments. He wore his white hair in a buzz cut whose sparse bristles sprouted from a freckled scalp, and he had grown a beard, perhaps in the misconception that it made him look rakish. In fact it gave him the appearance of a half-plucked rooster. He limped and carried a cane, and his shoulders sagged like a circus bear that's been flogged into submission.

Where my mother had a vicious mouth, Pat's father was the soul of affability, not just with his grandchildren and step-grandkids, but with Lenore and whoever else passed through the kitchen, where he held court at the Conroy apartment. With me he gabbed about basketball. "Pat tells me you could dunk," Don said.

"Pat exaggerates."

"No shit, Sherlock! Have you read his books?"

In Don Conroy's telling, his oldest son wrote fiction. Pure and simple. The portrait of his father as a child and wife abuser was a lie. Impure and simple. But the dispute between them had somehow evolved from an Oedipal argument into a burlesque routine. Don festooned his car with a Great Santini vanity plate, and the two of them traveled together on book tours, each signing copies and proclaiming competing versions of life in the Conroy household.

In Rome, whenever one of his children or stepchildren was within earshot of his father, Pat declared, "Here's the man I warned you about. The monster who almost murdered me."

The kids laughed and Don laughed along with them. I had no reason not to believe Pat, but there was something baffling about these claims. Pat didn't appear to be any more upset by Don's denials than Don was by his son's condemnations. How could the two of them charge each other with psychopathic behavior, then continue chumming around together? My best guess was that Pat kept Don Conroy in his life as a reminder of his unspeakable childhood suffering and to give the Great Santini a chance to redeem himself. Or was it a darker impulse, the cruelest kind of revenge? Maybe Pat embraced his abuser as he would a defanged, declawed pet, now forced to dance to whatever tune he piped?

7 Millions remember my fortieth birthday on February 19, 1983. This isn't egomania. Thanks to Pat Conroy, who re-created the occasion in his novel *Beach Music*, readers around the world probably retain a more vivid image of the evening than those actually there.

The party took place in our dowdy apartment where we served chips and dips, pizza slices, and jugs of red and white wine. Linda had baked a cake enormous enough to feed a flock of guests, which included fellows from the American Academy, diplomats from the American and Irish embassies, a number of my tennis partners, and a CIA operative, Freckie Vreeland, who, despite his pedigree as *Vogue* editor Diana Vreeland's son, displayed absolute indifference to style with his ghastly yellow-and-green-check sport jacket.

In those days, Pat Conroy had the bad habit of grousing, "I'm tired of being the most interesting person in the room." But that night he could relax; the place teemed with fascinating people. Donald Stewart, the editor of *Playboy International*, attended with his wife, Luisa Gilardenghi, a former *Vogue* cover girl. Mickey Knox, popularly known as the Mayor of Rome, put in an appearance and discovered he was a distant relative of Lenore Conroy. The two of them had been raised in Brooklyn as Red Diaper babies—in different generations, Lenore stressed. Blacklisted from Hollywood, Mickey had cobbled together a career as a dialogue coach, script translator, and dubber of Italian films into English. Never one to arrive at a party emptyhanded, he dragged along actors Eli Wallach and Anne Jackson.

Center stage, however, belonged to Gore Vidal, who stationed himself at the liquor table and let constellations of admirers revolve around him. In his habitual uniform of grey flannel trousers and blue blazer, he looked like the silver-haired U.S. senator he had hoped to become. After losing the 1982 California Democratic primary, he declared his political aspirations dead.

Vidal and Conroy shared more in common than either man was aware. Born in the base hospital at West Point, Gore was a military brat par excellence. His father, a legendary athlete, had played football and basketball at the U.S. Military Academy, competed in the 1920 Olympics, and excelled as an army pilot. He later coached football at West Point before resigning for a position in the private sector as a commercial aviation executive.

During World War II, Gore's family failed to land him a cushy assignment and he ended up as an enlisted man on the Aleutian Islands off the coast of Alaska. He survived the war with a frostbitten knee that plagued him for the rest of his life, but he also mustered out with his first novel, *Williwaw*.

Like Conroy, Vidal hailed from the South. Although you'd never know it from his accent or his patrician manner, he had kin in Tennessee and Mississippi and had grown up in the Washington, DC, home of his grandfather, Thomas Gore, a conservative senator from Oklahoma. After his mother divorced and remarried, Vidal moved to the Virginia estate of Hugh D. Auchincloss, subsequently Jackie Kennedy's stepfather.

Pat sported a party wardrobe of rumpled khakis and a plaid flannel shirt, and as I escorted him over to Vidal, I dreaded one of Gore's withering putdowns. "Where you headed, big feller, the 4-H Club?" Instead he said how much he had enjoyed *The Lords of Discipline*. "All that S and M stuff brought back nights in the barracks. Of course," Vidal added, "I would have liked it better if you had been honest about your theme."

Pat paused before asking, "What's that?"

"Those boys at that military school, you can bet they were having sex together. It couldn't be clearer that the narrator and his best friend were banging each other."

As a first encounter between celebrated American bestsellers, this scene could have been etched in stone with not a word changed. But Pat embellished it in *Beach Music*, dramatizing my birthday as a glittering Roman gala at the palazzo of a rich American couple, Paris and Linda Shaw. (The original manuscript names the couple the Mewshaws, but Pat's editor, Nan Talese, persuaded him to change that.) The protagonist, Jack McCall, a surrogate for Pat, shows up in a tuxedo, accompanied by his precociously verbal daughter Leah. Struck by the beauty of the little girl, the fictional Vidal gushes, "This child is lovely. She looks as though she were born in pearls." In fact, Gore loathed children and referred to Sean and Marc as the "dwarfs."

If my mother needed evidence of why Pat was a bestseller and I would never be, this was Exhibit Number One. Instinctively, he grasped what readers liked and the market demanded.

NOT LONG AFTER THE EVENING Pat met Gore, I visited Vidal at his penthouse overlooking Largo Argentina. Five floors below, rush hour traffic swerved around ruined temples like scavengers scuttling past meatless bones. Among the shattered stones, cats feasted on plates of pasta dished up by the city's *gattinare*, the mad women who ensured that the square smelled like a litter box. High above them we drank white wine, while around us gilt-framed mirrors reflected three Dutchmen slaying a wolf on an Aubusson wall tapestry and photographs of Princess Margaret and Jack and Jackie Kennedy.

Whenever he was asked why he had lived in Rome since the '60s, Vidal didn't do anything so obvious as gesture to his apartment or his majestic view. He didn't mention history or culture, the climate or the food. He compared himself to Howard Hughes, who had huddled in a darkened hotel suite, his hair and fingernails grown long, and his feet shod in Kleenex boxes. "It's just something I drifted into," Gore quoted the eccentric multi-millionaire.

But in an interview with Martin Amis for the *Sunday Telegraph*, he confessed that he fled the United States "because I didn't want to become an alcoholic . . . Fitzgerald, Hemingway and Faulkner are the classic examples, but it didn't stop with them."

When I met Gore in the mid-1970s, he restricted himself to drinking wine, and maintained that no amount of the grape was as harmful as hard liquor. Then after he switched to high-test alcohol, he lectured that timing was the key. "Think how many American men down two or three highballs before dinner and a bottle of wine with a heavy meal. Then they jump into bed, try to have sex, and have a heart attack instead. My father had a coronary in middle age and never really recovered. The trick is to schedule sex in the afternoon and save the food and booze for later."

These days, even though he drank as much as he liked of whatever he liked whenever he liked, Vidal mocked his contemporaries as sloppy drunks. Truman Capote, Tennessee Williams, James

Jones, Irwin Shaw—he dismissed them all as dipsomaniacs who dug their own graves with swizzle sticks.

"Last fall, when your friend Styron visited Ravello," Gore told me, "it was flabbergasting how hard he hit the bottle."

"That's funny. He said the same thing about you."

"I bet that's not all he said."

To tweak Gore's noble nose—in silhouette he resembled a Roman emperor stamped on a gold coin—I told him Bill envied his villa, La Rondinaia, but said that fags could afford such opulence because they didn't have kids to support and college tuition to pay.

"How true," Vidal mused in a glacial tone. "But then fags don't get to marry department store heiresses like Rose Burgunder. Every dollar I have, I earned myself."

He poured us each another glass of Episcopo, the vintage he hauled back from the Amalfi Coast in industrial quantities.

"Your friend Conroy interests me." This was a rare admission from a man not inclined to take notice of younger novelists. "He's onto something. He's tapped into a truth the rest of us never knew ran so deep. His novels about dysfunctional families indicate just how fucked-up our nuclear units have become."

"I'm sure he'll be happy to hear that."

"Let's not exaggerate," Gore hedged. "He interests me more as a type that the Quality Lit Biz slots into a category. Me, I'm in the fag pigeonhole. Ellison's still the Great Black Hope. Bellow's the designated Jew, with Roth breathing down his neck. And Styron's the Southern Comforter. But Bill's so slow, you never know when or if he'll finish another novel. That's where Conroy fits in. I think they're grooming him to replace Styron."

"*They*? Paranoia apart, do you really believe it works that way?"

"Of course it does. Bestsellers are manufactured, and Conroy's the perfect cornpone poster boy. The old South is dead. It's good-bye gothic mansion and miscegenation, and hello suburban tract houses and army bases and child abuse. If you care about him, you should warn him."

"Warn him what?"

"Warn him he's about to be swallowed by the great American success machine."

"I don't see that it's done you any harm."

"That's because I'm not a backwoods boy," Vidal said. "I'm a third-generation celebrity. My grandfather and father and I have all been on the cover of *Time* magazine. I was born into the world you and Conroy are so eager to crash."

"Leave me out of it. I'm happy right where I am."

"Well, Conroy has bigger fish to fry. He's bound to hit the jackpot sooner or later. And when he does, watch out! He'll never know what hit him."

It dawned on me that Gore might be mulling over his own publishing predicament more than Pat's. Lately he had had contractual disputes with Random House and creative differences with his editor, Jason Epstein, who badgered him to stick to historical fiction and drop his current project, *Duluth*.

"When publishers pony up a million bucks," Gore continued, "and manufacture a bestseller, they damn well mean to get their money back. The pressure can run a writer off the rails."

"I don't see Pat Conroy suffering from writer's block."

"No, his problem's the opposite. He's in love with his own voice. He wants readers to adore him, and a lot of them will. But there'll be plenty of reviewers and fellow writers who'll hate him, and he won't know how to cope with that except crawl into a bottle."

Vidal punctuated this pronouncement with a swig of wine. "You can already see it in his face, the bourbon blush."

"He has an Irish complexion."

"I rest my case. He's Irish."

"So am I. Do you think I'm an alcoholic?"

"There are two types—wet Irish and dry Irish. You're dry Irish. He's wet."

I lifted my wineglass.

"Don't be literal-minded. I mean your personality, your style, is dry. Conroy writes luscious prose like the lush he'll become. Every time I read Faulkner and he rambles on about 'the ancient avatar of the evening sun slipping down the crepuscular sky,' I know he was deep in the sauce. Ditto Conroy."

"I've never seen him staggering and falling down." It went unsaid that I had watched Gore lurch around Rome, buckling to his knees.

"Wait and you will. He reminds me of John Horne Burns, another novelist with talent, but no self-control. His first book, *The Gallery*, was brilliant, but success and booze killed him."

"I thought you told me it was fag-baiters who hounded Burns to death."

"That was a factor," Gore conceded. "But nobody would have known about his sex life or anything else if he hadn't gotten so much publicity. These days a writer has to sign onto a permanent campaign, like a politician. I'm built for that. Conroy's not."

AS WINTER PASSED INTO SPRING, it appeared that Vidal's admonitions about success might apply to me. My nonfiction book about men's tennis, *Short Circuit*, was scheduled for a June pub date, and showed promise of allowing me to stay on in Rome with significant upgrades. A newer car, for instance, without holes in the floor. An apartment in the *centro storico*, with an efficient heat-ing system. And for Linda, an American refrigerator with a freezer compartment.

The Book of the Month Club had chosen *Short Circuit* as a summer alternate selection, and first serial rights had sold to *Harper's Magazine* and *The Washington Post* in the United States, *Stern* in Germany, *Lui* in France, *Playboy* in Italy, *Sportsworld* in India, and *Smash* in South Africa. Negotiations with the London *Daily Express* had reached £40,000 for a pre-Wimbledon excerpt.

Pat was more exuberant than I and predicted a commercial bonanza. Then he asked a favor, one of the few times he ever appealed to me for help. Having finally managed to complete two hundred rough-draft pages of *The Prince of Tides*, he wanted an outsider's opinion.

I hoped to help, but feared that I'd hurt him. Pat had very thin skin and we had debated about writing often enough for me to realize that we approached novels from radically different perspectives. Thomas Wolfe was his greatest literary influence. Graham Greene was mine. Wet versus dry, as Gore Vidal might put it.

In a trattoria around the corner from Piazza della Pigna, we served ourselves at the antipasto table. For this working lunch, we chose light appetizers and mineral water, no pasta, no wine. It was warm and we ate outside, under a canvas umbrella that smelled like a sail. Pat said he had spotted eight lizards on the wall of his courtyard—a sure sign of spring. In the background a waiter unloaded wood from a truck, flinging it down a metal chute to a pizza oven.

Uncapping his Montblanc pen, Pat opened his journal, poised to take notes. Since we sat side by side, I could read every word he jotted down. I started off praising his novel's energy, its pace and propulsive story line. I said I was jealous of his knack for creating likeable characters. But as chunks of wood kept rattling down to the pizza oven, I was distracted and thought back to the antipasto table. More and more, it seemed to me a metaphor for the first seven chapters of *The Prince of Tides*. In the abundance on offer, one could, I told Pat, be overwhelmed by choice. "You know, there's fish, there's fowl, there's cheese, there's cooked and raw vegetables."

A slightly stricken expression crossed his face. So I switched to a different tack, telling him, "I don't like big moments in film or in books. I like small moments. I enjoy insignificant moments that have large reverberations."

Pat dutifully copied this down, but after that what he transcribed seldom corresponded to what I said. "There's a war in all your books between autobiography and invention," he scribbled on his own with no reference to my remarks, "between what you imagine and what you know damn well happens. You want to make all your characters wonderful—much more wonderful than yourself. To realize your full potential as a writer, you need to feel you have the right to your own emotions."

"There's no right or wrong way," I assured him. "But chapter by chapter, you introduce a seven-foot giant skulking around the suburbs of Atlanta. Then vicious convicts rape members of the Wingo family. Then a tiger escapes from its cage and kills the convicts."

I paused, and there was the thud of wood chunks. "This is just one man's opinion. But these all seem to me like opening chapters, the kind meant to grab a reader's attention. I wonder whether you shouldn't have peaks and valleys, not a straight line of Mount Everest summits."

Pat bore down on his notebook. I wished he would look up at me. But then I noticed what he scrawled and decided it was better that he had his eyes averted. "I cannot write the book Michael would write. The faults he discusses will always be my faults. I've monitored them carefully. They're not accidents."

I felt awful and wanted to order wine. "Take everything I say with a grain of salt. If it's not helpful, forget it. There's only one scene I wish you'd cut."

"What's that?"

"You remember the story I told you about a friend of mine who killed a kid during the Korean War to save his own life?"

"Sure," Pat said. "I changed Korea to World War II and didn't think you'd mind my retelling it."

"Normally I wouldn't. The problem is I already used that scene ten years ago in my novel *The Toll*. I wouldn't want anyone to think you lifted it."

"Thanks for the heads-up. Thanks for all your help." He closed his journal, capped the Montblanc, and called for the bill.

When *The Prince of Tides* came out, Nan Talese had tidied up the first two hundred pages considerably. A soldier still kills to save his skin, but Pat changed the little boy to a woman. Later in the novel, he named the nefarious corporation that designed, built, and operated the factory that threatens to pollute the rivers of South Carolina with weapons-grade radioactive waste the Y.G. Mewshaw Company of Baltimore, Maryland. Linda regarded this as a personal dig. I preferred to view it as an homage, and trusted that whatever we thought of each other's work, we'd always remain friends.

8 The gods of laughter, as Steve Geller dubbed them, deserted me that June and my high hopes for *Short Circuit* collapsed. *Harper's Magazine*, which had contracted to publish a 5,000-word excerpt, ran a 12,000-word abridgement of the entire book, cherry-picking the best passages from each chapter. Worse, they invented transitions and edited interviews so that questions no longer connected with the correct answers. Never consulting me, the magazine also eliminated the names of players and tennis officials I had quoted, and this led to charges that I had indicted pro tennis for corruption on the basis of anonymous sources.

The Washington Post emulated *Harper's Magazine*, deleting the names of my sources. *Newsweek* went a step further and airbrushed me out of the picture altogether, publishing what purported to be its own investigation of men's tennis. When I threatened legal action, *Newsweek* inserted the title, *Short Circuit*, into a footnote. Still, the article contained so much information from my book, the London *Daily Telegraph* scotched its plan to serialize *Short Circuit* for £40,000 and simply reprinted the *Newsweek* piece.

In Germany, *Stern* ran a chapter, which it credited to a staff reporter. In Rome, during the Italian Open, a tournament official dragged me out of the press box, roughed me up, and threatened far worse if I didn't recant what I had written. While none of the journalists on site deemed this incident newsworthy, BBC dispatched a crew to Rome and professed outrage at my mistreatment. Pressing me for the names and phone numbers of my sources, and borrowing a videotape interview with Arthur Ashe, they promised to promote *Short Circuit* in their broadcast during Wimbledon.

I made it onto the screen for a minute and was identified as "the most hated man in tennis." Never mentioning my book, BBC tracked down my sources, asked the same questions as I had asked, and passed off the answers as its exclusive exposé of pro tennis.

The editor of *Short Circuit* in France, a true *philosophe*, advised me to bow to the new paradigm in journalism. "You've enjoyed a *succès de scandale*," he said. "Be satisfied with that and resign yourself to the position of authors in today's marketplace. You're in the research and development wing of the entertainment industry. Your task is to produce raw material. After that everything is out of your hands. As far as the mass media are concerned, the content of *Short Circuit* doesn't belong to you any more than a diamond belongs to the black South African miner who digs it out of the bowels of the earth."

Pat loved this tranche of Gallic wisdom and did his best to cheer me up while I was in the States staggering through a gauntlet of early-morning and late-night talk shows. As one did in those days, he and I communicated by airmail, and what a colossally generous and gifted correspondent Pat was. On July 1, 1983, he commiserated about the publicity snafus but congratulated me on the fine reviews I was receiving. "Even you, Mewshaw, with your unassailable powers of finding horse turds hanging from magnolia trees, must be backflipping through your own rectum."

In Rome, he said he was suffering "world-ennui, soul ague,

spiritual cancer." He hadn't written a word of his novel since I left, and he stunned me by announcing that he was moving the family back to Atlanta. Not for a summer vacation, but for good, for bad, and forever. "My old hatred of moving and insecurity and money-doubt have all arisen to dance upon my heart," he wrote.

By telephone, Lenore explained that Pat's mother had relapsed and was undergoing another round of chemotherapy. Then, too, Alan Fleischer, having transferred to the University of Arizona medical school, had petitioned the court in Tucson for custody of Gregory and Emily. Tired of dealing with these troubles long-distance, they had called it quits on Italy. But before they drove to Antwerp to ship the BMW to the States, they distributed going-away gifts and delivered to Linda their high-end German refrigerator with its huge freezer compartment.

When Linda and the boys met me in America and tagged along on my book tour, Pat invited us to visit Fripp Island, South Carolina. After weeks on the road, I couldn't wait to unwind with the Conroys. First, however, I had an interview with CNN in Atlanta.

TV appearances, I had learned, followed a basic formula. A grinning commentator, who had never read my book, lobbed questions as fluffy as his hairdo. But these amiable exchanges had the potential to turn poisonous. The CNN correspondent thrust a letter on Associated Press stationery into my face and demanded why I had lied on my application for tournament credentials. AP's European Sports editor had notified the International Tennis Federation that the news agency had no relationship with me.

I blurted that the Rome AP bureau chief, Dennis Redmont, had hired me to cover two events. After that I was credentialed by different outlets.

"That's not what it says here," barked the CNN inquisitioner.

"This document"—suddenly it was a document, which sounded far more incriminating than a mere letter—"insists you never wrote for AP."

For the rest of the interview and the remainder of the summer I floundered like a man in quicksand. Although Dennis Redmont corroborated that I had freelanced for AP, the damage had been done. AP's letter continued to circulate in the tennis community through the U.S. Open, effectively killing *Short Circuit*.

By the time I arrived on Fripp Island, I felt half-dead myself, and Pat didn't appear to be in any better shape. Pale and paunchy, he might have spent the past month on a barstool rather than at the beach. Following the move from Rome, he admitted, he couldn't write, couldn't sleep, and couldn't quit drinking. Lenore carped that she missed Italy and she missed Gregory and Emily, who were with their father in Tucson on a court-mandated visit. "God only knows when or whether he'll let those two shitbirds come back," Pat said.

Pat had arranged for us to rent a condo that abutted what appeared to be a fetid swamp. He swore this splurge of spartina grass and cattails was actually prime real estate. "Only Yankees buy oceanfront property, and their houses blow away in hurricanes. You're safe back here."

Batting aside a scrim of sand flies and mosquitoes, he pointed to seagulls, sandpipers, and ospreys. "Keep an eye open for alligators," he told the boys.

On a tour of the island, his car crunched over oyster shells and tunneled beneath live oaks bearded with Spanish moss. He conceded Fripp was a slow-poke, politically conservative, culturally vapid place compared to Rome. "Everything's spanking new and as fake as a retiree's toupee. But I like it. I'd stay here full-time. But Lenore won't hear of living anywhere except Atlanta."

"I'm sure the kids'll be happier in a city," Linda said.

"The hell with the kids. I say leave Greg and Emily with Dr. Bonzo in Arizona."

The next day he and I traveled nineteen miles to Beaufort to stock up on supplies, and Pat spent the trip singing arias to the Eden of coastal South Carolina, the turquoise sea, the canopy of pines, the opalescent sky. But as we crossed the causeway to the mainland, he spotted a pick-up truck with a bumper sticker that read, "When you're tempted to sin, think about hell."

"I think about hell all the time," Pat said.

"Do you want to talk about it?"

"Talk about hell?"

"Talk about whatever's bothering you."

"Everyfuckingthing's bothering me."

He bleated about the slow bleed of words from his Montblanc pen onto yellow legal pads. He normally finished five or six pages a day. Now he was lucky to squeeze out a few lines.

Meanwhile, his mother had been hospitalized in Augusta, Georgia. Pat apologized that he needed to drive there next week and discuss her care with the oncologist. "I wanted to show you and the boys a terrific time. I wanted this to be R & R after your awful book tour."

"We're fine. Take care of yourself and Peggy."

"I promise this week we'll have fun every day."

True to his word, he taught Sean to bait crab traps and clean and prep their catch for dinner. He swam laps in the pool with Marco on his back. One night we watched a DVD of *The Great Santini*. Then, as a treat for me, he ran a tape of this past year's NCAA basketball championship game, Houston versus North Carolina State. Because NC State started two players from DeMatha, Pat figured I'd be interested—and I was.

Together we traipsed through the tree-colonnaded antebellum lanes of Beaufort where Pat's childhood flashed past as if on film ever fresh in his mind. We dropped by the high school gym where he had starred in basketball, introducing this somnolent outpost to the big-city game he had developed in Washington, DC. We walked the baseball diamond where, Pat said, a teammate had keeled over with a heart attack and died. After sightseeing at Tidalholm, the handsome white frame house where the movie of *The Great Santini* had been shot, Pat showed me the more modest home where he had lived with his parents and six siblings.

In August heat thrumming with insects, we toured the Marine Corps Air Station where his father had piloted fighter jets. At the entrance to Merritt Field, several planes were canted on stanchions, looking as fierce as sharks. Everything about the base—the crew-cut troops, the cropped lawns, the sun-drugged barracks, the sound of hard boots on soft asphalt—called to mind my summers at the Naval Receiving Station working for Tommy. Back then my every second thought had been to escape the military life, which Pat also professed to despise. Yet here he was, smack in the middle of it, claiming he would settle in Beaufort if Lenore would allow it. Already I was longing for Rome and regretted that Pat wouldn't be there with me.

One evening, the Mewshaw and Conroy families gathered on the beach to release baby turtles and watch them scuttle across sand that rippled like a weightlifter's belly. The sea tossed the turtles back once, twice, then sucked them out into the lemon-colored Atlantic.

After that, Pat disappeared for a couple of days to the hospital in Augusta where Peggy Conroy's prognosis had deteriorated. When he returned he invited us for a farewell dinner at their rented house in a thicket of pines. The summer was over, and we had, as

Pat said, to break camp. He made no effort to hide his foul mood. There was no banter, no kibitzing with the kids, just steady drinking and slow talking that sounded like a Southern sheriff with a fist on his holstered pistol as he read you your Miranda rights.

Lenore and Linda shooed the kids onto the porch and had them eat outside. Then they came in to fix plates for the adults. Pat poured himself a brimming tumbler of wine. "Tell you what, gang, I'm too tired to eat. Too tired and too drunk and too fucking fed up."

"You'll feel better," Lenore said, "once you have some food in your stomach."

"No, I won't. Not when I have to go to Atlanta in the morning and fly to Tucson, Arizona, while my mother's dying in Augusta."

Lenore broke into tears. "I'm sorry."

"Sorry's not going to cut it. Not this time. You always say you're sorry, then you keep doing what you've always done. Alan calls and tells you a lie and you believe him."

"Don't do this," she begged him. "Don't ruin Mike and Linda's last night."

"We'll leave and let you two work this out," I said.

"No, stay," Pat urged us. "You need to know what's happening. Alan Fleischer has sworn in court that I'm insane and not a fit parent. He's suing for custody of the kids again and won't send them home."

"He won't win," Linda assured him.

"Maybe he will. Maybe he won't." Pat's pose as a Southern sheriff was losing its taut control. "The one sure thing is I'll bleed cash from every bodily orifice. How can he trick you over and over, Lenore?"

Her sobs deepened, and she shrank in her chair, miserable to the core. Linda went to comfort her.

"I don't get it. Are you desperate to find some redeeming qualities in Dr. Bonzo because otherwise you couldn't justify being married to him?"

I moved between them, replaying a scene from my childhood, from Pat's childhood.

"The thing I hate about you, Lenore," he said, "is that you loved Alan Fleischer. It kills me that I could love the same woman as that monster. I can't stand that you stayed with him for twelve years, that you have such hideous taste."

"You're right," Lenore said. "I have no taste, no excuse at all. Just stop screaming at me. If you're going to bring up Alan every time we argue, you should leave me."

Pat lurched, as if to push past me. I had one hand on his chest; his heart pounded against my palm. I hadn't seen him like this since Susannah's birth, when he blamed Lenore for infecting him with herpes.

"I'm as dumb as she is, doing the same thing over and over."

"Please," I said. The kids leaned against the screen door looking in from the porch.

Pat drained his wineglass, blotted his mouth with a napkin, and tramped off to the bedroom.

"It'll be okay," Linda soothed Lenore. "He's exhausted."

"I know he wants me to leave him," she said.

"The important thing is to decide what you want."

"I want to die."

9 Back in Rome, we returned to the same apartment, camping out amid the landlady's belongings, subject to eviction at her whim. After sampling the seductions of America, Linda was disappointed with our helter-skelter existence, and the boys clamored for sugar-coated Cheerios and color TV.

I felt I had been found wanting as a provider, no better than a gypsy coercing his wife and children to ride aboard a claptrap wagon—toward a destination I couldn't guess. My publisher offered a $12,000 advance for *Year of the Gun*. When I complained that this was 80 percent less than I received for *Short Circuit*, he suggested I try elsewhere. My agent shopped the novel around to no avail, and we skulked back, hat in hand to accept the low-ball advance.

I wished Pat were around to swap tales of woe and laugh at ourselves. Instead we stayed in touch by airmail. Janet Malcolm has written, "Letters prove to us that we once cared . . . They are fossils of feeling." This was certainly true in Pat's case.

September 12, 1983:

I've sat down at my desk again to write—the first time I've done so since the last days in Rome when I could turn around in my chair and see the Campidoglio. Now there is kudzu growing in my window . . .

The trips out to Arizona have been disruptive, discouraging and expensive—Lenore and I have been alternately despondent and furious—but so far I have not leapt across the courtroom and ripped out Alan's thorax and larynx as [Mark] Helprin would have done . . . Having Fleischer call me crazy is like having a fly complain that someone has too many eyeballs.

The expense is the killing thing. We've now built up thirty thousand dollars in legal fees and I've yet to testify. Lenore has testified for ten minutes. So far our version of the events has cost us three thousand dollars a minute.

Pat confessed that he persisted with the court battle not at Lenore's behest, but because of his own combative nature. When the bell rang, he was like a punch-drunk boxer, unable to resist his fighting instincts. "Alan is bullying Lenore," he wrote, "is breaking the law, is arrogant beyond my tolerance to endure it and has pissed me off . . . I'm also not sure that Lenore can be happy if we don't make a fierce fight for her kids. Already she weeps for long periods of most days. 'Tis a lovely atmosphere in which to write novels which will never die . . ."

About Peggy Conroy, he said it's "possible that I will have to be a bone marrow donor for Mom if she gets critical. [Dad] cheered me up by saying that the surgery for both the donor and the recipient is the most painful of any kind of surgery. I would be in bed for a month, then spend the next six months learning how to walk again. My first cheery impulse is to say quite merrily, "Fuck you, Mom. Sorry you gotta die," but then the two-thousand-year-old guilt of the Catholic boy asserts itself and I offer my balls to be transplanted . . . wherever they might help. With my luck, Fleischer would be the visiting surgeon."

I didn't know whether to laugh or cry. Who among all of Dr. Freud's acolytes could possibly unpack the freight of these sentences?

"Mostly, we miss you, Mike and Linda," Pat concluded. "We have a nice thing going—a life-changing friendship that has four distinct parts like a weathervane, and it all moves in harmony and we know how all the winds of the world are blowing when we get together. The full diminishment of losing you has not hit me yet and I don't think I could stand it if I faced it fully now. But what magic the world is full of . . . I owe my love for you to Alan Fleischer. He also gave me the gift of Rome, and as I sit here, hoping to write again, I feel that old love of the Mewshaws flowing off this desk, lifting above this city, sailing eastward and lighting like a bird on your terrace overlooking the city. I want that bird to sing to you, Mike and Linda, to thank you for everything, to sing its little ass off and let you know how much we, I, miss you both."

There was a lengthy postscript:

My weakness is that I never mail letters the day I write them. Life continues and there's more to say. I was in Augusta [visiting Mom] . . . They took a bone marrow sample and discovered that the latest round of chemotherapy had failed—the leukemia survived . . . I then reeled in, dazed, to my mother's room to comfort her when she had just been delivered a kind of death sentence. She was lying in bed, her eyes tightly shut, with tears streaming down

her face. I cannot describe the tenderness and helpless-
ness I felt for her. The whole world seemed concentrated
in that room and I could feel our shared history surging
around us. I can remember sitting on Mom's lap when I
was Marco's age and I remembered it that moment as I
kissed her and felt her tears against my face. We talked,
both of us crying, until I watched the courage return to
her eyes. I could see it replacing the fear. But the fear
never left my eyes and I can't shake it. I thought I'd do
much better with this . . . *Basta!* You'll make me never
write again or pay me not to.

Actually, I would have paid Pat to write like this for the rest
of his life. The hastily scrawled PS, produced under duress, represented his prose at its best.

Before I had a chance to answer the letter, he sent another:

"I thought I probably had everyone fairly suicidal after my last
letter. I kept looking up and seeing the ass of the world sitting on
my head. But not this letter, gentle readers . . . Victory on all fronts.
Fucking victory with a capital F. Fleischer . . . lost everything in the
Arizona courts including legal fees and our expenses." Gregory and
Emily—Pat called them Judas and Benedict Arnold—were now
home in Atlanta. He continued:

Also, my mother survived the massive chemotherapy. It
was hideous but it seems to have worked and they think
she might go into remission again. Oh Lord, am I getting
good at the cancer lingo . . .

Conroy (we writers sometimes refer to ourselves in the
third person) is back at his desk but words eke out slowly
and I'm out of practice . . . I think it has a lot to do with

my overwhelming jealousy that Mark Helprin is on the best seller lists and I'm just sitting here writing about a guy catching shrimp. I'm not really jealous, just consumed with an Iago-like envy that will probably lead to manslaughter, except I don't want Mark to rip out my thorax.

In early November I replied:

Thanks for your two fine, long, newsy letters. I fear this will not be their equal. Far from it. Linda & the kids are asleep. I'm awake, fighting various demons with which you're familiar. If you can believe it I retain the capacity to be furious at [my publisher] . . . A sane & sensible man would put this whole thing—everything related to *Short Circuit*—behind him. But the doctor can't cure himself. Perhaps because I keep being reinfected by the virus . . .

Hey, this is sounding awfully negative—and I'm not a negative guy. Mordant and bleak maybe, but never negative. I want to be upbeat, I want to boogey, I want to be fun to be with, peppy, effervescent. I want to be a Seven-Up . . .

We had a dinner party—the Nagorskis [the *Newsweek* bureau chief and his wife], Jim Fallows's brother Tom and his wife Andrea Lee who wrote *Russian Journal* and Gore Vidal who has really porked out and talks of little except his advancing age and expanding waistline. He regaled the gathered masses with the news that he had been examining his naked parts in the mirror and had come to the conclusion that his cock—which he invariably referred to as his wee-wee or whang—was retreating into his body. He insisted that fat wasn't overwhelming his whang, but rather that his member was growing in the wrong direction. That's the kind of literary conversation we have in Rome . . .

I'm relieved to learn that your mother is recovering, I'm glad to hear Greg and Emily are back, I'm proud to know you're writing. But more than anything I'm pleased that you're all going to a family counselor. It should help to have someone to talk to on a regular basis. The hardest thing, as that old insurance salesman Wallace Stevens said, is to know how to live and what to do. It seems to me inevitable that you'll all feel better as you talk and work and let your nerves reknit.

Lenore wrote then to tell us that the family had returned from a "four-day, foul-weathered, child-infested weekend . . . in the N[orth] C[arolina] mountains where Pat has gone to write and to escape the multitudes of well-wishers, welcomers, needers, users, and of course tension producers . . . I thought Pat was doing pretty well until he broke down and cried in our family therapy session . . . It's his trick of putting distance between his feelings, filling time with too many strangers and drinking lots and lots of liquor to numb the pain."

She added that "while I am feeling constantly sad these days, I don't feel quite as helpless as I did before we started in therapy." Gregory and Emily appeared to her to have pulled through the custody conflict unscathed. "They have some crazy mechanism which enables them to fit in wherever they find themselves." But she feared that Susannah had suffered a "radical change." "We had to leave her every time we flew to Tucson so her former secure life suddenly got blown completely apart. After three weeks of being away she would not let us walk out of a room without becoming completely hysterical."

One positive development: "In four days' time Pat has managed to get 86 pages of manuscript done and I decided I'd do the typing. An economy move as well as a justify-my-own-existence endeavor. In addition to every other pressure, he has a big deadline hanging over him. But I think it's a healthy sign that words are flowing and he feels he can write again."

She closed: "I can't even remember the reason why we decided to come back." They both longed to return to Rome and were debating whether to do so.

More frequently than I am comfortable admitting, Linda and I discussed Pat's and Lenore's letters and wound up arguing. What began as idle talk about the latest news from Atlanta provoked wrangles about our future. If we had been in family therapy, a shrink might have suggested we were indulging in a screen conversation. Fretting about Pat and Lenore and whether they should return to Italy, we were really fretting about ourselves.

I always sided with Pat. I defended him. More than that, I identified with him as he and I coped with our cankered childhoods and negotiated a rapidly changing publishing industry. Balancing the demands of agents and editors against those of wives and kids, I believed I was better off overseas, in a city that nourished me. Now if the Conroys would come back, I thought life would be complete.

Linda disagreed and reminded me of the hassles in Rome, the brain-deadening bureaucracy, the tax laws that created perpetual terror for foreigners. How much longer, she wondered, would we live in strangers' houses? More than anything, though, she worried that the boys would always be interlopers here, and unless we moved back to the States soon, they'd wind up alienated there as well.

Like our arguments, which fell into a predictable call-and-shout, Pat's and Lenore's choral complaints were repetitive, but expressed in such amusing letters it was difficult to accept that they were as desperate as they claimed to be. Pat wrote that it depressed him that "Mark Helprin, who is now a major hero to me, had the cover story [in] last week's Sunday *Times* [magazine]. Because you will do tarantellas of pure ecstasy I give you the whole autobiographical squib rectangled below the article, 'Mark Helprin, whose latest novel is *Winter's Tale*, recently returned from a year's residence in Italy studying European security.' I recently returned from Italy after a year's study of the effects of a diet of tomato sauce on congenital hemorrhoids. I can't wait until the American Academy hears what Mark says he spent his time doing."

Never one to make his misery sound anything except hilarious, Pat added: "Alan [Fleischer], that moldy handful of rat's sperm, has called our family therapist and wants to enter therapy with us—you know—as part of the family. I should have been born a eunuch tending the orchids in the Sultan's greenhouse with airspace where my genitalia once modestly hung."

At Thanksgiving Lenore reported that she had "begun to have a delayed-reaction nervous breakdown. I actually don't have time for a lengthy, dramatic breakdown so I have these mini-breakdowns, between carpools or while I load the dishwasher."

On December 30 she wrote: "Christmas this year was hectic and I am in post-partum depression . . . We had our Christmas dinner at Barbara's [Pat's first wife]. The cast of characters is worth noting since it included so many extensions of family and odd matings. Barbara [and her three daughters by Pat], Tom [Barbara's current boyfriend and future husband], Tom's kids from his first marriage, Barbara's in-laws from her first marriage, Pat, me, Susannah, Pat's father Don and one of his many women friends, two of whom gave him wristwatches this year, causing him to have to change watches whenever he was with one or the other."

She closed, "Your life sounds charmed. And I'm fully aware of how frustrating it is [in Italy]. But would you settle for boredom? Iceberg lettuce? Carpools? Lawn fertilizer? Congealed salad?"

10 Sometimes lawn fertilizer and congealed salad didn't sound so bad to me, not when Linda was unhappy and the boys grumbled about having nowhere to ride their bikes except around and around Piazza Navona. It cut no ice with them that this was one of the most splendid urban spaces on earth, or that they wheeled past Bernini's incomparable baroque Fountain of the Four Rivers, or that ancient Romans had flooded the square and staged mock naval battles here. Even the afternoon sun inflaming the pumpkin-orange and Pompeian-red facades didn't stir them. They missed bland, broad American sidewalks.

When foul weather trapped us in the apartment, the kids scattered Legos across the tile floor of the living room and constructed castles whose parapets toppled over in thunderous crashes that prompted the lady downstairs to pound at our door. At such times I didn't know whether to lash out at my sons or at my neighbor. I remembered then what Hemingway wrote about Paris: "When the cold rains kept on and killed the spring, it was as though a young person had died for no reason." Nothing was sadder than Rome moldering under relentless March drizzle.

Then a letter from Pat raised my morale. He had just sent

off 580 pages of *The Prince of Tides* to Houghton Mifflin. "With luck I hope to finish the goddamn thing by May. I have promised myself never even to think about the south again, much less write a book about it, but I know that's an idle threat. I will be delirious when this book is finished, edited, polished off and made fun of by discerning critics.

"My mother continues to struggle . . . the overall prognosis still sucks, but her spirits remain high."

I promised to light a candle for Peggy at Santa Maria sopra Minerva, where an elephant sculpted by Bernini stood in front of the church bearing an Egyptian obelisk on its back. In exchange, Pat encouraged Emily to pray for the success of my novel—a good little Jewish girl murmuring Hail Marys as the nuns at St. Francis School had taught her to do. Shrugging off my congratulations for his progress with *The Prince of Tides*, he predicted that *Year of the Gun* would be my breakthrough book.

At first his prophecy seemed plausible. *The New York Times*, daily and Sunday, ran positive reviews, and *The Washington Post* compared it to the best of Alberto Moravia. *The New Yorker* declared, "Its depiction of the look and feel and fascination of Rome is almost beyond praise." But then inexplicably—at any rate, I couldn't explain it—*Year of the Gun* imploded.

I didn't have the luxury of indulging in what Lenore called a "mini-breakdown." Our landlady notified us that we had a month to pack our belongings and move out. We counted ourselves lucky to find an *attico* on Via Santa Maria in Monticelli, across the tram tracks from the Gellers in Palazzo Cenci. True, it was a 110-step walk-up, with a staircase as grim as a Piranesi prison sketch. True, the apartment was occupied until September and we had to stay elsewhere for the summer. True, the lease stipulated that we allow the landlady's daughter, a college student, to live upstairs during the Christmas holidays. But at last our address was in the *centro storico*, and the flat had a rooftop terrace where I could write with all the fabled geometry of Rome spread out around me.

We piled the boys into the increasingly decrepit VW and forged north, bunking with friends in Provence. Then we imposed ourselves on other friends in Paris and Brussels. By August, ashamed of living on sufferance—and on fold-out couches—Linda flew to the States with Sean and Marco to visit her parents in Pittsburgh. In no frame of mind to face my in-laws, I caught a ferry across the Channel and holed up in yet another borrowed flat in London.

There I watched BBC's coverage of the '84 Olympics in Los Angeles, where palm trees shook like a cheerleader's pompoms. As the women's marathon ground toward a ghastly finish, a Swiss competitor, Gabriela Andersen-Schiess, went rubbery-legged, missed the last watering station, and staggered on and on. By the time she stumbled into the LA Coliseum, Joan Benoit had won the gold medal twenty minutes earlier, and Andersen-Schiess's body, from black shoes to peaked white cap, looked as attenuated and twisted as a candle wick.

Alarmed TV commentators called for her to be rescued before she suffered a stroke. Medical personnel barged onto the track, but Andersen-Schiess waved them off; if they touched her she would be disqualified.

While the crowd clapped and chanted her name, the phone rang. It was Pat Conroy from Fripp Island. "Are you fucking watching this? She's me," he said, "I'm her, dying in the home stretch."

"No, she's me. Born to lose but still plodding ahead."

"Please, somebody save Mike and Pat before they're brain-damaged." He crowed with laughter. "Carry them off on stretchers and strap them into straitjackets."

"How'd you know where to reach me?" I asked.

"Linda called Lenore from Pittsburgh and said you were hiding from your in-laws in London."

"I didn't have the strength, the stamina, to make the trip."

"I love this," Pat hollered as Andersen-Schiess wobbled along at the rate of four hundred meters in five minutes, clutching her head, on the brink of utter collapse. When she crossed the finish line, medics swarmed her, and the Coliseum echoed with the ecstasy of the crowd.

"She's a role model for us," Pat said. "I don't know about you, Mike, but I've got goose pimples from my elbows to my asshole."

"I conceal my emotions."

"Come on, I bet your bladder's puckered like a pigskin. Look, the reason I called—"

"Are you saying the women's marathon didn't move you?"

"Not half as much as your novel. I wrote you a letter about *Year of the Gun*. But I didn't know where to send it. I'll mail it to Pittsburgh and have Linda carry it to you. Meanwhile, I salute you, as they say in the Corps, hand to helmet."

Weeks later, in Rome, I read Pat's letter, the longest response to one of my novels since William Styron's critique of the fledgling manuscript I wrote as a grad student.

"I cannot tell you if I loved the book because I love you, or if I love the book because I love Rome. Lenore moaned with pleasure as she read the book. I moaned orgasmically for the book sang with little moments that make a writer happy to be alive and writing in the English language. I mostly felt sad that we were not in the same city together. You made a good book wonderful. You made a city live on the page which has always seemed to me the highest precinct of art. It hurt me to see how fabulously you wrote about the city we both revere. I was proud and filled with awe. I wished that I had written every word of the book and you had lived in

St. Louis. I can't believe a better book will ever be written about the city of Rome and my jealousy is praise . . .

"Atheneum [the publisher] does not get high marks . . . the book was reviewed long before it was available [in stores]. The jacket also stank and was unexciting. The advertising was negligible and not inspired. I'm sure I'm not telling you anything you have not already noticed but all these publishing companies, Mike, seem to treat your fiction as though it were on a flight pattern over the Sudan. They treat it as though it was not important, not essential, or an event to be celebrated. Since the industry will always remain a mystery to me, I can't claim to be surprised but I can claim to be disturbed. Have you wondered what you can do to break out of this cycle of neglect, Michael?"

This wasn't an unreasonable question, even if it did abrade the raw spot that Mom always aggravated by asking why I couldn't produce a bestseller. I read on, hoping Pat had an answer.

"I have come up with nothing that will not cause you to reach for a vomit bag, but I have studied the American scene with uncommon repulsion since we returned to the States and I will offer you some of my observations. I think that you write well-crafted novels, Mike, that fall between the two twin Alps of mediocrity in American publishing. There is the Alp of Shit, the bad novel, which makes the most money and sells the most books because of the incomparable shallowness of the American reading public. You cannot join the expedition to the Alp of Shit because you are incapable of writing a bad sentence. These are the books of Leon Uris, Sidney Sheldon, Harold Robbins, Trevanian, etc. They have ridiculous story lines, Velveeta characterization, moaning plots, international locations (you have that too, but at your hotels the plumbing never works) and sex which causes tidal shifts across the planets. (In your sex scenes the women always have small breasts and can never come. Great breasts and orgasms in women, followed by douches of Lafitte-Rothschild are *de rigeur* in the Alp of Shit lexicon.) Now I think your novels lie in the long desolate valley between the Alp of Shit and the Alp of Significance. Gore is a genius in maintaining his condo on the Alp of Significance. So is Bill Styron. Look at Gore's last two books. *Creation*—about a Persian who tells the story of Greece as it should have been told if Herodotus wasn't a flak. Then *Lincoln*, a historical novel about the most glorious American created by God during America's severest test as a Republic. Bill wrote *Sophie's Choice*—about the Holocaust and its bitter aftermath when a young Southern writer meets a girl who lost her teeth at Auschwitz. Before that there was *Nat Turner*, slave psychic commanded by Yahweh to set his people free. Notice, Michael, that we are dealing with large themes, all of which can be summarized in a single line of ball-clutching advertising prose. These men write about giants who die grandly."

Pat neglected to break for paragraphs, but I broke to ponder how much of this applied to me and *Year of the Gun*, and how much represented an attempt to strategize as he completed *The Prince of Tides*.

"Yes, I know this is repulsive," he continued, "and alien to any good boy who learned to parse Latin at DeMatha High School. But when I read that light shit ad for *Year of the Gun*, so timid as to be invisible, I tried to figure out what could have been done to lift your novel out of the Valley of Neglect and balloon it up to the Alp of Significance. Finally I had it. The Pope had to be kidnapped, only not just any Pope. *The first American Pope.* The keys of St. Peter's had to be in the pocket of the guy who sat on the board of Chrysler. Who would do the kidnapping? Aha! The Red Brigades claim credit and demand that the church sell every painting and fresco in Rome to obtain his release. The Israeli secret service could have a hand in it, angered after the Pope had embraced Arafat in a group photo shot. Or a rightwing cabal of Cardinals who find out that the new Pope plans to allow priests to marry and sully their pee-pees on the happy pasturage of vaginas around the world. South African Commandos. Libyan expatriates. IRA dissidents. The list is endless and my profession makes me sick."

But not so sick that he didn't ramble on. "With every book I've ever written, the advertising department of Houghton Mifflin has asked me to come up with a single line describing what my book is about. I never can do it and am always jealous of writers who can. The one-line, I think, is absolutely necessary to scale the Alp of Significance . . . I'm wondering, Mike, if you and I should try it."

Pat was being disingenuous. He had already produced novels of the requisite bestseller size and complexity and raised himself far above the Valley of Neglect. But I cringed to think how he would react—how any publisher would react—if I presented a one-line synopsis of *Blackballed*, my novel-in-progress. It was about a Tuareg tribesman who conquers the tennis world, winds up in jail on bogus charges, then mounts a comeback wearing Islamic regalia.

"I'm worrying about myself in this letter," Pat finally confessed, "and in the back of my mind I'm trying to come up with a snappy one-liner to describe my new tome. Shrimping family, buggered by ex-cons, are removed from their ancestral lands by the Federal Government who wants to build a Nuclear Power Plant. Already I'm in trouble. Who gives a shit about a shrimping family? But if I said Southern Peanut Farmer who becomes President loses his ancestral lands because of the wily machinations of his Republican successor—I have mounted the Alp of Significance (or Shit) in a single bound.

"Anyway, these are the thoughts I've been thinking . . . since I read *Year of the Gun* and realized Atheneum was going to let the sucker slide. It's a terrific book and it deserves better than it seems to be getting.

"In my next letter I will deliver another sermon, a hysterical cautionary tale about not coming back to America to appease your children's lust for Burger Kings and Little League. But for now, I love you both and miss you terribly. I am proud of you, Michael. You done good. I return now to my toehold on the Alp of Shit."

I read and reread Pat's letter. Like a jeweler studying a stone through a loupe, I held it up to the light and turned it this way and that. Although written tongue in cheek, his remarks seemed far more than mere jokes. A good deal of thought and energy had gone into it. Coming from a different friend, his advice might have sounded offensive, but Pat had the saving grace of humor and a disarming knack for empathizing as he criticized.

For a while Pat let Lenore communicate with us while he finished *The Prince of Tides* and tended to his mother. Impatient with the Italian postal system, Lenore took to telephoning, and because of the six-hour time difference between Atlanta and Rome, she often called after Linda and the boys were in bed and I was up late reading. Lenore regarded our talks as therapy sessions and dubbed me Doctah, a nickname that stuck.

She phoned on November 17 to say that Peggy Conroy had died and Pat was crippled by grief. He remained incommunicado until December 26, 1984, when he wrote, underlining the date and stressing, "Fuck this year."

"This will be another whining report in mid-passage," he started off, but soon descended into self-mockery, reporting that his Christmas gift from Lenore was "some snappy Yves St. Laurent underwear designed for men half my weight, but blessed with twice my genital burden. Speaking of weight, I've lost ten pounds and now weigh what a smallish professional wrestler weighs. When next you see me, I'll look like a jockey and I'll shop for those neat Italian suits worn by svelte pimps.

"I bought for Lenore (and me) a ticket to Rome on June 10. Naturally all of you will have moved to Bonn or back to America and we will enter a strange city with no connections or prospects, but we plan to stay at least a month and will decide if we're going [to move back] or not. I'm glad I was back here when Mom died. The end was hideous but I had a whole year to make my peace with Peg. The last thing we did together was to attend a family reunion in Piedmont, Alabama. All my relatives had tried out for the banjo player in *Deliverance*. The kids were in a state of shock when they contemplated the ghastly gene pool in that room, but all of us came away admiring my mother for the giant step she made out of Piedmont. The funeral was very lovely and very moving. The five sons served as pallbearers and much of the town turned out. She was buried in the same cemetery where they buried Santini in the movie. Something about the whole thing broke my heart. Peg was 59. A kid."

It troubled me that Pat felt obliged to be funny about his grief. Perhaps it helped him cope. Maybe the alternating current of humor was all that allowed him to endure his sorrow. As he zigzagged from one emotion to another, he called to mind an ice cube on a stove top, skating as it melted, searching for a spot that wasn't scalding.

11 The 1980s were the heyday of New Journalism and hot magazines. Many a novelist supported his fiction by producing articles, celebrity profiles, and travel pieces. Impressed by my portrait of Rome in *Year of the Gun*, David Breul, the editor of *European Travel & Life*, offered me an assignment for the publication's inaugural issue. He wanted something light yet substantial, factual yet fanciful, writerly yet not overwritten. When I asked him to be specific—what should my first "Letter from Rome" be about?—Breul said, "It should be about two thousand words."

With that directive in mind, I banged out "Campari and Complexity at Center Court," which hailed the Italian Open tennis tournament as a microcosm of the city's hallmarks: "dazzling color and motion, dense golden light, copious food and wine, high fashion and low comedy, spontaneous friendship and rabid nationalism, grace under fire and ham-handed evocations of a real and imagined past."

Breul bought it, cementing a relationship that lasted seven years. When *ET&L* died, as all fine magazines inevitably do, there followed an even longer relationship with *The New York Times Sophisticated Traveler*, where Sarah Ferrell and Nancy Newhouse welcomed my article ideas, the more idiosyncratic the better. Skiing in Slovakia, exploring an obscure art installation in the Moroccan desert, sampling nightlife in post-apartheid Cape Town, reconnoitering the Silk Road cities of Samarkand and Bukhara—these and other outré assignments got me off my ass, out of my usual routine, and sharpened my eye for details that fed my fiction.

Then the *Sophisticated Traveler* expired, too, but not before it influenced Pat Conroy. Although he never wrote for the magazine, he was a conscientious reader of my articles and he made Jack Mc-Call, the narrator of *Beach Music*, a freelance Rome-based travel author whose favorite outlets were . . . *European Travel & Life* and *The New York Times Sophisticated Traveler*.

IN THE SPRING OF '85 Rome experienced a spate of extraordinary weather. Working in the blisteringly cold upstairs studio in fur-lined boots and a ski parka, I watched snow mantle the red tile roofs and snap the fronds off frozen palm trees. Meanwhile, in Atlanta, where azaleas and dogwoods bloomed, Lenore was preparing for a summer visit to Rome. She counted on me to persuade Pat to travel to Italy with her. "I think he stands a better chance of working there (anywhere)," she wrote, "than here. A lot of Pat's time is taken up giving advice to Cliff [Graubart] and Bernie [Sheine] on their writing projects which is great and generous . . . but not on a constant basis and not at the sacrifice of one's own writing?"

In mid-June, Pat showed up along with the rest of the Conroy clan, but overlapped with the Mewshaws for only a few days. The landlady had cajoled us—"cudgeled" is a better word—into vacating the apartment so that she and her daughter could stay there for July and August. Linda, the boys, and I spent those months in the States, in a borrowed flat on the Upper East Side, where the Conroys paid us a visit as they passed through Manhattan on the way home. Pat was ebullient about the movie prospects for *The Prince of Tides*. Our old friend Andy Karsch had found financing in Hollywood and hired Pat to write the screenplay. This figured to free them of debt and permit them to return to Rome in grand style.

As much as Pat, like me, was an operatic complainer, constantly decrying that he was trapped in a revolving door of misfortune, a case could be made that he, again like me, flew along serenely under the protection of a guardian angel. The difference between us was one of quantity. Whereas I had just signed a $12,000 contract for my new novel, *Blackballed*, Pat was poised to make millions from *The Prince of Tides*. Since I wasn't immune to human weakness, I should have been jealous as hell. But Pat wouldn't allow it. He simply wouldn't let it happen.

In a hydra-headed strategy of envy preemption that he employed not just with me but with any potential green-eyed demon, he downplayed his success. He maintained that it never made him any less miserable. He was cravenly grateful for crumbs of kindness, never bragged about his accomplishments, and was unfailingly generous with his praise of others. For a guy who had been a great athlete, he buried his competitiveness in almost every sphere except his court battles with Alan Fleischer.

That night in New York when Pat told us the good news about *The Prince of Tides*, I congratulated him and said I was happy. But I also couldn't resist a quip that had "passive-aggressive" stamped all over it. "Every time Conroy writes a letter," I said, "somebody turns it into a movie. Me, I write a novel and it instantly turns into a dead letter."

No one laughed harder than Pat. He liked the line and jotted it down in his journal. Days later, before Linda and I left for Rome, Andy Karsch called to say he had read the galleys of *Blackballed* and decided to option the film rights. I suspected Pat had put him up to it. Andy denied this and cut me a check for $10,000. A year later, he renewed the option for another $10,000, and although I challenged Pat, he professed to have had nothing to do with it. I thought I knew better. While it may not have been Pat's money, I think he primed the pump at Andy's production company.

ELATED TO BE BACK IN Italy that September, we trudged up the 110 steps to our apartment and discovered that the duplex had shrunk to a monoplex. The landlady had blocked off the upstairs studio and terrace because, she claimed, her daughter had contracted tuberculosis and was recuperating where I had counted on writing.

Wouldn't a sanatorium be a better place for the poor girl? I asked. Wasn't there a danger of contagion?

The landlady wailed that Americans were heartless. And when I suggested we deserved a reduction in rent since she had cut the apartment in half, she accused us of unconscionable avarice. Still, she agreed to a small discount.

That fall I worked in the living room in a wicker peacock chair with a lapboard on my knees. My schedule revolved around Sean and Marco's school day. The minute the Marymount bus picked them up, I began writing. When the bus brought them home, I closed up shop and played baseball with the boys in Piazza di San Salvatore in Campo. From the windows of a madhouse, patients and doctors watched in disbelief as three Americans shagged grounders bouncing crazily off cobblestones.

Overnight the tubercular girl on the top floor enjoyed a miraculous recovery and moved out, and a French couple moved in. When I complained—no, exploded!—the landlady huffily in-

Pat and Lenore Conroy, Joan and Polly Geller, Linda and Marc Mewshaw, Emily and Greg Fleischer (foreground). Rome, the day we met, September 1981.

Mike Mewshaw, Pat and Lenore Conroy,
Linda holding Marc Mewshaw,
Sean Mewshaw (foreground).
Christmas Rome, 1981.

Mike Mewshaw and Pat Conroy. Rome, December 1981.

Susannah and Pat Conroy. Fripp Island, South Carolina, Summer 1983.

Marc and Sean Mewshaw, Pat Conroy. Fripp Island, South Carolina, 1983.

Pat Conroy and Mike. New York City, summer 1985.

Pat Conroy and Linda Mewshaw. New York City, summer 1985.

Bob Kirby, Lenore and Pat Conroy, Linda, Mike, Sean and Marc Mewshaw, Susannah Conroy, Emily Fleischer Conroy. Naples, Florida, 1988.

Linda Mewshaw and Pat Conroy. Charlottesville, Virginia, Halloween 1989.

Marc Mewshaw and Pat Conroy.
Charlottesville, Virginia,
Halloween 1989.

Lenore and Pat Conroy, Linda and Mike Mewshaw, Susannah Conroy. Fripp Island, South Carolina, January 1990.

Pat and Lenore Conroy, Sean and Marc Mewshaw, in front of the Conroys' house. San Francisco, March 1991.

Susannah Conroy and Linda Mewshaw in front of Roman painting of Lenore and Susannah as a baby. Atlanta, Georgia, December 2009.

Lenore and Susannah Conroy. Atlanta, Georgia, 2009.

Susannah Conroy and Marc Mewshaw. Rome restaurant, 2015.

Mike Mewshaw at Pat Conroy's grave. St. Helena Island, South Carolina, 2017.

formed me that since I had forfeited the studio in exchange for a discount, she had the right to rent it to anybody she pleased.

Appeals to her fairness and decency failed, and I resorted to guerrilla tactics. I choked off the heat and electricity to the top floor, casting the French couple into shivering darkness. The landlady retaliated by jamming matchsticks into the door locks on the VW Derby, and it cost me $200 to have a specialist undo this slimy trick.

But that was small change compared to my legal expenses. In Italy an industry had cropped up around rental disputes, and because nothing about our lease was on paper, our attorney, sounding like a medieval casuist, argued for a "faith-based" contract, which depended, like the existence of God, on "evidence unseen." After months of gutter fighting, the case concluded with a negotiated settlement. The French couple stayed upstairs, the landlady dropped the rent by another hundred bucks, and we consented to relinquish the apartment next summer.

Marymount's Christmas pageant showcased Sean as a singing soloist and Marco as a silent shepherd. Afterward, Victor Simpson, an Associated Press editor, congratulated me on the boys' performance. Victor and Daniela Simpson's son Michael played soccer with Sean, and their eleven-year-old daughter, Natasha, rode the school bus beside Marco, acting as his surrogate big sister.

On December 27, the Simpsons were at Fiumicino Airport waiting for a Trans World Airlines flight to the States. Because TWA shared a counter with El Al, passengers headed for New York milled about with people bound for Israel. In the confusion, four Arabs with assault rifles and grenades turned the terminal into a killing field. El Al ticket agents, who doubled as security guards, vaulted the counter, shot three of the terrorists dead, and wounded the fourth—but not before sixteen travelers were killed and ninety-nine injured.

The boys, still in pajamas, were watching cartoons on TV when the news broke. Simultaneously with the assault on Fiumicino, Hezbollah had attacked the Vienna Airport, killing three and injuring thirty-nine.

Sean and Marco, having spent their young lives in Rome, had heard all too much talk about terrorism to get riled up over yet another incident. But when RAI reported that Michael Simpson had been shot in the stomach, and his father, Victor, in the hand, they were riveted. Then it came out that Natasha Simpson had died at the scene, and Marco fell apart. No matter how many times we tried to explain things to him, he asked over and over whether Natasha would be on the bus when school resumed after the holidays.

At this remove in time, when terrorism dominates public discourse, it seems unfathomable that this incident played no part in the discussion between Linda and me about whether to remain in Rome. Nor did it dissuade the Conroys from returning. Did we imagine that we were immortal? In Piazza Navona somebody had scrawled in chalk, "Americans, you will be sent home in boxes." But we went there every weekend to watch the boys ride bikes.

While terror didn't change our plans, it insinuated itself into my writing. The same held true for Pat Conroy. In *Beach Music* he re-created the Hezbollah attack on Fiumicino with such grisly specifics that friends of the Simpson family grumbled that he had exploited their tragedy. But everywhere Pat turned, the terror inside him found an objective correlative outside him, and all his novels, no matter how humorous, hinged on violence.

MY MOTHER-IN-LAW ALERTED ME TO an intriguing double murder near their retirement home in Naples, Florida. A young businessman, Steven Benson, allegedly planted a pipe bomb in his mother's Chevy Suburban and killed Margaret Benson (sixty-three) and her son Scot (twenty-one), and badly burned her daughter Carol Lynn Benson Kendall (forty). Prosecutors argued that Steven had an overpowering motive—the desire to inherit an estate estimated at $16 million.

The story had all the ingredients of a successful true crime book—wealthy flamboyant characters (boring criminals and poor victims needn't apply), a posh gated community (trailer parks held no appeal), and a secret scandal involving Scot Benson who was actually his sister's, Carol Lynn's, illegitimate son. I drafted a ten-page proposal, signed a contract, and over spring break Linda and I brought the boys to Florida, where we stayed with her parents. It could hardly escape me that this was a ghoulish vacation; while the rest of the family frolicked on the beach I studied autopsy photos.

Then the defense petitioned for a delay and the trial was postponed until summer. While Linda, Sean, and Marco flew back to Rome, my in-laws asked me to drive their car, packed with their belongings, to their home in Pittsburgh. En route, I stopped at the Conroys' in Atlanta, where Pat was alone with Gregory and Emily. A storm had just passed through, stripping the azalea bushes and strewing petals like snowflakes over Peachtree Circle. But the windows of the house were wide open and the three of them sat at the kitchen table in tee shirts as if on a sundeck. Not that they looked relaxed. They appeared tense, perhaps petrified by the cold. Pat told me to pull up a chair and listen to Emily. Now twelve, she recounted in an eerily calm manner how her father, Alan Fleischer, had sexually abused her since the age of five.

It all started, Emily said, with father and daughter snuggling in the same bed. Then he began kissing and touching her. Later he started masturbating on her and sticking his penis into her mouth. This past summer in Tucson, things had gotten much worse.

She painted a lurid picture that appalled me and enraged Pat and left Gregory looking sick. Pat roared that he would ruin Fleischer, would have him jailed, would kill him. The more theatrical his threats, the calmer Emily became. As she continued her clinical narrative, the two of them seemed like flint and straw; every word she uttered had a kindling effect on Conroy.

I couldn't judge the truth of what she told us, but everything about her affect struck me as odd. Of course, this wasn't the place and we weren't the people for her to talk to. She should have been speaking to a therapist or the police, not her overwrought stepfather, stunned brother, and me. But she had spent much of her childhood listening to Pat enthrall crowds with tales of his father's abuse. Was that what persuaded her to share such intimacies with an audience?

The phone rang, and Pat answered it. Andy Karsch was on the line from LA with an update about *The Prince of Tides*. Barbra Streisand was in negotiations to star, direct, and produce the film.

Gregory left the table; I sat there in the cold kitchen, gazing across at a child with curly dark hair and an astigmatic eye that gave her a slightly evasive look. I wanted to reassure Emily, offer solace. But before I could decide what to say, she told me what her father had done to her the last night in Tucson.

Along with shock, a great sadness settled over me. As deeply as I sympathized with Emily, I also felt sorry for Pat. I knew he would punish Alan Fleischer. You could depend on that. And in the process he would punish himself. Now that his first novel in six years was about to come out, now that he was ready to move back to Rome, I was sure he would take on yet another rescue mission. Although determined to talk him out of it, I had little hope that he would listen to me.

12 In June, before I decamped to Florida to cover the Benson murder trial, the Conroys landed in Rome in time for a farewell dinner and the next day helped carry our luggage down to the taxi for the airport. They had rented a duplex penthouse on Piazza Farnese, and from the rooftop terrace they had commanding views of the Campidoglio in one direction and in the other the dome of St. Peter's, which French author Henry de Montherlant called "the candle-snuffer of western thought." Pat savored that quote.

The front windows opened onto the piazza embossed like a silver medallion on the *centro storico*'s breast. Two Egyptian fountains, pilfered from the Baths of Caracalla, babbled as pleasantly as brooks. Off to the left loomed the Palazzo Farnese, a sublime example of Renaissance style, its upper facade designed by Michelangelo. Currently it housed the French Embassy.

The scene enjoyed by the Conroys was seldom static; it altered by the hour. In the morning, the Caffe Farnese set out tables, unfurled its umbrellas, and sold the best *cornetti* in town. Then an old man in a peaked hat pretended to be a parking lot attendant, pocketing a few lire from each motorist. By evening, weather permitting, young couples congregated on the ledge in front of the

French Embassy. At first they confined themselves to kissing and caressing. But as darkness fell, they stretched out full-length, convinced of their impregnability under the watchful gaze of armed guards and surveillance cameras.

In an adjoining piazza, Campo dei Fiori, Lenore did the daily shopping, undaunted by her comic-opera Italian. She spoke to merchants with great brio, and even though she suspected what she said was not just ungrammatical, but obscene, she generally brought home what she needed. She was devoted to an establishment she called Fratelli Ladri, the Robber Brothers, where the owners scolded her for pawing at the produce and smudging her fingerprints on the canned goods. She didn't care. She liked that they remembered her name and sang out, "*Ben tornata*," as if she were a family member.

While I was in Florida, we corresponded regularly, and to my dismay, Pat's and Lenore's letters sounded no less anguished than those they had sent from Atlanta.

"I believe having hit rock bottom," Lenore wrote, "with no place to go but up, we are on the mend. The biggest problem has been the frustration of dealing with our rotten two-faced landlord, but today the SIP people made a live appearance in our apartment to deliver 2 (count 'em!) new telephones. I'm confident that by the time we do have [a working phone] we will have fully adjusted to not having one and most of our friends' telephones will be *guasto*." (broken)

Some of her unhappiness, Lenore revealed, derived from the news that Steve and Joan Geller intended to divorce. Because life in Rome often resembled a marriage afflicted with hysterical shouting matches and passionate reconciliations, the last thing anyone could abide was for the turmoil in the streets to invade a home. That this had befallen a couple who meant so much to us, a husband and wife who seemed to have expat life figured out, deepened the distress.

Lenore mentioned nothing about the fortunes of *The Prince of Tides*, but Linda and I had read about its multi-million-dollar paperback and film deals. Pat also said nothing about his success. It was as if he feared that whatever he gained, he was bound to lose. Instead he indulged in orgies of humorous self-abasement.

The return address on his letter of August 5—"Piazza Farnese 51, Atlanta, Georgia 30309 (Oh Jesus)"—suggested his head and his heart inhabited different zip codes. "I'm sure you'll return soon, get me laughing again and put this horror in perspective. Forget that it's a hundred degrees inside the basilicas, that the *rondini* [*sic*] all died of the heat, that the telephone just came last Friday, that the landlord has begun eviction service, that the kids talked me into buying a turtle, that we've had 95 teenage visitors from Atlanta . . . Forget all that.

"We do know now why everyone leaves Rome in the summertime. Far too many people come through the city and we ought to move to Bonn or the Orkney Islands as a defensive measure . . .

"I always forget about the struggle of daily life in Rome but Lenore tells me it's all worth it. Lenore seems happy as a pig in shit to be back. Of course, she's about to be evicted from her home for non-payment of rent, so we'll see how she adjusts to living under a bridge on the Tiber . . . No, I've not written a single word of deathless prose since I got here. Yes, you need to worry about my Roman attitude, but I'll be cured by your prompt return."

STEVEN BENSON WAS CONVICTED ON two counts of first-degree murder. The jury spared him the death penalty and sentenced him to consecutive life terms. The courtroom had seethed with so many authors, agents, and screenwriters the trial might have been a cutthroat literary conference. The bloodletting hit slimy bottom when a reporter, pretending to be from *USA Today*, claimed he was writing profiles of the half a dozen writers who had book contracts. After milking each of us for information, he churned out a general backgrounder that made it appear he had covered the case from the start.

Once I returned to Rome, I had ninety days to submit a finished 500-page manuscript of *Money to Burn*. (Pat Conroy supplied the title.) Our new apartment, above a tire dealership and a TV repair shop, had a cubicle off the kitchen, barely adequate to accommodate a table and a chair. There I gobbled breakfast and lunch as I scribbled, frantic to meet my deadline. The publisher wanted my book to hit the market first. I suspected that all the accounts of the Benson murders would be reviewed together and kill each other off. Still I pressed on, well aware I wouldn't receive the last installment of my advance until I produced an acceptable draft.

In late September, the Conroys invited us to their apartment for dinner. Since the Communist Party was throwing a street fair in Piazza Farnese, it looked as though Pat had hired a cast of hundreds and a brass band to welcome us. The grown-ups sipped *aperitivi* on the terrace, marveling at the sky where scraps of salmon-colored clouds clung in a herringbone pattern. The kids ran downstairs to rub elbows with the comrades and play dubious games of chance. Gregory and Megan, Emily and Marco broke into applause when Sean won a skateboard at the chuck-a-luck wheel.

Ever alert for opportunities to demonstrate to Linda the wisdom of living in Italy, I asked where else in the world we could witness such splendor, allow our children such freedom, and rest confident that no harm would come to them even in the clutches of Godless communists.

Lenore concurred. Linda kept her counsel. Pat blew a lip fart. I assumed his grousing was good-natured. But it soon became apparent that he was seriously pissed off at all things *all'italiana.*

"I can live with a certain amount of aggravation," he said. "I've rented apartments here before and I know what to expect. I don't mind paying an extortionate price, and we'll eventually get the place furnished. But when we went to sign the lease, I found out the owner refused to list the actual price. He said this has to be a secret agreement between us. Yet I had to give him a signed assurance that I'd vacate the flat at three months' notice. In exchange he gave me a verbal promise that we'll be able to stay for three years. I feel like a guy who just bought an underwater lot in Port Alligator, Florida."

I laughed and thanked him for supplying my next "Letter from Rome"—"Real Estate in a Surreal State." But that didn't jolly him out of his malign mood. Like the rabble of starlings flying overhead, Pat noisily flittered from grievance to grievance, until he lit on Alan Fleischer. "He's the first person I've ever met with no conscience whatsoever. He'll do anything to hurt Lenore and me even if it means hurting his children. Especially if it means hurting his children. Know what Emily told me the other night?"

"Pat, please don't," Lenore said. "Mike and Linda are here to celebrate our return."

"How can I celebrate after what she said? It was bad enough that he beat off on her."

"Pat, you promised," Lenore wailed. "You swore to Emily it was safe to talk to you."

"She knows I'm going to file a report with the police."

"Mike and Linda aren't the police."

Grudgingly, he changed the subject, and almost as grudgingly he updated us about *The Prince of Tides.* He insisted he never read reviews, positive or negative. Once a book was out, he said he didn't care what critics thought. Nobody, he said, was more aware of his shortcomings as a novelist than he was. Anyway he had bigger things on his mind.

"Your worries are over," I tried to convince him.

"Not as long as Fleischer's alive."

Later Lenore confided how thoroughly Pat had immersed himself in Emily's troubles and assumed responsibility for what had "happened on his watch." Each day after school, he and Emily disappeared into the master bedroom, and while his stepdaughter stretched out and shut her eyes, he took notes. The rest of the family had strict instructions to steer clear, and only afterward learned that Emily now claimed Dr. Fleischer had raped and forcibly sodomized her.

Lenore couldn't bear to picture what her daughter had endured. But almost as disturbing to her as Emily's trauma was the image of her whispering secrets to her stepfather, like a patient in psychoanalysis. That Pat himself had been physically and psychically abused by Don Conroy, that he had doubtful objectivity about Fleischer, added to Lenore's anguish.

Was Emily telling Pat what she imagined he wanted to hear? Had he elicited from her what he wanted to believe? Lenore acknowledged that Emily was susceptible to suggestion. The two of them had attended a rally in Alabama for sexual abuse victims, where Emily spoke with a number of women who described satanic rituals. On the ride home, she claimed that Alan had driven a little girl into the desert outside of Tucson and killed her. Lenore had no doubt this was a fabrication, not something that deserved to be reported to the police. But she couldn't decide what to make of the stories Emily told Pat.

IN OCTOBER PAT TRAVELED TO the Frankfurt Book Fair, then proceeded to the States for a coast-to-coast promotional tour. In his absence, Lenore had us over for Thanksgiving dinner, and by then the penthouse was furnished. An immense marble coffee table looked heavy enough to crack the living room floor, Pat's library had been shelved on three freestanding bookcases, and a life-size statue carved out of a single slab of wood appeared to stand poised to slice the turkey. The landlord had assured Lenore that the statue would be better than a husband. When I proposed a toast, I spoke as if the wooden nobleman *were* her husband, and expressed gratitude to Pat for a meal he paid for even though he wasn't on hand to eat it.

AFTER HIS WEEKS ON THE road, bloated by hotel dinners and cocktail parties, Pat couldn't be coaxed onto the tennis court. He carped about the hollowness of his life in Italy, shut off from friends in the States and alienated by his poor grasp of the language here. He started repeating the lamentation I remembered from his first stay: "I'm tired of being the most interesting person in the room."

Because I loved him, I didn't fire back that the more often he said this, the less interesting he sounded. I thought I understood his predicament. Now that he was wealthy and well-known, he felt no better than when he had been poor and obscure, and he behaved as if he had been gypped—literally cheated out of what should have been his. Don Conroy had stolen his childhood. Now Rome was robbing him of the recognition he had earned.

Lenore believed Pat had been on his own so long, it was difficult for him to adjust to domestic life. For months he had lived like a hermit on Fripp Island finishing *The Prince of Tides*. Then he had plunged into promoting the book. "Rejoining the family," she said, "was something he didn't relish. In Atlanta he could go to Cliff Graubart's bookstore or leave town for a few days. In Rome, he has no place to escape. Nobody makes a big deal about him or asks for an autograph. He feels stuck and dependent, and because he's miserable, he makes the rest of us miserable."

Laughingly, she added, "He even misses American junk food. He made a mess of the kitchen cooking up a batch of salt-and-vinegar potato chips."

I did what I could to convince Pat he was better off away from the personal and professional stresses in the States. I introduced him to the new fellows and residents at the American Academy, I got him on the list of guests at the screenings of English-language films hosted by *Variety*'s bureau chief, and I took him and Lenore to a St. Patrick's Day party at the Irish Embassy, where everybody wore green except a contingent of Cardinals in scarlet robes. I arranged a dinner with Galway Kinnell, a poet and tennis partner of mine, who knew Pat's sister Carol Ann, herself a poet. Whenever a new correspondent arrived or an old one departed, I invited Pat to catered events where we freeloaded off the extravagant entertainment budgets of international journalists. We watched NFL games on late-night satellite TV and went to boxing matches in Parioli. One weekend, with the help of connections in the travel industry, I got the Conroy family comped at the Gritti Palace Hotel in Venice. But none of this broke his funk.

As I strolled the city on the lookout for fodder for my *ET&L* column, Pat sometimes accompanied me. One day while crossing Largo Argentina, I pointed out Vidal's palazzo, and Pat asked, "How's the divine Gore doing these days?"

I thought it might help for him to realize he wasn't alone in his unhappiness. "Gore's only sixty-one," I said, "but he tells me he wants nothing more now than to die. He's fed up with the publishing business."

"I know the feeling," Pat replied.

"This was at a party at Donald Stewart's place. Gay and Nan

Talese were there, and Gore was upset because Gay accused him of sucking all the air out of the room."

"What is it about writers that makes them hate each other? And makes me hate them all?"

"I don't hate you, Pat. And I hope you don't hate me."

"Gore has everything a writer could ask for," he said. "Why the hell does he want to kill himself?"

"Suicide's not his style. He says he'll just keep drinking a bottle of Scotch a day and let nature take its course."

"The trouble is Scotch isn't quick," Pat said. "And unless you have a cast-iron stomach it stops being fun."

"Yes, there must be more interesting ways to make yourself unhappy," I said.

"When you find them, let me know."

After that, he begged off our walks, and we met mostly in the evening when he was drunk and manic and enticed me into dueling tales about our grisly childhoods. Sometimes Pat "Tastee-Freezed," as we put it. He laughed so hard alcohol foamed from his nose like soda from a nozzle. This deluded me into assuming that as long as he had a sense of humor all wasn't lost.

But one night at dinner he badgered his family to make up its mind: Should they remain in Italy or return to Atlanta at the end of the school year? Lenore voted to stay, and Susannah supported her mother. Everybody else voted for Atlanta.

As he explained the decision to friends, Pat stressed that he missed his daughters. Joan Geller countered that going "back to America to be with three teenage girls was crazy." I brought up the letters he had sent me lambasting everything about life in the States. I even risked his ire by observing that by dragging his kids back and forth across the Atlantic, he was replicating the rootless life that he had hated as a child.

As if falling back on his last line of defense, Pat revealed that he had signed a million-dollar contract for his next novel and was nearly paralyzed that he'd never produce a book worth that much. To complicate matters, *Beach Music* was another book about the South. He said he felt the need to be on home soil while writing it.

How could I blame him? Although his departure struck me as a painful defection when I was already dealing with the split between Steve and Joan Geller, I couldn't begrudge him the adulation that awaited him in the States.

 Gore Vidal had long acted as a combination border-guard and social arbiter in Rome. But with Pat Conroy's star in ascendancy, the city acquired a second magnetic pole, one that reflected the power shift in the States to the Sunbelt. Corporate execs and correspondents from CNN's headquarters in Atlanta flocked to Piazza Farnese, as did Hollywood screenwriters and producers eager to bid on the film rights to Pat's next book. Between Christmas and New Year's, Nora Ephron and Nick Pileggi swanned into town, and because Pileggi was related to Gay Talese, he called Pat, who put together a lunch at La Maiella, Nora's favorite restaurant.

Nick and Nora were sometimes described as the reincarnation of F. Scott and Zelda Fitzgerald. But they weren't the type to get falling-down drunk and dive into fountains. Nor did they trade on beauty and sex appeal. In fact, Nora wrote hilariously about her physical imperfections, launching her career with a threnody about her small breasts and later fretting about the crepey skin at her neck. As a college coed she had been a White House intern during the Kennedy administration, and she quipped that she was mortified that JFK had never made a pass at her. As a humorous self-deprecator, she rivaled Pat Conroy. Even after her novel *Heartburn* was made into a film starring Jack Nicholson and Meryl Streep, she had no inflated notion of herself.

Nick Pileggi was, if anything, more low-key. Craggy-faced and bespectacled, he had the slightly bemused expression of an English professor, not an investigative reporter who had penetrated the inner sanctum of the Mafia and published *Wiseguy*, later filmed by Martin Scorsese as *Goodfellas*. Now Nick was fascinated by terrorism. Recently the PLO had hijacked a plane, separated the passengers with Jewish-sounding names, and threatened to execute them.

Nora confessed that she wasn't a conscientious Jew. "You can never have enough butter—that's my belief. If I have a religion, that's it," she had famously wisecracked. But that day at lunch in Rome she swore if terrorists seized her plane and demanded that Jews step forward, she would march with her tribe.

The following summer, when I flew to the States to promote *Money to Burn*, the field was so chockablock with books about the Benson murders, my publisher pulled the plug on my publicity tour, stranding me in New York City. Because I couldn't afford to stay in a hotel until Linda and the boys joined me, I crashed in an un-air-conditioned sweatbox that I vacated early each morning when the owner arrived to work there. Most days I moped around Central Park, searching for a shady bench un-encrusted by pigeon shit and unencumbered by loquacious madmen.

Then out of the blue—or rather, out of a molten grey sky— Nora Ephron called. The Conroys had alerted her that I was marooned in the city. Since she and Nick were flying to London, I'd be doing them a favor, she said, to babysit their apartment. She instructed me to catch a taxi to the Apthorp.

Nora hung up before I could betray myself as a rube and ask

for the address. But the cabbie knew the building and drove me to Broadway on the Upper West Side to a mock Renaissance palazzo that boasted a massive iron gate and a courtyard that would have suited the Medicis.

Nora greeted me in tight black stirrup slacks and a loose white tee shirt, looking like a waifish cleaning girl overwhelmed by the chores ahead of her. Max and Jacob, her sons by her second husband, Carl Bernstein, had littered the apartment with toys, socks, underpants, and baseball mitts before hurrying off to visit their father.

"Don't mind the mess," she said. "Just shove stuff aside. I don't intend to touch a thing."

I didn't believe that, no more than I believed it when she urged me to move in the next morning and sleep in the master bedroom. Nick and Nora and I had spent a total of two hours together.

I asked what I could do to reciprocate her kindness. She said, "Take me down to the deli and buy me a Popsicle."

She chose cherry. I liked lemon-lime. Jostled by pedestrian traffic, we lollygagged on Broadway slurping ice-lollies that melted almost quicker than we could suck them into our mouths. I had no idea what to say except, "Thanks."

Like the cashier in the deli, Nora said, "Enjoy." Then, dropping her Popsicle stick into a trash bin, she added, "Leave the keys with the doorman."

I NEVER STARTED OUT TO spend long stretches of my life in strangers' apartments. I counted on there coming a day when Linda and I could afford to buy a house of our own. But at the age of forty-four, after twenty years of marriage, I feared that we would forever be economic nomads. Still, I tried to look on the bright side and regarded each new place as an opportunity to act like an anthropologist and sift for clues about the owners.

At the Apthorp, things were just as Nora had promised she'd leave them. In the kitchen sink, breakfast dishes soaked in tepid water. In the bathroom, damp clothes dangled from the shower rod. In the master bedroom, the pillows bore the imprints of Nick's and Nora's heads, and in the twisted sheets nestled a little black book, open to Meryl Streep's phone number. Thumbing through the pages, I spotted listings for Diane Keaton, John Gregory Dunne, and Joan Didion. If I got lonely, maybe I'd invite them over for drinks.

Although I resisted reading the open letters lying about, I read the contents of the apartment like a book, fascinated by the arc of lives different from my own. Nick and Nora appeared to have spent a fortune to furnish an urban flat as if it were a shabby-chic farmhouse. This was the opposite of what people in Italy did—upgrade rural hovels into sumptuous villas.

My snooping was interrupted by one of the twentieth century's most illustrious sleuths. Carl Bernstein rang and right off the bat demanded, "Hey, who the hell is this?"

I mentioned my name, which meant nothing to him, and explained that I was house-sitting. "Nora didn't tell me anything about this," Bernstein said. "How do I know you're not a burglar?"

"Call Nora in London." I recited the phone number she left.

"If you're bullshitting me," Bernstein said, "the cops'll knock down the door in five minutes."

I guess Nora calmed him down. Carl never phoned again. But a garrulous gentleman rousted me out of bed the next day. The instant I answered he recognized that I wasn't Nick, and rather than threaten me with the police, he began cracking jokes. Like Pat Conroy at his most manic, the guy treated the telephone like a stand-up comic's mike. I had to interrupt and ask who he was. "Henry Ephron," he said. "Nora's father."

Drunk dialing from Hollywood, where the sun had yet to rise over the Angeles Crest, Henry was eager for an audience. In me he had found one, and he phoned every morning, as reliable as a wake-up service. I depended on those calls to get my day off to a rollicking start, and as my time at the Apthorp wound down, I told Henry I would miss him.

"Well, if you're ever on the West Coast," he said, "gimme a ring and I'll buy you a drink." Then he asked, "What are you going to buy Nick and Nora for a house gift?"

"What do you suggest?"

"Wine. Not a bottle, a box."

At Zabar's I chose a selection of Super Tuscan vintages, which I deposited on the dining table, along with a thank-you note that issued an invitation to treat them to dinner. I never heard back from Nick and Nora, and feared I had committed some unforgiveable faux pas. Although I had gathered the underpants and socks off the floor, and washed the dishes in the sink, perhaps I had erred in not ironing the clothes on the shower rod. Or did Nora object to my daily chats with her slightly soused father?

When I asked Pat Conroy, hoping I hadn't ruined his friendship with the Ephron/Pileggis, he told me, "Forget it. Letting you live in their place was no big deal to them." From which I inferred it had been their favor to Pat.

Speaking long-distance from Atlanta, he confessed he had a case of reverse culture shock. Once again he and Lenore regretted bolting from Rome and planned to spend next summer there— assuming Nan Talese didn't tie him to a desk until he finished *Beach Music*, assuming Alan Fleischer didn't drag him into court again.

Like a bulldog with a bone, Pat wouldn't let go of his mad-on at Lenore's ex-husband. In the spring of 1988, he granted two interviews to the *Atlanta Constitution*, both of which disclosed that Fleischer had been indicted in DeKalb County, Georgia, for molesting Emily. Maintaining that his stepdaughter had given him permission, he revealed much of what she had confided to him during their sessions in the penthouse on Piazza Farnese.

Pat contended that he had moved his family to Rome in 1986 to thwart Fleischer's court-mandated visits. And he had returned to Atlanta because the charges against Fleischer had been dropped to spare Emily the trauma of a trial. This, he said, had convinced Fleischer to quit fighting for custody of his kids.

None of this was, strictly speaking, true. Without publicly contradicting Pat, the DeKalb County prosecutor notified Fleischer that he was still under indictment and subject to arrest if he returned to Georgia. But Fleischer never abandoned his attempts to gain custody of his children and continued to petition the court for relief.

IN THE SUMMER OF 1988, determined to make progress on *Beach Music*, Pat rented an apartment from a Polish woman who had aristocratic pretentions despite her address, which was next to Regina Coeli (Queen of the Heavens) Jail. Every evening, as inmates exercised in the yard, women congregated on a hill behind the prison wall and cried out to their husbands, lovers, and pimps. The chorus of names they shouted put Pat in mind of Gregorian chant, a plea to all the angels and saints to intercede and free their souls. He loved listening to the women and wrote about them in *Beach Music*, but otherwise did little work in Rome.

Instead, a passel of his kids and their friends overran the apartment. Then Cliff Graubart and his fiancée pitched up, and Pat and

Lenore organized their wedding on the Campidoglio. Droves of Southern novelists and cookbook writers who frequented Cliff's bookstore in Atlanta attended the ceremony and had to be fed and feted. At a reception on the Conroy's terrace, Gregory shot a film of the party, complete with footage of Lenore in a slinky black cocktail dress.

Among the many interruptions to his writing, he received an invitation from Mickey Knox to join Linda and me for a Mexican dinner. Because Mickey was notorious for serving meatless, beanless chili, Pat was inclined to pass on the honor until he learned that Elliott Gould would be there. Gould had been married to Barbra Streisand, who was deeply involved with the film of *The Prince of Tides*, and Pat hoped to glean a few tips about his feisty ex-wife.

Gould harbored his own motives for meeting Pat, just as Mickey Knox did for bringing them together. A tireless networker, Mickey survived by sheer chutzpah as a go-between and general fixer. A major source of his income derived from his rent-controlled apartment, which he sublet at an inflated price to actors on location in Rome. Perhaps he had Gould pegged as a future tenant and customer for his personal services. Mickey admitted to me how far he went to keep his houseguests happy. "Do you have any idea how hard it is to get Burt Lancaster blown every night of the week? It'd be one thing if he was willing to pay. But Burt thinks he's still a star and chicks should go down on him for free."

Elliott Gould owned the movie rights to Bernard Malamud's novel *A New Life* and pitched the idea of Pat's doing the screenplay. He praised the cinematic scene in *The Great Santini* where Ben Meechum beats his father in one-on-one basketball. Pudgy and bearded as an Elder of Zion, Gould said he played the game himself. As a matter of fact, he bragged, he had gone up against Michael Jordan and cleaned the all-star's clock.

Although a shameless spinner of tall tales, Pat had his standards and never crossed the line about his basketball exploits. I expected him to tell Gould he was full of shit. Instead he said, "You know, Elliott, I'm the wrong guy for your project. If I remember correctly, *A New Life* is about a love affair between an English instructor and a faculty wife. Mike Mewshaw's your man. He taught at the University of Texas."

Deftly palming Gould off on me, Pat collected Lenore and departed without a bite of Mickey's beanless, meatless chili. I stayed on. If there was a chance, no matter how remote, of a movie payday, I needed to listen. The next day I tracked down a copy of *A New Life*, read it, and as they say in the business, took a meeting with Gould at his hotel. A family of gypsies joined us in his room. They were considerably cleaner and less flamboyantly dressed than Gould, who wore the sort of overalls favored by grease monkeys, a Mr. Goodwrench uniform. His feet were bare, and around his neck was looped a necklace of human teeth—his children's teeth, he said. As for the gypsies, they had worked as extras on a film with him and he liked to have them around for good luck.

The beautiful French actress Nathalie Baye swept into the room with a photographer in tow. She and Gould were scheduled to shoot publicity stills, and Baye objected that Elliott wasn't in costume. He insisted that Mr. Goodwrench was his favorite fashion label. With sour misgivings, Ms. Baye allowed the photographer to pose them on the bed. But rather than embrace her face-to-face, Gould began slobbering on her feet. Whereupon she flounced up screaming, and I bid the gypsies adieu and slipped away.

Pat expressed no contrition for sticking me with Elliott Gould. "Michael Jordan, my ass," he fumed. "I can't believe Barbra Streisand ever married that asshole."

•

WITH THE CONROYS BACK IN Georgia, the cobblestones in Rome began to quake under our feet. Linda's mother was diagnosed with early onset dementia and confined to what doctors referred to as a "structured environment." Because she had no siblings, Linda needed to be near Pittsburgh, not a nine-hour flight away. Hastily, we decided to move to the States at the end of the current school year.

Then Italian authorities launched a crackdown on foreign tax dodgers, arresting an American lawyer who managed the financial affairs of numerous expats. While he cooled his heels behind bars, the *Guardia di Finanza* seized his files and audited his clients. To escape the dragnet, people stampeded to the airport. The alternative was to do what Gore Vidal conceded he had done—pay up a $100,000 bribe to bury a potential tax squabble. Lacking Gore's assets, Linda and I lowered our profile like crocodiles until only our nostrils remained above water. Even so, I was interrogated by both U.S. and Italian auditors, and I realized we were living in Italy on borrowed time.

DONALD STEWART HAD AN OFFICE near Campo dei Fiori where he edited *Playboy International*. In the afternoon, while he enjoyed a long lunch at home, he let me write at his desk amid snapshots of prospective Bunnies. Each day as I hiked down from the Gianicolo, through the dense mesh of alleys in Trastevere, across Ponte Sisto and past the blackened statue of Giordano Bruno, who looked as if he had been martyred by fire that very morning, I was conscious of the city sinking into my bloodstream. Now that I knew I'd be leaving, I wanted to carry away a map of Rome in my heart.

Even as I stored up impressions of Rome, I stoked up memories of Pat Conroy. Though he was no longer present, I clung to him as best I could. If I were an artist, I suppose I would have painted his portrait. But what I had were words, and I cloned him in my new novel, *True Crime*, without realizing that at the same time he was including me in *Beach Music*. Both of us borrowed key phrases, anecdotes, and incidents from the other. My book was set in Maryland, much of the action on a marshy island in Chesapeake Bay, which could have been coastal South Carolina. The plot revolved around events that had shaped Pat and me as surely as DNA. A drunken violent father, adolescent devotion to basketball, a college girlfriend who gets pregnant by another guy—every story point of *True Crime* sprang from conversations that Pat and I had had as we walked the streets of Rome surrounded by lapidary lines carved in Latin on stone. I depicted the narrator's brother, a burly, wisecracking public defender, as much like Pat as wish fulfillment and my talent would allow.

OUTSIDE OF THE *PLAYBOY* OFFICE autumn advanced in such slow increments I scarcely noticed any change until one afternoon grape-colored clouds closed over the city and hail hammered down so hard I feared it would crack the window. The storm lasted for hours, piling up drifts of icy pellets. By the time it stopped and I set out for home, the air was cold and my footsteps crackled on the cobblestones. Beneath low dripping tree branches, the 44 bus sprayed slush as it fishtailed up Via Dandolo. Astonished and saddened, I felt the seasons had vaulted ahead and *ottobrata romana* had vanished into deepest, deadest winter.

THAT CHRISTMAS WE VISITED LINDA'S father in Florida, so he wouldn't be alone now that Linda's mother was in a nursing home. To our delight, Pat and Lenore drove down from Georgia with Gregory, Emily, and Susannah and registered at a hotel in Pelican Bay. Pat was on the wagon, following a strict health regime. He and Lenore hiked miles on the beach each morning, and he had already lost so much weight he wore suspenders to prevent his pants from falling off. A medical check-up had shown "some bad numbers," he said, and doctors ordered him to stop drinking, start exercising, and cut back on coffee. Not that he had gone cold turkey on caffeine, but he no longer consumed twenty cups a day.

"It's taught me a lesson," he said.

"About mortality?"

"Fuck mortality. I've learned I can't write any better when I'm sober than I could when I was drunk or high on espresso."

Still, he was resolute. At cocktail hour he refused to be tempted. With dinner he turned down even a tipple of wine. But one afternoon while everybody else was out at the pool, I stepped into the kitchen and stumbled over Pat, crouched on his heels, chugging vodka straight from a bottle.

The following day, he told me now that Gregory was headed off to the University of California at Santa Cruz, he and the family planned to live in San Francisco. Pat was sick of Atlanta, its provincialism, its redneck mind-set. His friend William Kovach had been ousted as editor of the *Atlanta Constitution*, and Pat was abandoning the city in protest.

Then, too, he had a good friend, Tim Belk, dying of AIDS in San Francisco. He felt compelled to help care for AIDS patients who had been ostracized by their families. He said he knew what it was to be a pariah.

Lenore encouraged Linda to believe that in California our two families could re-create the best aspects of Italy. Emily and Sean could enroll in the same high school, Susannah and Marco in the same grade school. I'd have plenty of tennis partners, and Pat would have me as a role model of sobriety and self-discipline.

I interrupted with the news that I had accepted a visiting writer's position at the University of Virginia. "Charlottesville's where Linda and I met," I said. "We loved the place."

"You'll hate it now," Pat said. "And they'll hate you. That's what I learned by going back to Atlanta."

"It'll be different for them," Lenore protested. "They don't have your insane family and memories of being beaten half to death by your father."

"Right!" Pat laughed. "Linda's mother is in an institution. Mike's mother's the one who beat him. That'll make all the difference."

14 As Pat had predicted and I secretly dreaded, our re-entry to the States was a disaster. A university town of thirty-five thousand smug citizens, Charlottesville seemed slow-poke and self-satisfied. As William Faulkner, himself a visiting writer at UVA, once remarked, Virginians are snobs. A faculty wife welcomed us with the warning that we would have to wait ten years before people made up their minds whether to accept us. The English department appeared to have decided immediately, billeting me in a cubbyhole without windows, without a phone, without a single grace note.

The boys, too, suffered a bumpy landing. Sean, who had clamored to return to America for high school, discovered that his Roman street smarts didn't translate into the local country-club style. His classmates called my lanky, clean-cut son "a big hairy Italian."

In the fourth grade, Marco was perplexed by black kids with Muslim names. At Marymount he had had plenty of friends from Islamic countries, but they were the sons and daughters of diplomats, not kids from the projects who declared they hated him because he was a honky. What was that all about? In Italy, Honky was a sportswear brand.

Marco's teacher assured us he was adjusting nicely to his new environment, but Marco insisted, "*Questo è uno scherzo.*" That's a joke.

"Your teacher wouldn't have said it if it wasn't true," I reasoned with him.

"I fooled her." Then reverting to Italian. "*Questo paese mi fa schifo.*" This country disgusts me.

"Don't say that. America is your country."

"No, *io sono quasi italiano.*" I'm almost Italian.

I trusted that time would change his mind and perk up my mood. Reluctant to admit I was depressed—the term carried too many calamitous associations with my mother and William Styron—I fantasized that fleeing to Rome would solve my problems.

Meanwhile, the Conroys had settled in San Francisco and purchased a house in Presidio Heights. They also now owned a place on Fripp Island, where Pat isolated himself, attempting to write. This didn't strike me as a healthy family dynamic. But I was grateful when he sneaked a break from *Beach Music* and drove up to Virginia.

"I know this type of Southern town," he said of Charlottesville. "I grew up in one like it. Everybody festering with envy and resentments. The creative writing program just makes it worse. You should join us in California."

Together we explored the rural roads of Albemarle County, west toward the Blue Ridge Mountains. Orange, red, and purple leaves spangled the two-lane blacktop. On this clear, apple-scented day, no place on earth could have been more beautiful. But neither of us was in a fit state to appreciate the autumn foliage.

At the Miller School, where Pat had coached basketball at Camp Wahoo for two summers during college, we traipsed around the campus, seeing no one and hearing nothing except the crunch of dead leaves beneath our feet. I hadn't a clue where Pat's head was at. Mine was in Rome, somewhere between the Pincio and the Borghese Gardens.

He talked about his time at Camp Wahoo, fondly recalling friends. "I got to play with Art Heyman," he said. "An All-American at Duke. He called me Peanut. 'Just pass me the ball, Peanut.' I must have had a million assists."

"That sounds like fun."

"The greatest fun was being far away from Dad."

Because I had to teach an afternoon seminar, we headed back to UVA, and Pat volunteered to sit in as a guest lecturer.

"My students would love it," I said. "But the department won't pay you a measly dollar."

"Don't worry about that. It's worth it to have more time with you."

The seminar lasted three hours, and Pat spent every minute of it speaking. He said nothing I hadn't heard before and repeated sprawling stories about his childhood, his hazing at the Citadel, and his first callow attempts at writing. Much as these recollections amused the class, they appeared to amuse Pat even more. He was like a child rubbing a scrap of silk between his fingertips, soothing himself and salving the pain behind these anecdotes.

Afterward, my students strolled with Pat across the Lawns toward the Rotunda. People recognized him and fell into step. Some asked him to autograph their spiral notebooks. A few raced to fetch paperbacks for him to sign. I had walked these brick paths at UVA with great authors—James Dickey, Robert Lowell, Reynolds Price, William Styron, Peter Matthiessen, Philip Levine, James Salter—none of whom ever attracted such a flash crowd. Everybody loved Pat Conroy—except, perhaps, himself.

On Halloween, Pat took the boys trick-or-treating. Costumed as a zombie, Marco plastered his face with red grease paint, which at first didn't look like blood. But a sudden rainstorm streaked his cheeks as if they had been clawed by a cata-mount. In his baggy khakis and tight shirt with the sleeves rolled up over his muscular forearms, Pat resembled Popeye, lacking only a corncob pipe.

Back at the house, he hugged Marco on his lap and once more implored the Mewshaws to make common cause with the Con-roys in California; the mayor of San Francisco was already his good friend, and Pat promised to have him issue an official invita-tion to the city. Sure enough, a week later a letter with an impres-sive seal urged us to relocate to the culturally diverse and literarily sophisticated Bay Area.

Linda wouldn't hear of it. She was flirting with the real estate market in Charlottesville, citing the prevailing wisdom that pay-ing rent was moronic; accruing equity was the key to financial independence. While she pored over the For Sale ads, I fumed that the independence I craved was the kind I had enjoyed in Rome and foolishly squandered. Restless, my heart was a helium-filled balloon about to slip its string and drag me along for the ride. Teaching only two days a week, I often flew to Italy, ostensibly on magazine assignments, in reality on futile excursions to cure my middle-age craziness.

UVA invited me to stay for a second stint as visiting writer, and by now the boys had found their footing. At soccer matches Sean still shouted coaching instructions to Marco in Italian. Otherwise the two of them had become convincing replicas of American kids. Sean, who had never seen a football game before, made the var-sity as a sophomore, and by the time he was a six-foot-five senior he started at tight end on an undefeated team that won the state championship. Marco, in decisions calculated to drive me mad, started drum lessons and acquired a lethargic python and a hostile boa constrictor.

After a family referendum, I resigned myself to another year in Virginia. I drew the line, however, against buying a house. We rented from a professor on sabbatical and postponed any discussion about the future until fall.

On the last day of the spring semester, the chairperson of the English department summoned me to her office. Since the creative writing program was a separate fiefdom, this was the first time the chair had spoken to me. Skipping the pleasantries, she informed me that my reappointment as visiting writer had been rescinded. Instead of a full-year position, she offered to hire me as "a community resource" for a single semester at a reduced salary.

As cooly as I could, I explained that I wasn't just some day laborer who happened to live in Charlottesville and was available to teach at the University's convenience. My community was Rome, Italy. I was here at the pleasure of the creative writing program, and had consented to a second year with the promise of a raise. On that basis, I had rented a house, I had re-enrolled my children in private school, I had—

The chairperson wasn't listening. She had delivered her edict and had more pressing matters to attend to. At this point I went postal. Not that it ruffled the chairperson's aplomb. She was unbudgeable.

The creative writing program sympathized. They conceded there had been a mistake. They had renewed my appointment without consulting proper channels. Now it was too late to change the chairperson's mind.

A wiser man would have calmed down and reflected that Simon & Schuster had bought my latest novel, *True Crime*, and I didn't need to teach. At no great cost I could have broken my lease and recovered the deposit from the boys' school. But like Pat, who admitted that he fought Alan Fleischer in large part because the man pissed him off, I was seized by an irrational appetite for battle. The English department chairperson and the pusillanimous creative writing program had picked on the wrong guy. I prepared for combat, ready to do everything in my power to force the University to reinstate me for a second year in a town where I didn't want to live in the first place.

I met with the dean of Arts and Sciences and demanded satisfaction. If I didn't get it, I'd take my case public. In a snarky piece for *The Washington Post*, I fired off an early salvo, recounting the University's history of exiling writers who didn't fit the mold at Mr. Jefferson's academical village. The list was long and illustrious, ranging from Edgar Allan Poe to Paul Bowles.

UVA capitulated. In short, I won. In truth, I lost and alienated everyone on the faculty. Pat Conroy compared my plight to cadets at the Citadel who violated some unwritten code and were subjected to "the Silence." After I was shunned in Charlottesville, he again urged me to join him in California.

Curiously, almost all his phone calls in favor of San Francisco came from Fripp Island, where he was writing little, drinking a lot, and surviving in what he described as solitary confinement. With Nan Talese bugging him to finish *Beach Music* and Lenore hounding him to come home, he declared that he hated our profession.

"Forget the profession." Low as I felt, I assumed the role of cheerleader. "Go back to the basics. Remember how you were a gym rat shooting hoops for hours?"

"It's not the same. I loved basketball."

"You used to love writing when you did it for yourself. Forget your editor and your agent and the million-dollar contract. Write for the pure joy of it."

"I wouldn't recognize joy if it bit me in the ass."

"You will if you channel your feelings onto the page."

"I don't feel anything," he said. "Check that. I don't feel pleasure, but I feel plenty of pain."

"Maybe what you need is to get away from it for a while."

"I *am* away from it. I haven't written a word in weeks."

"Why not tag along on my next magazine assignment? Remember the trip to Munich?"

"I'd love to travel. The trouble is I'd have to bring me along and that would ruin everything."

"Jesus, Pat."

"Sorry. Am I bumming you out?"

"No," I lied, smothered by the weight of my own dejection and now his. "But you've got to take care of yourself."

"Every time I think about taking care of myself, nothing comes to mind except pouring a tall drink."

"Maybe you need to go back on the wagon."

"That wagon has passed."

As the two of us thudded along like a phonograph needle in a dusty groove, I started to question for the first time whether this choral complaining did us any good. The hours of mutual commiseration, the quips and comic riffs were supposed to bolster our spirits. Instead they sent us spiraling lower. We needed to change the conversation. But to do that I'd have to change the discussion, the tumult of talk, in my own head.

AT NIGHT I DREAMED OF Rome—the view from different bridges, the honeycombed arches and cupolas, the murals of angels and saints swimming on ceilings. Often I woke and gazed out the bedroom window at pinprick stars over Charlottesville and felt the vertiginous sensation of being sucked up into darkness. The agony of this out-of-body experience was almost strong enough to crack my ribs.

Still, I resisted calling the condition by its name. For months I endured full-blown, clinical depression and didn't acknowledge it until terrifically good news drove the truth home like a nine-inch nail. Half a decade after its publication and interment on remainder tables, *Year of the Gun* was made into a $16 million movie directed by John Frankenheimer and starring Sharon Stone. Because some dimwit in Hollywood had let the option on my novel lapse, my agent renegotiated the film rights, doubling the purchase price, putting me on the payroll as a $3,000-a-week consultant, and flying Linda and me to Rome first-class.

Rather than euphoria, my reaction was one of profound regret compounded by currents of fury. I couldn't help thinking, If this had happened a couple of years ago, if I had had the slightest inkling, I would never have left Italy, never lived in Charlottesville, never fallen into such a toxic funk. Like Pat bleating about the misery of his million-dollar advance, I railed against the cosmic unfairness of my good fortune. The sight of Frankenheimer shooting a scene on Piazza Farnese in the very same building where Pat and Lenore had lived left me lukewarm. Meeting Sharon Stone and Valeria Golino left me completely cold. Something was seriously wrong.

Hurrying back to Charlottesville, I saw a therapist and was prescribed the then new antidepressant, Prozac. For a week my engine locked in neutral. I couldn't lurch backward or forward no matter how hard I gunned the gas. Then suffused with what I presumed to be a placebo effect, I turned energetic to the brink of mania. After a month I leveled off, as if a floor had been inserted between my feet and the abyss. I could wake from dreams and stare out the bedroom window and not fear my soul had been sucked away into an indifferent universe.

My first instinct was to relay the good news to Pat. I called and told him how it had helped to speak to a therapist.

"I'd rather talk to you," he said.

"I like talking to you, too. But I can't give what you need."

"All I need is for you to listen." His voice turned testy.

"I'm listening and I hear you. I hope you hear me too. This antidepressant—Prozac—has been a godsend."

"I'm not taking any fucking chill pill."

"What's the harm in trying?"

"I'll tell you the harm. You dope yourself with happy pills, and you'll wind up writing Hallmark greeting cards." For the first time in our friendship he hung up on me.

Pat was a man of many faults, all of which he confessed and apologized for so effusively, it was impossible not to forgive him. In this instance, he mailed me what amounted to a Valentine:

"I realized I'd never written you two a love letter and it was high time to do it. I don't know how my life would be different if we had not moved to Rome and met you, but I do know that I'd be deprived of two of the best friends I've made on earth. I was waiting my whole life to meet someone like Mike and then I realized that he had [to] marry someone as fine and beautiful as Linda to make it work all around. I'm still amazed at your generosity and hospitality to all your friends in Rome. You taught me things about generosity and love that I never knew and I've tried to incorporate them into my life simply because I admired them in you first. I never like my life as much when I'm not with you, when we're not living in the same city, when we're not talking about books and friends and the cities of the world and the great damaged families that produced us. I've never had friends as splendid as you two and I've never thanked you for this inestimable and freely given gift. I cherish you and I love you and I say this without a single reservation."

Nobody had ever written me such a letter. Not a lover. No one in my family. Certainly not a male friend. Its unabashed emotion moved me deeply. Who wouldn't rejoice to hear, "I was waiting my whole life to meet someone like you?" My one fear was that Pat had set himself up for disappointment and set me up as another person he loved who would let him down.

15 As a featured speaker at the PEN/Faulkner
Reading Series at the Folger Shakespeare
Library in Washington, DC, Pat invited
Linda and me to his lecture and to dinner afterward. Because legions of Conroy
fans overflowed the original venue, his talk was transferred to a
nearby church, lending the event the electric charge of an evan-
gelical tent-meeting. On the altar, at a pulpit-like dais, Pat didn't
depend on priestly vestments to transfix the congregation. He wore
an oatmeal-colored sport coat, a shirt with the collar unbuttoned,
and a knit tie loosely knotted at the neck. His charisma came from
his words, and like Othello with Desdemona, he wooed the crowd
through the ear.

A rambunctious contingent of African American high school
kids frisked amid the sedate NPR subscribers and soccer moms.
Late arrivals loitered at the back of the church, which is where
Linda and I landed. But Pat asked, "Are the Mewshaws here?" and
when we waved sheepishly, he motioned us to reserved seats in the
front row.

With no prepared script, he plunged ahead: "You maybe are
expecting or fearing I'm about to drone on for an hour, reading
from my books. But to me nothing's more boring and worthless

than a novelist spouting his own work. You can read me at home. Why waste time and fight traffic and pay to park your cars just to hear my deathless prose? Instead, I'll tell you a little about myself and my family and how I got started as a writer."

He might have been at a table in a Roman trattoria or on the front porch on Fripp Island as the origin legend poured out of him like the *Iliad* from the lips of blind Homer. He invoked his parents, as though they were the God of War and the Goddess of the Hearth battling for his soul. Like listeners eons ago who committed tribal lore to heart, I could have declaimed all these stories myself. No doubt, so could many in the audience who had read Pat's books or caught him on radio or TV. He spoke of the wrath of Don Conroy, who dropped napalm on Asians for a living and spent his leisure hours battering his wife and kids. Pat's role in childhood, as he described it, was to be beaten, dragooned from one forlorn military base to the next, and cautioned by his mother that for the good of the nation and the survival of his family, he should keep his trap shut about the violence at home.

It was a Horatio Alger tale on steroids. Where other cultures had *Künstlerromans* dramatizing sensitive boys coming of age through the annealing power of art, Pat's American crucible boiled over with cruelty—which paradoxically he played for laughs, as if he suspected nobody would care if he told it straight. He repeated the vignette about his father taunting him that if he had realized that abuse would transform Pat into a bestselling author, he would have hit him harder and made him a better writer. To which Pat replied with a well-honed punch line: "Dad, if you had beat me any harder I'd be Shakespeare."

Funny, obscene, provocative, transgressive as current academic jargon would have it, Pat's performance worked a cathartic effect on the crowd. As for its effect on him, he stumbled offstage lathered with sweat, his comb-over askew. He hugged Linda and me and apologized that the PEN/Faulkner Committee had organized a sit-down dinner in his honor and the guest list was restricted to board members. "Let's have lunch tomorrow," he said.

"We have friends in town," I told him. "Two women from Arkansas."

"Bring them along. I'd love to meet them." Then he was swept away on a swell of people and applause.

AT THE GEORGETOWN INN, PAT awaited us in a dim corner of the Grill Room, wary of exposing his red-rimmed eyes to sunlight. Dressed in the same clothes—his sport coat had dried the color of congealed cereal—he was badly hungover. But he bucked up when Linda and I arrived with Helen Harrison and Katherine Downie, a couple of sisters we had known since the '60s. While Helen lived in Little Rock, Katherine, a divorcée, had a house across the Potomac River in Alexandria, Virginia, with her young son.

That Helen and Katherine were attractive and intelligent, that they had honeyed Southern accents and delightful laughs might have charmed any man. But Pat was particularly susceptible to Katherine and her plight as a single mother. He paraphrased his article about divorce being the death of a small civilization, and added that while he understood a boy needed a father, he also knew there were times when it hurt, rather than helped, to have a man around. Still, he guaranteed Katherine, "You're going to meet somebody who'll love your bee-hind and marry you."

Somehow it was a short step from that to the subject of child and spouse abuse, and the lunch seamlessly meshed with last night's PEN/Faulkner lecture, complete with sound effects of Don Conroy's fist smashing Pat's face.

Perhaps I had listened to these tales too often. Maybe Prozac had chemically altered my POV or impaired my sense of humor. Something had changed, and overnight his shtick had turned into a tired joke. His admissions of inadequacy had previously struck me as signs of strength, his confessions of failure as secret triumphs. Now he simply sounded sad and sick, and instead of feeling an impulse to swap lachrymose yarns about our youth, I stayed quiet.

Pat always claimed he told stories to understand himself. But it hit me that day at the Georgetown Inn that this might actually be an avoidance mechanism. Rather than seal a bond between friends, his anecdotes seemed to open a distance between the teller and his tales. He didn't need another fan, I thought. He needed help.

AFTER LUNCH, PAT WALKED US to our car and suggested we bring the boys to San Francisco over spring break. I promised to think it over.

A trip to California appealed to the family, but nobody cared to settle there permanently. Sean had two more years of high school and was eager to graduate with his class. Now that Marco had quit trying to remake Virginia into Rome, he was happy in Charlottesville, and Linda said she needed to be near her mother.

That ducked the question of what I should do. I took a stab at a novel set in contemporary Prague, a retelling of *The Sun Also Rises* with a female narrator replacing Jake Barnes as the sexually dysfunctional reporter. But no matter how often I revised it, publishers agreed with Pat Conroy that readers preferred multi-orgasmic women.

Dreading that I'd plunge back into depression unless I found a project, I decided to do another book about pro tennis, this time the women's tour. While Linda and the boys were in California visiting the Conroys, I shopped a proposal around in New York and landed a contract that kept me on the road for months.

The Women's Tennis Association's circuit concluded at Madison Square Garden in November, which coincided with the premiere of *The Prince of Tides*. Pat put Linda and me on the invitation list, and although no cast members appeared, Gloria Steinem, Liz Smith, Gay Talese, and prima ballerina Heather Watts provided sufficient glamour.

Pat had co-written the script, and I wanted him to be happy and wanted him to know I was happy for him. Still wrestling with *Beach Music*, he said he appreciated my high opinion of the film, and as we strode together up Fifth Avenue after the screening, the skyscrapers, strung with Christmas lights, seemed to raise his spirits.

Pat and Lenore's suite at the Pierre was banked with poinsettias and had a view over the Central Park ice-skating rink, where golden couples circled in silver light. Caterers had arranged a bar in the living room, and uniformed waiters bodysurfed through a sea of family and friends, serving flutes of champagne and baby lamb chops.

Three of Pat's brothers introduced themselves to me, and the one named Mike joked that a childhood with Don Conroy had been great preparation for his current employment at a mental hospital. Pulitzer Prize–winning cartoonist Doug Marlette jogged my memory about our meeting eight years ago on Fripp Island. His syndicated series, Kudzu, continued to be popular, but increasingly, he told me, he was concentrating on writing fiction.

"Somebody's got to stop him," Pat said. "There's already too much competition and too little money to go around."

"I'm in it for the glory," Marlette gleefully needled him.

"That's worse."

Red wine had stained Pat's teeth and blurred his blue eyes. Lenore slipped an arm around his waist and steered him toward a *New York Times* reporter whose article in the next day's paper described him as groping for cheer and "tentatively" exclaiming, "What a night. What a city. What a life. I'm telling you, this is the life."

In private, Lenore explained why Pat was so frazzled and distracted. Emily had stayed behind in San Francisco. Now seventeen, she had had a horrendous year, and for fear that she would harm herself, she was under psychiatric care. No sooner had Pat and Lenore registered at the Pierre than Emily called—to make sure they were safe, she said. But Lenore sensed something was drastically wrong.

The next day, Emily sneaked out, and the housekeeper followed her to Union Square, where Alan Fleischer was waiting for her. Emily refused to divulge the purpose of this rendezvous, but she promptly unraveled, and on the night of *The Prince of Tide*'s San Francisco premiere, she swallowed a bottle of Tylenol and had to be rushed to the emergency room. For the rest of '91 and well into '92, Emily was in and out of the adolescent psych ward.

Usually at his most compassionate and loving when other people were falling apart, Pat snapped as his stepdaughter fell apart. He told me he had witnessed too many suicide attempts in his own family and couldn't bear to watch another person self-destruct. Fleeing to Fripp Island, he said he had to save his sanity and salvage *Beach Music*.

In Charlottesville, while I finished *Ladies of the Court: Grace and Disgrace on the Women's Tennis Tour*, an acquaintance took a chainsaw to a tree in his yard and brought the trunk down atop himself, severing his spinal cord, paralyzing him for life. To my astonishment, he showed up in a wheelchair for a Christmas party and professed to be in high spirits. He granted that his recovery required many changes and the cooperation of everyone around him. His home and office had had to be refitted with ramps and grab-bars and widened doorways to accommodate his chair. He didn't go so far as to refer to himself as "differently abled," but he refused the label "handicapped." He drove a hand-operated automobile, he taught his classes, he lived his life, and while he conceded he wasn't the man he had been, he insisted he was the same person.

This led me to picture Pat on Fripp Island, in his own kind of wheelchair. He could function, I thought, but you had to cut him slack and make allowances for what he had suffered, starting in childhood and ongoing today. Lenore and the family couldn't count on him to rescue them. They had to help rescue him, and he had to learn to accept his situation. But when I ran this past him during our next phone call, Pat dismissed it as "Prozac talking."

"That's better than Jim Beam talking."

"To each his own."

Again that year we celebrated the holidays with Linda's father in Naples, Florida. Not that there was anything festive about the occasion. He had contracted Guillain-Barré syndrome, and although he regained the ability to walk, he tired easily and stayed indoors, bundled in sweaters and gloves. Despite the sweltering heat, he swore he was freezing.

On the trip north, we laid over in Orlando, where my biological father, Jack Mewshaw, was visiting. I hadn't seen him in twelve years, not since Marco was an infant. We met for a meal in a franchise restaurant at an anonymous strip mall. Perhaps compared to where he lived in Las Vegas this spot near Disneyland struck him as a homey setting for a family catch-up. But I staggered out of Denny's sick at heart.

The plan was to stop in South Carolina to spend New Year's

Eve with the Conroys. In winter Fripp Island was leached of all color except for strands of gaudy lights braided into the lank flags of Spanish moss. Pat greeted us at the front door, a glass of champagne in one hand, an oyster in the other. He wore a white pullover, and because I had on a dark blue sweatshirt, we might have been opposing images on a photo negative. Draining the champagne, inhaling the oyster, he set the glass aside and flung the oyster shell into the road. Rather than embrace me, as he customarily did, he fell to his knees and spread his arms wide like a crucified Christ.

"Don't tell me," he said. "Lemme guess. You met your father after all these years and it went just like one of the Hallmark cards you're writing."

"Stand up, Pat," Lenore said. "Help them with their bags."

Pat stayed on his knees, pretending to be Jack Mewshaw. "Please forgive me, son. I've been a terrible parent. You deserve better. You deserve to be loved. I hope it's not too late. I've thought about you every day, every minute we've been apart. Let's never lose touch again."

After lapsing into momentary silence, he asked, "How am I doing?"

"Please, Pat," Lenore signaled for him to get up. But she was laughing. So were Linda and I.

"You're slightly off the mark," I said.

"Tell me where I'm wrong." He labored to his feet. "Tell me where I've failed as a novelist, an expert at reconciliation scenes."

"It wasn't a reconciliation. It was more like a chance meeting between high school classmates who had never been close friends. He gave me a curt handshake and said, 'How's it going?'"

"But then I bet you talked about your feelings for hours."

"Not exactly. Maybe it's because we were at Denny's. Great place for a Reuben sandwich. Not so hot for father-son reunions."

Pat threw back his head and shouted into the darkening South Carolina sky, "Fuck all fathers!"

"You're a father," Lenore pointed out. "Or have you forgotten?"

 Tennis authorities did not take kindly to *Ladies of the Court.* As the Miami Open got underway on Key Biscayne, news broke that the book revealed the frequency with which coaches sexually abused underage girls on the tour. The tournament cancelled my press credentials and revoked its permission to sell copies on site. *The New York Times* grumbled that this violated the First Amendment, which was something I gabbed about on a coast-to-coast promotional tour.

When I reached San Francisco, the Conroys wouldn't hear of my staying anyplace except their house in Presidio Heights. Fresh in from Fripp Island, Pat let me sleep in his top-floor office. If that weren't enough to make me feel like a valued member of the family, Susannah, now eleven, announced that she was converting to Catholicism and wanted Linda and me to be her godparents. Without mentioning that her maternal grandmother might already have baptized her in a Roman bathtub, I happily accepted.

Pat had no comment about his daughter's conversion. He had little to say about anything. After his long absence, he seemed like a stranger in his own home. I put this down to our profession.

Novelists lived mostly in their heads, which were often thronged with imaginary characters who made it difficult to deal with flesh-and-blood people and their mundane demands.

The family pet, a King Charles spaniel named Jimmy, suffered from fly-catcher's syndrome, an obsessive-compulsive disorder that caused the dog to snap at imaginary insects. It pleased Pat to report that the veterinarian had prescribed a selective serotonin reuptake inhibitor for Jimmy. "Wouldn't you know it? I've got a depressed dog on Prozac to go with my depressed friend."

"I've quit catching flies," I said. "I've also quit chasing my tail."

"Congratulations. Lenore's on my case for chasing a different type of tail."

It had crossed my mind that Conroy might not have lived alone all those months on Fripp Island. But I asked no questions, figuring he would tell me if he cared to. When he suggested we take a walk, I guessed he meant to discuss his marriage. Instead we tramped up and down the steep hills in silence. To tourists on cable cars we must have looked like a duo of white-haired gents trudging on a StairMaster.

Pat eventually began limping and told a scarcely credible story about being hit by a car. "I came back from the liquor store one night carrying a sack full of bottles. A car sideswiped me at an intersection, and my fat ass flew over the hood. I landed on my feet, still holding the bag. There was a woman at the wheel, and her husband or boyfriend was smacking the shit out of her. I assumed he blamed her for the accident. But he was shouting for her to step on the gas and get out of there."

"Did you call the cops?"

"Nah. I staggered home and got no sympathy from Lenore. She didn't believe a word I said."

"I hope you saw a doctor."

"I did. He diagnosed me with a herniated disk. I already knew that. I've had one for years. My problem now is neuropathy."

The condition damaged the peripheral nerves, Pat explained, and numbed his feet. Some patients improved if they reduced the stress in their lives—a suggestion that Pat pronounced "ridiculous." He had no more hope of relaxing than he did of following the doctor's other recommendation: Quit drinking.

"How am I supposed to live without booze? Who the fuck wouldn't freak out with a wife like Lenore and a suicidal stepdaughter and a publisher breathing down my neck to deliver a novel or pay back an advance I've already spent? But I'm happy you're here. Finally I have a friend."

"You've got hundreds of friends. From what Lenore says, they'll all be at the party you're throwing for me."

"They don't matter, Mike. Not like you do. I can't write here. Then I go to Fripp and get so damn lonely, I can't write there either. It'd be different if you were around. We could work in the morning and talk in the afternoon."

"We talk on the phone almost every day."

"That's not the same."

At a restaurant in Ghirardelli Square, we ordered fried calamari, as succulent as any you'd eat in Italy, we agreed. Pat had a bottle of wine, an Italian, not a California vintage, and finished it himself. "I wish we had never left Rome," he said.

"I realize this is heresy, but I've lost a little of my faith that the Eternal City is the answer to every question. You've lived there twice and bailed out both times. Me, I'm staying in the moment," I added lightheartedly. "Tennis coaches tell me that's the key to success."

"How's that working for you?" He pushed unsteadily to his feet. "I want you to meet Tim Belk."

As we hiked through the Castro District, Pat's limp grew more pronounced. "Tim's supplying the musical accompaniment for your party. I rented a grand piano."

Tim and Pat had taught high school together in Beaufort, each an outcast in town, the one because of his sexuality, the other because of his liberal stance on race relations. Now in San Francisco, they acted as caregivers for AIDS patients whose cases were more advanced than Tim's.

"If you moved here," Pat said, "you could help us."

"How can I be sure you won't hole up on Fripp Island? Or uproot the family and ditch me for some other city?"

"Question my stability all you like. But never doubt my loyalty."

I didn't doubt that or his kindness. No sparrow ever fell in any dark forest that Pat didn't volunteer to help. But all too often he failed to notice that the woods were on fire and his own house was in flames.

At Tim Belk's apartment, the two of them embraced, then promptly traded insults. It was male bonding, Southern style. As a sign of their intimacy, they said the unsayable, the unspeakable. Tim, who was pale as parchment and skeletally thin, referred to Pat as a fat slob. And Pat wisecracked that his buddy had so few T cells, he should give each of them a name.

I told Pat that if I were sick, joking was the last thing I'd want from him.

"What would you prefer?" he asked. "Poetry?"

"I'd prefer tongue-tied grief."

Then they began bantering about the night Pat dropped by a local bar where Tim played piano. Who should cruise into the dive but Marlene Dietrich who broke out singing "Lili Marlene"?

"It was a drag queen," Tim insisted. "Marlene Dietrich spent the last ten years of her life confined to bed in Paris."

Pat refused to believe him and repeated the story in his posthumous oral biography, *My Exaggerated Life*, calling the occasion "one of the magic moments of all our lives."

BACK AT THE HOUSE, I asked Lenore about Pat's hit-and-run encounter with a car.

"I think he walked into it," she said. "Since I wasn't there, I don't know the real story. The bottles of bourbon were in the bag unbroken. He didn't have any blood or bruises on him, or we would have gone to the ER.

"He had had back pains for years. This seemed no different. Finally he had surgery and spent a lot of time in bed. He drank a huge amount, starting with wine at lunch and a tumbler of bourbon he took to bed after lunch. Then at 4 p.m. when he woke up from his nap, he'd start his serious drinking."

It upset her that he mixed alcohol with his medications, and that he bribed the kids to run to the store to buy liquor. "I was done enabling him," Lenore said, "and he was furious about that. He called me Carrie Nation. I brought him his meals in bed, but no alcohol."

She bet me Pat would never mention her room service. "He has a very selective memory. You can't take everything he says literally."

AT A CHINESE RESTAURANT ON the flats below Presidio Heights, Melissa and Megan, now in their mid-twenties, met Pat, Lenore, Emily, Susannah, and me for brunch. On a large round table with a lazy Susan at its center, dishes of dim sum circulated while a heated discussion flared up about the party that night. Someone had to stay home to wait for the grand piano and the flowers to be delivered. Then there was a debate about valet parking. How many drivers should be hired? And where should they stash the cars?

"These are Gucci Problems," Pat said. "Trivial shit that rich kids worry about. I'll take care of everything."

"Take care of it how?" Megan demanded.

"I'll write a check."

"That's how you always deal with problems. Take the easy way and write a check."

Melodramatic as a roulette wheel, the lazy Susan spun slower, then it stopped. "What do you think, Mike?" Pat's voice had dropped into a gunfighter's drawl. "Is writing checks the easy way out?"

"That depends on whether you have money in the bank."

"Goddamn right!" He walloped the table with the palm of his hand. "Wait until you girls start paying your own bills, then tell me how easy it is."

His wife and daughters looked stricken. This wasn't, I recognized, a dispute about money or who paid the bills. It was about love and how deeply the women in his life resented his regular withdrawals into his own remoteness or across the continent to Fripp Island. That he didn't understand only added to the sadness of the situation.

THAT EVENING, THE OVER-THE-TOP LAVISHNESS of the party deepened my own distress. The food, the wine, the floral displays, the servants, Tim Belk's rendition of the American songbook—everything suggested a profligate occasion whose purpose was anybody's guess. Pat looked as out of sorts as I felt. It struck me that with the exception of his place on Fripp Island, all the houses and apartments Pat lived in were an awkward fit—much like the gorgeous shells that spiny hermit crabs inhabit.

He kept his distance from me, standing at the bar and draining glass after glass of bourbon. I couldn't help suspecting that he blamed me for all this wasted effort and expense.

Incumbent mayor Art Agnos and former mayor Joe Alioto worked the room, backslapping as if at a fundraiser. Actors Peter Coyote and Michael O'Keefe, who had played Pat in the film of *The Great Santini*, were handsome faces in the crowd. O'Keefe's wife, Bonnie Raitt, an eight-time Grammy winner, hung back as though she feared someone might ask her to sing.

A pride of San Francisco writers—Herb Gold, Amy Tan, Armistead Maupin, Blair Fuller, and Mark Childress—stuck together, talking shop. I tried to strike up a conversation with Herb Gold, who, like me, had been a Fulbright fellow in France. That subject soon petered out, and I turned to Blair Fuller, whose daughter Mia I knew from Rome. Fuller asked if Luisa Stewart was still beautiful, and let it go at that.

Calvin Trillin sidled up to me and whispered, "What are we celebrating?"

"My new book."

He asked no more questions, not my name, not the book's title. I didn't blame him. His glazed expression was that of an author who had already met too many interchangeable egos.

I ended up helping Lenore, Emily, and Susannah distribute hors d'oeuvres and collect empty glasses and plates. Long before the last guests departed, I climbed the stairs to my room and watched boat traffic sluice beneath the Golden Gate Bridge, whose far end was lost in the foggy hills of Marin County. Guilty at hiding here, I decided I'd thank the Conroys in the morning before my flight to LA.

At 8 a.m., as I lugged my suitcase downstairs, the dregs of last night wafted up my nostrils—the smell of cigarette butts, wilting flowers, and spilled whiskey. Lenore had brewed a pot of coffee and taped a note to a cup. "Had to run Susannah to soccer practice. Pat's in bed. Wake him before you call a cab. XOXO."

I knocked at the master bedroom and got no answer. I knocked louder and Jimmy barked and Pat groaned. Swaddled in sheets like a half-risen Lazarus, he lay spraddle-legged next to the dog, who was snapping at imaginary flies. "Sorry," Pat said. "I'm too hungover to get up."

"It's me that's sorry for not thanking you and Lenore last night."

"Don't fucking mention last night. I had nothing to do with it. That was strictly a Lenore Fleischer production. The most humiliating night of my life!" There was an uncanny echo of the time he told Linda and me that Lenore had infected him with herpes. I hated to leave on this note, but Pat's head had sagged back on the pillow and Jimmy was licking his face.

On the plane to Los Angeles, I couldn't stop replaying the past few days—the most disquieting stretch I had ever spent in Pat's company. Had he insisted on my staying with him so he could persuade me to move to San Francisco? Or was it the opposite? Did he believe if I sampled his life here, I'd understand why he hid out on Fripp Island?

At LAX, I learned the city was on emergency alert. The publisher's rep said all my interviews had been cancelled in anticipation of riots after the verdict in the Rodney King case. Rather than pay for a hotel, the rep booked me a seat on a red-eye flight east. It came to me that on our trip to Munich, Pat and I had admitted we both feared flying. Now that I spent so much time up in the air, I had worse things to worry about.

17 On a travel magazine junket, I later crossed paths with Lenore in Paris and invited her to tea at Angelina under the arcade on rue de Rivoli. It was an old-fashioned café with a décor as deliciously confected as its pastries. Although supercharged with caffeine and sugar, we quickly subsided into a discussion of our grievances—my desire to live in Europe and start writing novels again, and Lenore's desire for Pat to finish *Beach Music* and resume living with her. He had sent hundreds of yellow legal pages for her to type, but she couldn't guess where the plot was headed or how it would end. Why, she wondered, couldn't he work like me, at home with his family, keeping regular hours, not driving himself and everybody else nuts with his need for isolation, special pens, a particular chair, and his favorite music playlist?

I defended Pat and confessed that, far from the low-maintenance, high-producing author she imagined, I wasn't writing anything these days apart from articles. Although I shared her concerns about his drinking and his health, I stressed that she had to understand that after all he had gone through during childhood, his first marriage, and his breakdowns, she couldn't expect him to behave like a conventional husband.

Lenore swore she expected nothing more than that Pat be present in his children's lives and emotionally available to her.

"Be honest," I said. "You expect him to fight Alan Fleischer, protect your kids, especially Emily, and pay the bills."

Lenore spoke as bluntly as I did. "You have no conception," she said, "of how hard it is to get him to make reasonable choices. He's great at solving other people's problems and ignoring his own. He should be talking to a therapist, not wasting hours on the phone with his friends. If something's wrong in our marriage, we should fix it together, not with him on the other side of the country doing who the hell knows what. You're his best friend, Mike. What am I supposed to do?"

"For starters, quit throwing parties like the one in San Francisco."

"*I* threw?" Her dark eyebrows spiked. "You mean *we* threw. It's what Pat wanted for you. He said to invite everyone we know. We drew up the list together. It was his idea to hire a piano and have Tim play. We discussed the menu with the caterer. This is his usual passive-aggressive routine. He makes decisions—or doesn't make them—then blames everybody else when he doesn't like how things turn out."

"I'm sorry. I have no right sticking my nose into your business."

"I value your opinion, Mike. But like I've told you before, don't take everything Pat tells you as literal truth."

THE SUMMER OF 1994, ALONG with the rest of America, Pat and I obsessed about the murder of Nicole Brown Simpson. O.J. denied he had slit her throat and killed her friend Ron Goldman. But on the day he was supposed to surrender to the police, he bolted in a white Bronco SUV with his friend, A. C. Cowlings, at the wheel. Surrounded by squad cars and tracked overhead by TV helicopters, Cowlings supplied a running commentary; O.J. had a gun at his head and threatened to commit suicide.

Pat identified with both men in the Bronco—Cowlings, ready to risk his life for a friend, O.J., the ruined hero, half longing to die, half hoping to be saved. "He's going to do it," Pat exclaimed by phone. "We're about to witness America's first televised suicide." Then he added a line that chilled my blood. "Wouldn't you love to check out with the whole country watching?"

"I may not be at the top of my game these days," I said. "But I'm not ready to commit suicide, with or without millions watching."

"Lucky you."

Weeks later, in what sounded like a postscript to our previous conversation, Pat called in tears and told me his brother Tom, age thirty-three, had jumped off a fourteen-floor building in Columbia, South Carolina. The baby of the family, Tom had been a schizophrenic, in and out of institutions, on and off his medications most of his life. Pat sobbed that the death had wounded his father so grievously, he feared the Great Santini would never bounce back.

The story of Tom's short, tragic life poured out of Pat with such vividness and power, it sounded ready to be set in type. He described the time that Tom, in a fugue state, had disappeared into the forest and been discovered lying naked on a bed of leaves. He had lain there so long and deathly still, Pat said, deer had licked salt from his body. Enthralled by this image, I didn't question until later, when Pat wrote up the scene, whether it could conceivably be true.

Then in late October, shortly before he turned forty-nine, Pat called again from Fripp and told me, "I've never been closer to killing myself."

The subject of self-harm played such a constant part of our conversations, I asked, "What's wrong?" in what I hoped wasn't an overly casual tone.

"Lenore's flying to South Carolina for my birthday."

"That's hardly a reason to kill yourself."

"No bullshit, Mike, I'm in bad shape. I can't write. I can't sleep. I can't stop drinking. Having Lenore around will make everything worse."

"She's seen you like this before. Why not take a break from the book and celebrate with your wife?"

"I'm in no fucking mood to celebrate. I'm in the mood to slit my wrists." He started crying. "You have to help. If I tell Lenore not to come, she'll talk me out of it. But she'll listen to you."

"I doubt that. Anyway, it's not my place to tell her."

"You'd rather I kill myself?"

"I'd rather you stop talking like a crazy person."

"Listen, Mike, my marriage is over. It's been over for years, and Lenore won't accept that. I swear to Christ, this'll end either with you convincing her not to come or me killing myself. Your choice."

"I'm not doing your dirty work. If you want a divorce, it's up to you to let her know."

"You don't have to tell her I want a divorce. Just tell her not to come to Fripp. Tell her we'll talk once I have my head screwed on straight. Is that such a big favor to ask? If I can't depend on my best friend, who can I count on? I don't have anybody else."

If there was the slightest chance he was serious and I could save his life, I couldn't say no. Still, I struck a bargain. I'd speak to Lenore if he promised to see a therapist.

Pat gave me his word and even gave me the name of the therapist—Marion O'Neill. Her office was on Hilton Head, an hour's drive from Fripp, and she had treated him in the past. Weeping in gratitude, babbling about his abiding love, Pat pleaded for me to call back after I spoke to Lenore.

Within minutes, I traded Pat's sobs for Lenore's. She skimmed from emotion to emotion in rapid succession—shock, embarrassment, pain, anger. "I don't understand, I just don't understand."

"He said he'll explain later. Right now he's all over the map."

"Explain what? It's obvious he wants out of the marriage. What am I supposed to do? Wait here, take care of his kids, and type his manuscript while he makes up his mind? What am I supposed to do with all the food, his favorite dishes, I was fixing for his birthday?"

I found myself apologizing for Pat, apologizing for the male race. She, however, demanded solid information and I had none. The best I could offer was to stay in touch.

I hung up and rang Pat, and the call kicked over to voice mail. I left a message for him to let me know he was all right. When hours passed and I hadn't heard from him, I dialed Fripp Island and left a second message, this one more urgent. Call me!

Though I feared the worst—that he had killed himself—I thought it more likely that in drunken exhaustion he had blacked out. Dialing him a third time, I got a recorded announcement that Pat's mailbox was full.

In autumn, half the houses on the island were locked up until spring, and loneliness settled in along with a dank sea mist that turned the swamps the color of onion soup, thick with floating debris. Pat professed to love it there in this season—a strange preference for such a gregarious soul. But in an emergency, who would notice that something had gone wrong? I had numbers for Cliff Graubart in Atlanta and Doug Marlette in Hillsborough, North Carolina. But neither of them was in any better position than I to race over and ensure that Pat was safe.

At daybreak, I dialed his number again, and he picked up immediately, as if expecting a different call. "I'm in a hurry," Pat blurted. "I have an appointment with the shrink on Hilton Head." He hung up so abruptly, I had no chance to ask questions.

The next day we had another aborted conversation. "Catch you later," he said. But there was no "later." As October vanished into November, Pat never called back, no matter how many voice mails I left. I wrote several letters, and he didn't answer them either. Once more, I feared he must have killed himself. What else could explain his silence?

In panic, I phoned Cliff Graubart at the Old New York Bookshop; he assured me Pat was at least alive. But he was a physical and emotional wreck. Cliff promised to pass along a message, and have Pat contact me once he recovered.

"When do you think that'll be?" I asked.

"I have no idea."

"Has he spoken to Lenore?"

"I stay away from that subject," Cliff said. "Anything to do with her or their marriage sets him off."

A NOVELIST NEEDS THE PATIENCE and stamina of a long-distance runner. After thirteen books I should have been an expert at waiting, confident that the plot would pan out. But I couldn't shake a woeful sense of abandonment and couldn't fathom why, after appealing to me for help, Pat had disappeared. For fourteen years we had had what he called "a life-changing friendship." Why would he turn his back on me?

Because there had been no warning, I was utterly unprepared and wondered what I had done wrong. How could I repair the damage? I considered flying down to Fripp. But if he refused to phone me back, how could I be sure he'd agree to see me?

Lenore had scarcely heard from Pat herself. After cutting off contact, he cut off the money, and as mortgage payments, school tuition, and household expenses piled up, she had to plead with his agent for interim support. Occasionally he surprised her with bouquets of flowers from Bloomers in San Francisco. Otherwise he communicated through his lawyers.

During Thanksgiving dinner, which Lenore fixed for Melissa, Megan, Susannah, and Pat's brother Jim and his wife and daughter, Pat called and asked to speak to Susannah. Confused and angry, his youngest daughter asked why he wasn't there with them. He told her he had to go shopping for a gun. Frantic, the family feared he meant to blow his brains out.

Suicide, some have remarked, is an unanswerable accusation leveled like a gun barrel at surviving loved ones. But what Pat was doing felt worse. Though still alive and talking to other people, he refused to tell his family or me why he had ghosted us.

Then I discovered something that hurt almost as much as his absence. I wasn't the first person Pat had pleaded with for help. He asked a former colleague of Alan Fleischer's at Emory University School of Medicine to tell Lenore the marriage was over. The doctor had declined to do so, because he knew something I didn't: Pat was involved with another woman. Now in addition to feeling ill-used, I felt like a fool.

Still, I didn't stop hoping, and after six months Cliff Graubart said Pat was ready to speak to me. He provided the name of a hotel in New York City and a room number. "He expects your call."

"Why doesn't he call me?"

"He's embarrassed," Cliff said. "He's afraid you side with Lenore and you'll guilt-trip him about the divorce."

The hotel phone rang and rang, then a robot instructed me to leave a message. I was tempted not to bother. Instead, I said I missed him and was worried about him. Linda's mother had died and we now felt free to leave Charlottesville. We were moving to London, I told him, and I'd hoped to see him before we left.

Pat never replied.

In June, Cliff passed through Charlottesville with a signed copy of *Beach Music* and called to say Pat had asked him to hand-deliver it. I told Cliff not to bother.

"But there's something in it you should read," Cliff said.

"I can't believe you'd be his messenger boy again after fucking me over before."

While I was out of the house, Cliff left *Beach Music* with Linda. In the acknowledgments, Pat praised "the novelist Michael Mewshaw and Linda Kirby Mewshaw who taught me the meaning of hospitality and made the Roman Years the great ones."

I might have been touched had I not been so bewildered. Was this the final kiss-off? In no mood to read *Beach Music*, I put it aside. But I followed the reviews, and every synopsis of the novel reminded me of the letter Pat had composed about *Year of the Gun*, blaming its failure on its lack of bestseller ingredients. By contrast, *The New York Times* remarked, *Beach Music*'s narrator, Jack McCall, "seems to have been mysteriously on hand to suffer the psychological bruises of almost every historical tragedy of the century."

As *Beach Music* climbed the bestseller charts, the paperback, film, and foreign rights sold for a king's ransom. Yet Pat sounded despondent in interviews and decried his separation from Susannah. To *People Magazine* he confessed, "I was a distant father. I'd just go off and write. I did the thing that screws up kids more than anything else in America. I went and got myself a little bit famous."

Tabloids and mainstream newspapers, slick magazines and literary quarterlies, television talk shows and NPR spread the accusation that Lenore had stolen his daughter from him. Pat referred to Susannah as his "lost child," suggesting the image of a waif on a milk carton.

In public Pat expressed melancholy. In private he dispatched menacing letters: ". . . you're going to see me fight for you Susannah. I'm entering the fray now and I'm going to write about my marriage to your mother. Several magazines, including *San Francisco Focus*, have asked me to write about my divorce . . . I do not want to do it, but I see no other recourse. The Lenores of the world hate exposure. I'm going to give her some . . . It has gone beyond mere cruelty. I miss you with every pore of my body. The marrow aches when I think about you. You're being raised by Fleischers, not Conroys . . . Please come this summer to Fripp for a long visit. If this thing ends, there will be no article about the divorce."

Much as I worried about the damage he was doing to Susannah, I also worried he was hurting himself. He didn't sound like the man I had known. It was as if he believed he could solve his personal difficulties the same way he resolved scenes in his novels, with a deus ex machina, like the tiger in the *Prince of Tides* that miraculously saves the Wingo family. Or with an ultimatum, like Tom Wingo threatening to throw a Stradivarius violin out a window. But he could never force Susannah to fall in line.

IN THE END, LEARNING TO live without Pat, I attempted to see things from his perspective. While I had lost an irreplaceable friend, he had lost his marriage, his youngest daughter, millions of dollars, and, by his own admissions, his mind for a time. It was hard to stay furious at someone who had squandered so much.

I recalled our discussion of the college coeds who had ditched us. Pat's girlfriend explained that he reminded her of a shameful period in her life, and she had abandoned him out of self-preservation.

Perhaps that was why Pat disappeared from me. Maybe it humiliated him to have asked for my help. No son of the Great Santini would want to be reminded that he hadn't been up to telling his wife he wanted a divorce.

This drew off some of the pain. It was better than the alternative theory that gnawed, rat-like, at my brain. To a man of Pat's effusive emotions, my behavior might have seemed withholding. He was wet Irish, as Vidal put it. I was dry. Had I failed to take on board how my refusal to move to San Francisco hurt him? In interviews he claimed he divorced Lenore because he believed she no longer loved him. Did he believe the same about me?

Boyhood had beaten Pat into a strange shape, like a horseshoe forged in fire. Don Conroy had left hammer marks on his son, just as my mother had on me. Long before Pat cut me off, Mom had withdrawn from all contact except for the occasional phone call. Although we lived less than 150 miles apart, she saw me only once in six years, and when I showed up unexpectedly at her house, she wouldn't open the door, reducing me to speaking to her through the mail slot.

Whenever I suggested a get-together, she said, "I'm too old and ugly. I don't want anyone to see me like this."

"I don't look so hot myself. But wouldn't you like to get to know your grandsons? You haven't laid eyes on Sean and Marco in years."

"Send me their picture."

As I had done with Pat, I attempted to piece together her reasons for rebuffing me, and in the lead-up to Linda's and my departure for London, I was determined to say goodbye in person.

My sister Karen told me Mom couldn't understand my insistence.

"I'd like to talk to her face-to-face," I said. "She's seventy-eight years old. We may not get another chance."

Mom, Karen, her husband, John, and I rendezvoused at a restaurant between Baltimore and Washington, DC, like warring armies powwowing in a demilitarized zone. Mom's hair was still dyed black and cut in bangs straight across her forehead. With age, she had shrunk and wore glasses with lenses of radically different strengths so that she appeared to be scrutinizing me from a distance and in a disconcerting close-up at the same time. At a secret signal, Karen and John excused themselves, giving Mom and me privacy.

"I hope you're not here to tell me something awful," she said.

"Like what?" I asked.

"Like you have a terminal disease. Or you and Linda are getting divorced."

"You don't sound like you'd be very sympathetic."

"Don't keep me guessing."

"Does there have to be a special reason for me to want to say goodbye?"

"You could have done that over the phone. You had me worried sick."

"I'm sorry. I offer an unqualified apology. There's no bad news—unless it's that I love you."

"Now you're being a smart-ass."

Karen and John rejoined us, and we ordered crab cakes and debated why they never tasted as good outside of Maryland. Was it the state water? Blue crab lump meat? Bay leaf? Afterward Karen and John drove Mom home, and I checked into a motel, starved for company. In the past I had called Pat whenever I was overwhelmed by strangled feelings toward my family. One of the worst aspects of his loss was this desire to speak to the very person who has abandoned me.

I wound up thinking about my mother, who for better or worse had passed on so much of herself to me. She had encouraged me to become a writer and had typed my first stories. It struck me that she had an artistic sensibility. The tragedy was she had no art form—no outlet, no means of expressing her inner chaos except through anger. How could I not love her? How could I not leave her?

WE LIVED IN A TOP-FLOOR walk-up in Hampstead that used to be a church priory. Among its astounding views of London, the only landmarks I recognized were the BT Tower and the dome of St. Paul's. The rest of the city remained, as Churchill said of Russia, a riddle wrapped in a mystery inside an enigma.

At first, we were all miserable. Marco and Linda resisted letting go of life in America, and even I, who had pushed hard for the move, had difficulty acclimating. A pinched nerve in my neck—a perfect symbol of deeply buried pain—disabled me and required months of physiotherapy and rehab.

Then like a convalescent risking baby steps, I began jotting notes, lines of dialogue and narrative fragments. Slowly, over half a decade, these coalesced into a novel, *Shelter from the Storm*, set in Central Asia, and a memoir, *Do I Owe You Something?* about various authors who had influenced me.

In 2000, to mark the new millennium, I sought new representation at the IMG Agency, where Carolyn Krupp took me on as a client and only afterward revealed that she was now Pat Conroy's agent. He had often spoken about me, she said. She knew the story of our estrangement and suggested it was time we got back together.

She must have told Pat the same thing in the same peremptory manner. He rang me in London and left an emotional message. I called back several times, but never got through to him. Desperate not to hit another dead-end, I wrote him:

Carolyn Krupp gave me your email address, but warned me that you don't often check it. In fact, you depend on your wife to do it for you. Let me confess I don't know diddly about this medium either and I depend on Linda to send, receive, etc. But I did want to avail myself of another channel of communication in the hope of reestablishing contact with you. It was painful for the past five years. I can be honest about that, can't I? I don't mean to guilt-trip you. I'm simply trying to say that you matter, and from what you said in your message we matter to you. So I'd like us to be back in touch.

Pat answered in a great tumbling breathless email whose subject line read "only connect." It lacked paragraph breaks or capital letters, but brimmed over with love and lamentation, bitterness and profound misremembering:

dearest michael. a funny thing happened on our road to reconciliation. my friends and family protested mightily and their point was mostly: the mewshaws chose lenore over you then fuck them. their point carries some resonance. it was only when i announced i was leaving lenore did i come to realize how loathed she was by everyone I loved except the mewshaws . . . you and linda have no idea what happened in that lousy marriage because you have been listening to the most untrustworthy narrator. do you remember that unbelievably ostentatious party we threw for you in san francisco, mike? i think it was the most embarrassing night of my life. by then i was beginning to understand her shallowness and vanity, but underestimated her cruelty and her evil. yes, evil and i do not use the word often or lightly. need an example? try this one: i have seen my beloved daughter, susannah, for only thirty days in the last seven years. i bet you have seen her more. at this moment i do not know if she graduated from the high school i paid fifteen thousand dollars a year to attend. i do not know if she is alive or where she is nor does any member of my family, including sweet megan. the last time i saw susannah she was yellow and lenore had given one more daughter an eating disorder. did lenore ever mention that she stole every penny i ever made from my writing career? did she report to you that she originally asked for a mere $38,000 a month for alimony? poor kid had to settle for a measly ten grand a month and for two years she has been making more money than i've made. luckily i will soon be filing for bankruptcy but am trying to stave it off until january. michael have you ever had a better friend than me? i'm serious, who has loved and cherished you more than i have? who has done you the honor of liking your work more than me? what other friend has tracked down your books and read them as carefully and lovingly as i did yours? do you have lots of famous friends in london? let me guess . . . martin amis, salman rushdie and all the usual suspects. do they love you more than i did, mike? i adored you mike and everyone in my world knew it and that love for you was as pure as anything about me . . . but i do not desire a spy in my camp who makes periodic reports to the malignant lenore. unless she appears at my bankruptcy proceedings, i plan never to lay eyes on that woman again. i will lead cheers when i read her obituary which will include not a single accomplishment. i lost two friends and two only in my divorce from lenore. the mewshaws. the rest rallied around me. because of my fame one might think? could be. but i couldn't tell at the time because i had a breakdown and was suicidal and had a tough time of it. my friends and family rallied around me. then they began telling me their lenore stories and what i put those people through because i married that woman causes me to shiver in remorse and shame . . . so let this be a start, mike. i needed to say some of these things because your withdrawal seemed like a betrayal at the time. but lenore was the one telling me what you were saying and how do i know you were saying those things? she's like the kgb. you never know what part of the evil empire you've entered . . . think about these things, michael, and talk it over with linda. i'm sorry I can't type and it just took me hours to peck this out. but you hurt my feelings. i can see linda choosing lenore, but not you. write me. great love pat conroy.

I was gobsmacked that he thought I had withdrawn and betrayed him. But he was right about one thing: I had never had a better, more generous friend. Still, I wrote back: "I don't feel that I chose Lenore . . . I don't feel I was given any leeway to make a decision. It struck me at the time that you simply withdrew from me . . . You stopped calling me and you stopped returning my calls."

I reminded him that I had had to phone Cliff to find out whether he was alive or dead. I reminded him that for five years, ever since he asked me to call Lenore, he had cut me off. "I never said anything to Lenore that I wouldn't say to you, Pat. My constant advice to her was to forget the past and if the marriage was over to get on with her life, to involve Susannah in it as little as possible, and to defuse the emotional pressure at every opportunity . . . But to get back to you and me for a moment, as '94 turned to '95 and months passed and I still didn't hear from you, I do know that my disappointment and bewilderment deepened . . ."

I explained that my motive for keeping in touch with Lenore was mostly to stay connected to my goddaughter Susannah. "I assure you that I'm not a message carrier or a spy . . . despite all the time that has passed, I'd like to reestablish contact. More than that I'd like to see you and talk to you. I've never forgotten you for a moment. I've dreamt about you repeatedly, and it's always a question of my encountering you unexpectedly and not knowing whether to embrace you or pass you by. I'm convinced it would be an embrace. Let me hear from you."

Pat replied that while my email was "beautiful and powerfully moving," it didn't address "the thing that has almost killed me in the five years of estrangement from you and linda. it is the hideous lenore's stealing susannah's childhood from me."

He challenged me: What if Sean and Marco didn't acknowledge gifts, such as the necklace he bought for Susannah last Christmas? It galled him that he had been so generous when "my father never got me anything my whole life."

> you're her godfather. tell me, michael, did my pretty daughter graduate from high school or not? . . . something else, godfather, did my daughter apply to college or not? where is my daughter right now? is she okay? the last time i saw her she was yellow and obviously suffering from an eating disorder. why do you wish to remain friendly with a woman who stole my kid from me, mike? my brothers think she is a common criminal for how she stole my money and [they're] trying to get me to have her arrested.

I answered that with Sean now living in California and Marco away at college, I missed the boys terribly. "There's something ineffably sad about losing contact with a kid, all the more so in your case where you've seen Susannah so seldom, haven't gotten the feedback you deserve and lack basic information."

> To remedy the situation to some extent, let me assure you that [Susannah] did graduate from high school. But the jaundice she seemed to be suffering the last time you saw her was actually an early symptom of chronic fatigue syndrome. She's been fighting that for the past year, seeing specialists, receiving treatment and mostly resting as much as possible . . . [This left] her with little energy to apply for college. So that's been postponed for a year. Health permitting, her plan is to go to Rome this fall, attend St. Stephen's School for a year, concentrate on painting and art courses, and get down to the business of applying to colleges.
>
> Much as it must torment you to be estranged from Susannah, I hope we can keep the discussion of our estrangement and, I hope, our reconciliation a separate issue. Regardless of whether I had cut off all contact with Lenore and had kept in constant touch with you, I don't believe I could've had much or any influence on the situation with Susannah. I could, of course, have offered sympathy, something I would have been more than willing to do had I been able to get through to you . . .

I pointed out that while Pat claimed, "'I cut you and Linda off because of the terrible things you were saying about me to Lenore,' you now allow for the possibility that we weren't saying those things, or that whatever we said had been exaggerated or twisted in the transmission. I trust that with hindsight you can understand how hurtful it was to Linda and me that you would believe that we were saying terrible things. More especially that you would believe them without allowing us an opportunity to respond and set the record straight."

> You've gone through a great deal of suffering and misery in the last decade, and I'm sorry for that and even sorrier that I wasn't in any position to offer support. In many ways, most of which don't really bear going into, I too have been hurting . . . for the past decade, and have only in recent years recovered a bit and begun to take tentative steps toward trying to live more or less sanely and as happily as possible [in] whatever time I have left to me. It isn't easy and never will be. How could it be otherwise? Given the start you got in life, you're lucky to be able to chew gum and walk at the same time. I feel the same about myself. I'm trying to take simple survival and the occasional accomplishment for the miracles they seem to me to be. I hope I don't sound, as you once said I would when I began taking Prozac, like a writer of Hallmark cards. I don't have the sort of bravado that would lead me to say that anything that doesn't destroy me strengthens me. Nor would I agree that we become stronger at the broken places that have healed. Frankly I feel pretty bruised and scuffed up, but I refuse to let that fuck up the rest of my life and prevent me from enjoying the things I look forward to, which include seeing you and having a chance to talk face to face, to reflect on old times and to have some new ones.

Pat responded with a seething email that would have offended me had it not made me fear for his mental health:

> that you do not feel any outrage for me or what has happened to me makes me wonder why you are attempting to

resuscitate one of the great friendships of my life . . . your missing sean and marco has nothing to do with the tragedy that befell me and susannah. it cheapens and belittles the agony i have endured because of that shitbird i once married. you cannot understand how painful my estrangement with susannah has been and you should never write a sentence like that . . . for whatever reason, mike, i lost you and linda during my divorce from lenore. i lost no one else of consequence. in fact i found something out. i discovered that i'm greatly loved, that i'm generous spirited and that spirit makes people want to be around me. i was with a group of old friends from high school recently and one of them asked the group if they got in serious trouble who would their first phone call go to. i was considering the question when i found the whole room pointing at me.

Then in an abrupt about-face, he wrote:

i sent your letter to doug marlette and cliff graubart and both agreed that you wrote me a love letter. i thought you did too. you are also right that I should not have believed anything lenore told me you had said. she is satanic in her use of lying. because of that, mike, you and linda know nothing of what happened in our marriage and I repeat the word nothing.

Just as he seemed to be softening, however, he veered back on the attack:

don't do the i made this phone call and you didn't answer my message and i told cliff i could be of this service or i

tried to open up these lines of communications . . . when
the smoke cleared you stood with lenore. i would trem-
ble with shame to tell a father that his child had graduated from high school when that father had paid for that
diploma . . . that's how horrible lenore is, mike, and mike,
mike, mike, what has she done to my child?

It came to me that Pat might be right. Maybe there was nothing to be salvaged from a friendship that had sunk to such a low
ebb. The Pat Conroy who had been my friend would never have
referred to himself as "much loved"—not without laughing.
    I replied:

Clearly, you're very upset and very, very angry, and just as
clearly a great deal of that anger has splashed over on me.
Some of this may have been deserved. I've granted that
in my previous e-mails. I've attempted to account for my
actions, apologize for my shortcomings and place things
in context. But at the risk of adding to your distress and
making you still angrier, I'm afraid I have to say that I
cannot accept the blame and responsibility that you seem
determined to heap on me. The simple fact is—you repeat
it with emphasis in your last e-mail: 'You and Linda know
nothing of what happened in my marriage, and I repeat the
word nothing.' As a matter of logical consistency, how can
we be held culpable for things that we neither caused nor
knew about?
    I'm not privy to the details of your divorce, your ali-
mony agreement, your child support, your visitation rights
etc etc. . . . I never had any reason to know that Lenore
had 'stolen' Susannah from you. Frankly I still don't quite

understand that. Since I assume that legally you have visitation rights, even if Lenore refused to send Susannah to see you, I don't understand why you didn't take legal action to remedy the situation or simply fly out to California to be with your daughter . . .

The problem seems to come down to one thing. You feel extraordinarily aggrieved by what happened in your marriage and by much of what has occurred after the divorce. But if I accomplish nothing else, I'd like to convince you that I don't stand with Lenore. I stand where I've always stood. I stand on my own. I don't agree with or approve of all that Lenore does and what she seems to value. But to tell the truth there's much that you do and seem to value that I don't agree with or approve of either . . . I don't believe that loving someone or being close friends demands complete congruency of values, morals, ethics or, dread phrase, lifestyle . . . With difficulty, I've learned that we live in a highly flawed world, that I'm flawed myself and that there's no way of surviving and retaining one's sanity unless one accepts that. You, however, appear to be an absolutist in certain areas. I accept this about you and still want to be your friend. But in fairness and in the hope that it might prompt you to examine your own conscience, and simply for the record, I feel compelled to point out that you've played fast and loose with some essential truths . . .

It's not crucial to our relationship for you to iron out the inconsistencies in your explanation of why you cut me off. I assume you had your reasons and they seemed justified to you at the time . . . I'm prepared to pick up and move on from here. But I get no sense that you're willing to move on . . . The suggestion that comes up over and over again is that you can't forget what's happened, you can't forgive. To me that doesn't sound like love, much less friendship. It sounds like a child who insists on unconditional love, unqualified acceptance and unquestioned agreement. I'm afraid I can't give you that, Pat. It's no more in my nature than in yours to accept ultimatums.

After saying all this, I fear you'll cut off the dialogue. That would make me very sad and would be, I believe, a great loss for both of us. But you've been frank and forceful in stating your views. I accept that as the price of friendship and trust that you do too. When we were at our closest, candor seemed to be the essence of the relationship. I wanted always to be honest with you. I wanted to be the person in your life who wasn't in business with you, or borrowing money from you, or doing a script with you. I simply wanted to be your friend. I still do.

Pat held off answering for nearly a week. Then, weary of wrangling, he denied that he was issuing ultimatums. "Let me make this easier," he wrote. "I take full responsibility for the break-up of our friendship . . . Now what, mike?"

For a month we remained in desultory contact. I inquired about progress on his new project, a book about basketball, and described my life in London. "I have a very good physiotherapist—as ever my back aches—and a psychoanalyst—as ever my brain aches."

In a move that wrong-footed me as deftly as a crossover dribble, Pat wrote back:

i have an idea that I wanted to run by both of you. i would like you and linda to act as intermediaries . . . between susannah and me. i do not know where she is on this planet at this moment. i've talked to sandra [his new wife, the novelist Cassandra King] about this at length and if susannah is indeed going to school in rome this year we would be more than happy to move to rome this january. i need to get to know my kid again and she certainly needs to get to know me . . . you are the only two friends on earth who even know where she is right now . . . i have been sickened over this thing with susannah. i implore both of you to consider this and i would simply beg you to help me with my daughter.

Recalling the last favor he had asked of me and how catastrophically it ended, I hesitated to serve as a go-between again. I even wondered for a moment whether his accepting the blame for our break-up had been to soften me up for this request. Why get involved?

But in fact I didn't require much softening, and I was already involved. For her good and for his, Susannah needed to reconnect with her father.

When I agreed to help, Pat was lavish with gratitude. Still he cautioned me: "i thought you should know this. you will hear from susannah that i sent her harsh emails. I sent her fatherly ones. she does not take criticism well."

He offered to copy me on their correspondence. I replied that that wasn't necessary. "My hope is that . . . you'll both start from ground zero and not have to thrash over the past. I don't want to get caught between you and Susannah any more than I want to get caught between you and Lenore. My hope is to open a door or two, and have you take it from there."

"You're under no pressure at all," Pat wrote. "If you have any success, it will be a great victory and tremendous opportunity for me to reunite with my beloved daughter. if you have none at all, i will be ever grateful for your gracious [attempt] to put humpty-dumpty back together again."

Pat went ahead and sent me their correspondence anyway, and as I read the letters and emails to Susannah, I couldn't say what shocked me more—Pat's venomous tone or his delusion that he sounded "fatherly."

Shortly before Susannah's birthday in December 1997, he had written,

> Susannah:
>
> Sixteen is a big year . . . I had my sixteenth birthday in Beaufort, South Carolina, my first in the town that would change my life. It was the year I scored 28 points in my first basketball game against Ridgebrook, was elected President of the Senior Class and watched Randy Randal die on the baseball field. It was the year my brother Tom almost died when a penny lodged in his throat, the day Dad's squadron flew to Cuba during the Missile Crisis, and the year that Gene Norris [his English teacher] gave me *Look Homeward, Angel*. Make it a great year for your own sweet self. Try to include me in the year.

If he had left it at that, his letter would have been a gift any child would treasure. But Pat switched gears and began grinding at Susannah

> Lenore can do this for two more years and then it'll stop. You yourself can see the injustice of my not seeing you— not seeing you but paying every penny that makes that

household in San Francisco possible. I am supposed to write the check every month, but not supposed to see the daughter I love with all my heart. I trust your sense of justice, dear-heart. What has been just about this?

Great Love,

The Big Dad

Because he believed Lenore was the puppet-master, he held his daughter blameless and thought that once Susannah turned eighteen, she would choose him over her mother. When that didn't happen, he often lashed out at her several times a day. By April 23, 1999, she had had enough:

Okay, who is the mean, disrespectful one here? Tell Sandra to read the e-mail you sent me, or any of them for that matter and after that ask her to review your conduct towards me over the past couple of years. I wouldn't allow anyone to speak to me as you [do], but I have swallowed it because you bear this title 'father.' But I have come to realize that this kind of passive behavior is ignoble and non-productive, and challenging your distorted view and offering alternatives to your condemnations is pointless as well. I say with confidence that you are an incredibly irrational person and in the interest of my health I am not going to fight with you, nor take to heart your words and judgments proffered only to hurt me. I am equally confident that I am not at fault here and years of enduring your brutality makes me owe you nothing at present. Yet still, and I must be insane, I will willingly come together with you if you decide that you want to begin to heal our relationship. I would love to love you but you hate me way too much."

Unmoved, Pat demanded by email that Susannah attend Megan's wedding in June. Under no circumstances would he permit her to put in a brief appearance, then depart for France, where she was enrolled in a summer language course. At 2:30 a.m., the night of Susannah's senior prom, he wrote:

> Some ground rules about the wedding. My brothers and sisters noted with great displeasure that you and Gregory hung back and apart at my father's funeral. They did not get to talk to you. That will not happen at Megan's wedding. Both of you will mingle among Megan's and my friends. Get the word to your brother. You are going to act like Conroys at my daughter's wedding, not Gurewitzes . . .

Susannah re-sent her earlier email: "Who is the mean, disrespectful one here?" and Pat fired another volley in what became a two-day fusillade.

> You do not write worth a damn because you don't think worth a damn . . . But congratulations for finally getting up the guts to write back. Quit trying to outwrite me. I'll kick your ass every time you do. Send me your plans. You hear that. Got a problem with that? Send me your plans. Having trouble reading that? I've asked about eight times . . . Where are you thinking about going to college? In your mother's rapacious greed to rob me of every penny I had ever made, she forgot to include your college tuition. She gets enough from me every month to send three kids to college but she likes spending all that money on herself . . . If I see you and your brother even talking together at Megan's wedding there will be a scene. One day,

Susannah, when you are no longer a prisoner of war, you are going to hate Lenore for this. Before I die you are going to adore me. I love you more than your mother ever can or will. Because I can love, Susannah. Another writing lesson. Be clearer. Be sharper. If you wish to attack me, which you clearly do, get better. Get far better. You are simply insolent and petulant, not incisive and cutting. Be an assassin who goes for the jugular. You kill by being sharp, not windy . . . I know your squirrelly mother engineered France and this summer. Tell her this. While she is in France I go for her throat in San Francisco. A mass letter talking about her divorce from me and what she has done to me and you . . . You do not know what Lenore did to me but you are about to find out. Everything you have or eat or buy or own I have paid for, Susannah, including the tickets to France this summer. I'm going to cut your mother up for bait for not allowing you to see me. I'm furious. I rage against this. It is wrong, it is totally wrong and you know it is wrong. You self-righteous little urbanite. I will win this eventually, Susannah, and that is a promise. Why your mother is getting you out of the country is she knows you will fall in love with your father if you ever spend any time around him. And you will, Susannah. That's a promise . . . I adore you, the Big Dad.

Susannah replied:

I do not want to fight with you. I am committed to Megan's wedding . . . and I think that it is imperative that I attend. It will only be more difficult if you continue to abuse me because I am not going to retreat from this wonderful occasion. Please try. I am giving you no reason to be mean to me, and furthermore, there is no reason why you should ever be so hurtful.

Pat reacted like a creative writing teacher chastising a deficient pupil:

I just reread your last three e-mails. Lenore has not only eclipsed your ability to write she has murdered your ability to think. Your e-mails are nasty things which is OK by me since I am very aware I'm not exactly sending you Valentines. But . . . I have never seen a girl in a divorce treasure or honor her father less than you. Your cowardice has been breathtaking. Lenore makes eunuchs of all her children. Who the hell are you? Do you stand for anything? . . . why can't you even raise your voice for that poor Southern boy who rose out of the South without much education but only a dream of becoming a writer? I have never seen a check that a publisher has ever sent me, Susannah. I'm the easiest person in the world to steal from. I never have money in my wallet and I don't care about it. I don't even care about the millions your mother stole from me. Money is her demon, not mine. It cheapens her spirit. You are her last weapon against me and you let yourself be so used. Shame on you, Susannah. You are half me, yet you do not love that half . . . Gloves are off now. You shame me and you shame my family. My father fought for his country in three wars . . . I'm famous all over the world for my struggles with and love of family. How did Lenore kill yours? What did she do to you? How did she make you so mean that you could do this to me?

In answer, Susannah repeated her previous email, the one ending "there is no reason why you should ever be so hurtful."

Pat shot back:

My third letter of the day. You are not going to do this to me. I will not suffer the utter humiliation of you attending my daughter's wedding and then going to France. Got it. You come to the wedding and I'm taking my lawful visitation. You come here you stay here. Got it clear enough, bigshot? You will stay here and get to know me and learn to love me and honor me . . . If your mother thinks Gregory can get you to the airport after the wedding tell her I will move against her son as the son of the Great Santini. I have never laid a hand on Gregory but I know how to. I will rearrange his handsome face if he tries to interfere with my seeing you this summer . . . You'll learn to waterski this summer instead of French grammar.

As the day wore on Pat's vituperation never diminished, but his self-control did. Ranting like Lear at a perfidious daughter, he forgot the King's impassioned plea, "Let me not be mad." Poor Pat sounded mad in both senses of the word.

This is total warfare now. Lenore is wrong, has always been wrong about not letting me see you and will be wrong about everything she does or thinks the rest of her life. If you come to Megan's wedding I intend for you to stay for the entire summer. It is because I love and adore you. If you do not come I'll expose your mother publicly . . . No two days in Beaufort, then France. Got it. Am I being clear . . . A writing lesson . . . You have yet to discover the awesome power of verbs, especially the short punchy an-glosaxon ones. They're the ones that sing and burn and rip and scar. Write me and let me know what you're thinking. If you attack me, do it better. I adore you, the Big Dad.

Reading this, I refused to accept that Pat Conroy, the icon of the abused child, had become an abuser himself. As he mocked Susannah's writing, I decided it was his own grasp of language that had let him down and deluded him into believing he could browbeat his daughter into loving him. Here was an author, who had swayed millions with "the liquor of language," now wielding words like meat cleavers.

Pat's career had always been predicated on self-exposure, on an almost religious impulse to confess and seek forgiveness. Was that why he let me see their correspondence? To show himself at his worst and obtain absolution? My first instinct was to refuse him. He sounded sick, dangerous, and I wanted to protect Susannah. But then I hoped that if I could unblock the logjam between them, maybe he'd regain his bearings.

19 In autumn 2000, Sean, who aspired to direct films, was a production assistant on Martin Scorsese's *Gangs of New York*, then shooting at Cinecittà in Rome. Linda and I rented an apartment on Via Giulia, to be near him and Susannah, who was at St. Stephen's School. Now eighteen, she looked no more than thirteen, and her dark hair and eyebrows exaggerated the pallor of her complexion. Frail and underweight, she had a voice so faint I had to keep asking her to repeat herself.

Lenore alerted us that doctors had diagnosed Susannah with neurally mediated hypotension. A condition sometimes confused with chronic fatigue, it was caused by an adrenal gland malfunction which, in her case, might have been exacerbated by the stress of the divorce and a four-month bout of mononucleosis. In addition to extreme exhaustion, her symptoms included dangerously low blood pressure and a discrepancy between her lying-down and standing-up pulse rates. Despite the side effects of nausea and dizziness, she took Fleurinof, a corticosteroid; Dexedrine; and DHEA, a hormone replacement.

I put off speaking to her about Pat until she had re-acclimated to Rome. Then in October, once her health and spirits improved, the two of us strolled downhill from the Aventino through the Circus Maximus, over gravel still dusty from the summer. In black slacks and a black turtleneck, Susannah might have been a Left Bank artist; she told me she was writing poetry and taking painting courses. She hoped to edit the school literary magazine. As we trudged around the track where legend had it Ben-Hur raced his chariot, she asked if I knew the Italian word for "goddaughter." Shamefully, I didn't, even after living in Italy off and on for decades.

She forgave my ignorance, observing that since I hadn't been a godfather before, I couldn't be expected to know that she was my *figlioccia*. "And you're my *padrino*," she said.

With no subtle way of broaching the subject, I explained that after years of estrangement, her father and I had struck up an email correspondence. It remained uncertain whether we could repair the rupture between us, but Pat had asked me to give her a message. He and his wife, Sandra, were willing to live in Rome that winter and work to resolve his differences with her.

Thin and pale as she was, I had expected it to be easy to read Susannah's reaction. But her face was a blank white page. We advanced to the foot of the Palatine Hill and sat on a stone wall.

"Have you read the emails he wrote me?" she asked.

"Yes, he sent me copies."

"It's like he wants the whole world to read everything he writes."

"I'm sure the emails hurt you," I said. "But when Pat loses his temper, he doesn't realize how he sounds."

"I guess you read where I wrote I must be insane for still loving him. But he hates me too much."

"He doesn't hate you. He loves you."

"He has a funny way of showing it."

I didn't push Susannah. I didn't press my thumb on the scale.

I sat quietly on the cool stone with the massed ruins behind us radiating the last of the day's heat.

When she spoke again, it was with a strength of purpose out of proportion to her size. She promised to meet with Pat, but only if he swore he would quit writing terrible things about her and her mother.

When I phoned Pat with what I regarded as good news, he sounded less than enthusiastic. He said he'd have to check with Sandra and consult Nan Talese about the publishing schedule for his book in progress, *My Losing Season*. Then he added, "I want Susannah to fly to South Carolina for Christmas so we can discuss things before I move to Rome."

"My impression . . . Actually, it's not an impression. She told me outright she'd meet you here, but that's on condition that you stop writing about Lenore and her."

"Let me get this straight. My kid, who I haven't seen in years, who's living off my money, wants to set the rules?"

Into the teeth of his truculence, I might have thrown raw meat, saying, Take it or leave it, Pat. Or I could have tossed him a tranquilizer, pleading with him to compromise. I did neither. I listened to the oceanic static of the long-distance line. Or was that Pat's angry breathing?

"Fuck it," he finally said. "If she won't come here for Christmas, I'm not going there."

"Is that what you want me to tell her?"

"Say whatever you like."

Filled with despair, I reminded Pat that I had done exactly as he had asked, and Susannah agreed to get together. Why had he changed his mind?

He couldn't or wouldn't explain.

Pat and I didn't correspond for more than six months. Then in

May 2001, bubbling over with bonhomie, he emailed me, marveling about a cruise he and Sandra had taken from Cairo to Lisbon. Almost as an afterthought, he wrote, "Again, Mike, thanks for your intercession with Susannah. I knew how it was going to come out but you had to learn for yourself. Lady Lenore has to quit pulling the puppet strings before there can be a resolution to this sad affair. Ah, but you had to learn that too. It touched me that you tried."

Pat appeared to have forgotten that he, not I, had suggested I intercede with Susannah. Lenore had had nothing to do with it.

For a while, Pat and I corresponded about my memoir, *Do I Owe You Something?* His enthusiasm for it and his offer to write an introduction raised my hopes that this would lead to a meeting between us. But when the publisher, LSU Press, declined to include a chapter about Pat, he lost interest, and another long silence ensued.

I broke it shortly before Christmas 2001 to say I had visited Susannah in San Francisco and found her in good health and happily enrolled at UC Berkeley. Linda and I were spending the winter in Key West and invited him and Sandra down for a visit.

Pat replied that there were too many writers in Key West for his taste.

Two years later, at the Virginia Festival of the Book, Sandra popped up after I participated in a panel discussion and introduced herself. She said Pat had encouraged her to pass along his greetings. I asked her to join Linda and me for dinner, and Sandra accepted. An attractive ash-blond with a lovely Southern accent, she spoke of the four of us getting together in spring. She promised to give Pat our love.

This led to nothing.

And so I resigned myself to never seeing him again except in dreams where we crossed paths, with me uncertain whether to hug him or let him hurry by. The idea of a reconciliation had come to seem so remote, I could scarcely remember the point of it. Still, I never stopped hoping and never stopped thinking about Pat, and I never stopped puzzling over how a love story had turned into a tale as troubling and mysterious as any of the true crime tragedies I had written. A shrink might say—a shrink *did* say—that this all tied in with infantile separation anxiety and had reawakened memories of other significant figures who vanished from my life. Not that this insight salved the pain. "Loss," as Pat wrote, "hurts and bleeds and aches. Loss is always ready to call your name in the night."

Graham Greene remarked that a writer's childhood is the bank account he'll draw on for the rest of his career. In this respect, Pat inherited incredible riches, and like any heir to a fortune, he faced the difficulty of deciding what to do with his wealth. His natural impulse was to splurge. During the last two decades of his life, he produced only one more novel, *South of Broad*, but turned out books of nonfiction that continued to tap into the same vault and pay out the same currency as his fiction. Regardless of what he wrote, it revolved around familiar characters and central traumas—his mother and father and the damage they had done to him, the duplicity of women, the victimization of children, and his lifelong effort to coax order out of chaos.

Even *The Pat Conroy Cookbook: Recipes and Stories of My Life* served up second helpings from his childhood. It also served up a couple of curious comments about his literary career. Discussing the background to *The Prince of Tides*, Pat said there was no early indication that it would be a great success. He named me as a discourager: "The novelist, Michael Mewshaw, read it in Rome and suggested I cut it into twelve novels." But Pat's recall of this episode a quarter of a century ago was shaky. I responded to the first two hundred pages of a rough draft, not the full finished manuscript, and I never suggested that Pat cut it into twelve novels. His journal entry from that day in 1983, when we reviewed the first few chapters, contains a correct version of events.

In *My Losing Season*, a chronicle of his senior year on the Citadel basketball team, he devoted almost as much space to rehashing his father's cruelty as he did to dramatizing his thwarted hoop dreams. For me, a fellow aficionado of the game, the book was better when it focused on his adolescent fervor to achieve through sport what had been denied him in other arenas. The hard yards he put into practicing his jumpshot foreshadowed the labor Pat later applied to his books, lifting a wounded boy into world prominence.

But a journalist attacked *My Losing Season*'s truthfulness, a serious accusation against any memoir, especially in Pat's case, where his credibility, not to mention his popularity, depended on his being a reliable narrator of his misery. A *Washington Post* excerpt from the book dwelled on Pat's days at Gonzaga High School, playing junior varsity basketball. At the annual athletic banquet he claimed Don Conroy had flown into one of his violent rages and hit Pat in front of an auditorium full of students and their fathers. According to *My Losing Season*, this set off "a free-for-all" as "dozens of dads . . . came roaring to my defense."

The scene prompted Dave McKenna, a reporter then at the *Washington City Paper*, now at *Deadspin*, to start digging. After *The Washington Post* acknowledged it hadn't fact-checked the story, McKenna interviewed witnesses Pat had cited by name. None of them had any memory of the brawl. William Bennett, former secretary of education, had been at the banquet, but said, "I can't recall that scuffle."

Pat Buchanan, a Gonzaga graduate, conservative TV commentator, presidential speechwriter, and former Republican presidential candidate, tried to verify the story with his six brothers who had all gone to Gonzaga. Not one of them had ever heard of the incident. Buchanan puckishly observed that Conroy's "some writer, isn't he?"

McKenna unleashed "an armada of emails and phone calls" to the author, his agent, and his publisher. Finally, Pat responded through his agent, "No one saw him get hit, and he did not discuss it with anyone."

McKenna concluded, "if nobody saw Conroy get hit by his dad, then the whole passage about Gonzaga dads coming after the elder Conroy is bogus. And that means the whole brawl is bogus. And that means any lasting emotional impact suffered as a result of the brawl, meaning great chunks of *My Losing Season*, is bogus."

In a follow-up article, McKenna placed this matter in the context of the recent controversy caused by James Frey's memoir, *A Million Little Pieces*, which had started off as a novel but had been marketed as fact. McKenna pointed out that Pat had blurbed Frey's fraudulent memoir, and moreover Pat's editor, Nan Talese, had edited *A Million Little Pieces*. This raised the question, at least in McKenna's mind, of what kind of fact-checking the books had undergone.

Apparently undaunted by this minor controversy, Pat repeated in his oral biography the episode of his father beating him the night of the Gonzaga athlete banquet. The scene now occurs on a parking lot, not in an auditorium. But that didn't change Dave McKenna's mind. In an article for *Deadspin*, he mocked Pat for lying from the grave.

Pat's next book, *My Reading Life* (2010), a collection of autobiographical essays, contained charming reminiscences about his baptism in the priesthood of literature. He dedicated it "to my lost daughter, Susannah Ansley Conroy. Know this: I love you with my heart and always will. Your return to my life would be one of the happiest moments I could imagine." No one would guess that

Susannah was now a grown woman of twenty-nine who long ago agreed to reconcile with her father.

How much of the book can be accepted as truth, I don't know. When Pat claimed to have bumped into Italo Calvino in a café and enjoyed a sprightly conversation with him, or when he described a tour of Rome with Gore Vidal as his private guide, I had my doubts. But these were minor quibbles compared to my reaction when Pat later maintained that he had often eaten out with Vidal, Linda, and me in Rome, and that Gore liked him because Pat always picked up the bill. To my recollection, Pat met Vidal precisely one time, at my fortieth birthday party, and Conroy's diaries note no dinners with Vidal.

AS I STARTED THE STEEP descent toward seventy, with Pat in a glide path behind me, time seemed to speed up. Other things slowed down. Still others slipped out of kilter. Doctors diagnosed me with a heart arrhythmia and cured it with a catheter ablation. An oncologist warned me that my prostate needed close monitoring.

My mother died, professing her love by telephone, but refusing to allow me to visit as she faded away. In Maryland at her funeral, none of my siblings cared to speak after the requiem Mass. But I extemporized for a few minutes, startling the congregation and myself by paraphrasing the Koran. Even in death, I said, Mom would remain as close to me as Allah was to his children—as close as the vein in a man's neck.

Pat, no surprise, was a far superior eulogist. Family and friends frequently beseeched him to speak at obsequies of their loved ones. A number of these tributes were published in a posthumous miscellany, *A Lowcountry Heart*. At Doug Marlette's memorial service he declared that their friendship was founded "on an untouchable loneliness" and "oceanic rage," and he demonstrated his loyalty by stridently defending Marlette's second novel, *The Bridge*, which had been criticized in some quarters as slandering a fellow North Carolina novelist. Speaking directly to his dead comrade, Pat proclaimed, "For you, Doug, in honor of you, my next book is to be named *Bring Me the Head of Alan Garganus*. In memory of you, Doug Marlette, each year I am going to bring a hundred of my novels and conduct a seminar on the burning of books."

Not satisfied with refighting a literary feud at a funeral, Pat maligned Lenore. A dozen years after their divorce, he advised mourners that he and Marlette always referred to his second wife as "the Taliban."

Yet another memoir, *The Death of Santini* (2013), opened with an invocation of the family's deities—Don Conroy "every inch of him a god of war" and Peggy Conroy "goddess of light and harmony." The last book published during Pat's lifetime, it was in parts as poignant as anything he ever wrote: "I was the oldest of seven children; five of us would try to kill ourselves before the age of forty . . . Love came to us veiled in disturbances—we had to learn it the hard way, cutting away the spoilage like bruises on a pear."

But other sections of *The Death of Santini* were as pugnacious as a brandished fist, and in his portrait of his suicidal brother Tom's madness the dialogue called into question Pat's own stability. "Hey, baby Tom, the games are over. Your oldest brother has arrived. And you know what big brothers do best? We love to kick the asses of our baby brothers because they're weak and pathetic and can't defend themselves."

With Tom sprawled on the floor, Pat planted a foot in his face and taunted him: "If you fight me, I'll kill you. If I kill you, I'll be sad for a day or two, but that's all."

Although Pat made no attempt to excuse his behavior, he offered an explanation: "My father's DNA assured me that I was always ready for a fight and that I could ride into any fray as a field-tested lord of battle."

For the first time he suggested that he inherited some of his belligerence from his mother. Rather than portray her again as the hapless martyr of her sadistic husband and of Marine Corps sexism, he quoted Peggy Conroy boasting, "I ruled the house and everything that went on in it. I could make [your father] dance like a puppet whenever I wanted. I was the boss and the police chief in every town we entered."

Revising a scene from *My Losing Season* where his mother grabbed a butcher knife to defend herself, only to have her husband slap her to the floor, Pat now insisted that she had stabbed Don Conroy, and pledged her son to secrecy as they rushed him to the emergency room. Pat conceded that no one else in the family had any recollection of this episode. But then his brothers and sisters, he said, suffered from seriously flawed memories. When they recalled their childhoods they sometimes recited passages from his fiction rather than personal experience.

In *The Death of Santini*, one thing hadn't changed. He continued to pound away at Lenore. "On a devastating, inexplicable rebound," he wrote, "I married Lenore Fleischer who would teach me everything about life and love that I didn't want to know . . . in the next ten years she would ruin my life and lead me into a suicidal spiral that I thought I would never recover from." He accused her of "unadulterated hatred of her daughter Emily, the victim of incestuous sexual violation," and said that Lenore "failed to tell me she had gone off birth control three months before our wedding, then surprised me by getting immediately pregnant, maybe even on our wedding night."

While a memoir is clearly an author's side of the story, and no one would argue Pat's right to cannibalize his life for his books, it bothered me that he kept doing what his daughter had entreated him not to do. Was this the humiliating exposure he had threatened if Susannah refused to bend to his will?

BY NOW PAT WAS VERY sick, and during the summer of 2012, stricken with Type 2 diabetes, soaring blood pressure, and liver failure, he nearly died. Again, doctors cautioned him to quit drinking and to follow a strict health regime. Almost a hundred pounds over his college playing weight, he was dangerously obese, but he checked out of the hospital determined to get well. Never one to do things by half measures, he hired a nutritionist and bought a business interest in a fitness center staffed by his personal trainer.

Even under duress—especially under duress!—Pat remained funny and eminently quotable. He joked to a *Washington Post* reporter, "If there was a loving, just God, foie gras would have one calorie and bean sprouts would have 1,400." In photos of him working out, sweating prodigiously in a tee shirt and shorts, his legs looked as robust as tree trunks, his belly as big as a basketball. He didn't appear to be sick, just gargantuan as if he had to be huge to survive all that had befallen him.

On the blog he had begun posting, he acknowledged, "There's nothing on my résumé that indicates I'll be successful . . . but I'm doing it because there are four or five books I'd like to write before I meet with Jesus of Nazareth—as my mother promised—on the day of my untimely death, or reconcile myself to a long stretch of nothingness as my non-believing friends insist."

One thing he had never managed to reconcile himself to was Susannah's absence. On St. Patrick's Day 2013, he sent a letter to her and Lenore, admitting that his health scare had forced him to recognize how fleeting life is and how pervasive his sense of loss. "Lenore, I'd like to beg you to let me make it right with Susannah."

As an inducement to his daughter, he promised to find her a job in publishing and pay for her to finish college. Then he added, "Because I don't reward bad behavior you're now cut out of my will. This seems ridiculous and easily fixable to me." All Susannah had to do was allow him a "chance to be your Daddy before it's too late . . . It's free money that'll come to you at the time of my death . . . This is a serious offer and I hope you take it seriously."

Susannah found the letter so insulting and hurtful she didn't bother answering it. Thirty-two years old, living now in Atlanta and employed at Emory University Hospital, she resented Pat's misapprehension that Lenore made decisions for her. It had been her own choice to detach from her father, and in this she had acted against her mother's wishes. Lenore actively encouraged her to reconnect with Pat, not least because she hoped a reconciliation would create family peace and stop Pat from taking potshots at them in print. It saddened Susannah how little her father understood her.

A year later, anxious for Susannah to attend his seventieth birthday party, he pressed her to talk to him face-to-face. So on a day of breath-catching high humidity and heat, they met at an Atlanta restaurant named Bones. A steak house frequented by businessmen and politicians, it had been Susannah's choice, and Pat considered this a propitious sign—he and Lenore used to eat here in the '80s.

Because Susannah hadn't seen him in sixteen years, she worried that she'd be shocked by his appearance. To prepare herself, she reviewed photos from recent interviews. Still, when he stepped into Bones wearing a red baseball cap and a dark blazer over a tee shirt, he looked diminished, even as he bragged that rehab had lowered his blood pressure to the normal range and got his weight down to 230 pounds. Bundled in his arms were books he had bought for her at a Barnes & Noble. As ever, she thought, Pat equated pedagogy with paternity.

He had studied the menu ahead of time online with his nutritionist, selecting dishes that suited his diet—a salad, sautéed mushrooms, and grilled vegetables. Neither of them drank alcohol. While Susannah nervously pushed a Caesar salad around her plate, separating croutons from the anchovies, they talked about people from Rome. Pat said he had read *Sympathy for the Devil*, my memoir about Gore Vidal, and praised its picture of the old days. Then they spoke of family members, living and dead, and as Pat moved from name to name, it was a bit like reciting the Sorrowful Mysteries of the rosary. No matter how painful, no matter how remote the relationship, it was important for him to caress every bead on the linked chain.

After lunch, he offered her a lift to her office in his new Volkswagen Passat. She opened the door on the passenger's side, and a batch of CDs slid off the seat. They both laughed. Pat had changed in lots of ways, but he still drove a messy car.

Though that lightened the mood, Susannah made sure he understood that she hated being defined by the falsehoods he wrote about her. She hated it that when she Googled "Susannah Conroy," she got "lost daughter." She wasn't "lost," she insisted, and if he kept claiming that she was and berating Lenore in his books, "That'll be a deal breaker."

"I get it," Pat said.

By email he stressed how delighted he had been to see her, "an Atlanta woman on the go." Apologizing for the "hurt over the years because of my writing," he explained, "it's an old habit and a hard one to break. It is part of my credo as a writer to tell the truth as I see it . . . If you think I've been unfair to Lenore in my books, you have not been introduced to Dr. Lowenstein in the *Prince of*

Tides or Shyla in *Beach Music*. I took the best parts of Lenore and celebrated those parts of her character."

He offered no apology for the less than celebratory things, or the flatly inaccurate ones, he had written. He encouraged Lenore and Susannah to cooperate with Catherine Seltzer, the biographer he had appointed. "If my biography does not tell the whole truth about me, Susannah, then my whole life will have been a lie. If you and Lenore choose not to tell your stories about me, then the book will be weaker . . . the book will read much stronger and more authentic with your voice alive and rolling afire with your own voices. Besides, you're both beautiful, articulate and funny as hell."

PAT CONROY'S SEVENTIETH BIRTHDAY WAS a three-day gala, thronged by 350 guests who paid to attend panel discussions and readings at the University of South Carolina Center for the Arts. An immense cake, baked in the shape of a shrimp boat, floated on a bed of white chocolate oysters and shrimp. Though hardly an occasion for father-daughter bonding, the party gave Susannah a chance to become reacquainted with her extended family, and to marvel at Pat's ability to field multiple demands. The front door to his house in Beaufort, she noticed, had a formidable combination lock, but since everyone in town knew the code, privacy was non-existent in Casa Conroy.

Afterward, Pat volunteered to chauffeur Susannah to the Savannah Airport for her flight back to Atlanta. They had barely cleared the driveway when he stopped to chat with a neighbor's child. Then he paused to speak to a boy on a bicycle. When Pat pulled over a third time to greet a friend, she reminded him that at this rate she'd miss her plane.

Among her father's exuberant fans, where was she supposed to fit in? Pat had always claimed that if she spent more time with him, she'd come to adore him. But where Pat was uninhibited in proclaiming his love, Susannah was shy and soft-spoken. It troubled her that she couldn't match his ardor; it left her feeling inadequate. She had deep emotions. She just hadn't discovered how to express them to him.

She related all this in Rome where she flew shortly after Pat's birthday. It pleased me that they had at last reconciled, and that Pat sent warm wishes to Linda and me. Susannah told us how much she admired Pat's persistence. "If someone cold-shouldered me for twenty years, I'm not sure I would have kept trying. So a tip of the hat to him for that."

OVER THE CHRISTMAS HOLIDAYS, PAT fell off the wagon with a splat and was soon gravely ill. A local doctor diagnosed pancreatitis, a condition Pat had suffered in the past, and treated it with Tylenol. But by New Year's his symptoms—acute abdominal pain, nausea, and extreme fatigue—hadn't improved, and Susannah, who worked at the Winship Cancer Institute at Emory University, thought her father needed a second opinion. After consulting oncologists in her office, she arranged for an ambulance to transport him from Beaufort to Atlanta.

Normally this would have been an easy, if boring, five-hour trip on the interstate. A snowstorm, however, turned the drive treacherous, and as Pat lay strapped to a gurney, listening to the siren scream, he ached at every icy bump in the road.

By daybreak, the city shimmered under a crust of crystalline ice, and the streets to Emory University, usually crowded with students, were deserted as Susannah set off at 9 a.m. to visit her father. She had delayed leaving home to allow him more time to rest. En route she bought *The New York Times*. She had no idea whether Pat was in any condition to read it. But the newspaper had always been a part of his morning routine, and she decided it would be reassuring to stick to it.

This was the way Susannah expressed love—not with grandiloquent pronouncements or bold gestures, but with small favors and acts of kindness. Show, don't tell, was her father's literary mantra. She would keep him company, keep him comfortable, and monitor his medical care.

For forty-five minutes, she had Pat to herself, except for a nurse with whom he was already best friends. Then a tide of well-wishers flooded into the room and reclaimed him as public property. He reveled in this role, perhaps because it diverted him while he waited for his test results.

Susannah left, hoping the crowd would leave too. But when she came back that evening, the rogue's gallery of friends and family hadn't budged, and everybody was up to date on Pat's diagnosis. Doctors had broken the dire news that he had Stage 4 pancreatic cancer. Under the best circumstances he would have had a few months to live. But "best" didn't apply in his instance. Because he also suffered cirrhosis of the liver, standard procedures to prolong life would be futile.

Straining for words and stymied in the attempt, Susannah didn't know what to say. Not in this mob. Not with everybody listening. Not with Pat, apparently in high spirits, holding court as if at a dinner party, flushed with laughter. "Here I was getting healthy with the help of a personal trainer and my own gym," Pat said, "and suddenly I'm dying."

The phone rang, and Pat told the caller, "I just learned I have terminal cancer. It's the best day of my life."

Susannah didn't understand this, no more than she had understood it as a little girl when he phoned on Thanksgiving and declared he was going out to buy a gun. It didn't sound like a joke. On the other hand, it didn't strike her as a cry for help either. It was more like he meant to serve notice that he accepted his fate and so should others.

The next morning, his mood changed and he went into warrior mode. On Facebook he posted that he had pancreatic cancer and vowed to fight it. "I owe you a novel," he told readers, "and I intend to deliver it." This prompted a reply from two million fans.

Each day, a nurse updated Pat's chart, and in the space after *Goal?*, she followed his instructions and filled in, "Finish novel." It sounded like one of his 1982 New Year's resolutions. "Work hard on writing every day."

Released from the Winship Cancer Institute, Pat returned to Beaufort, where his condition quickly deteriorated. Palliative care no longer coped with his pain. Still, he refused to give up. Swimming in and out of consciousness, he submitted to an agonizing drive to Jacksonville, Florida, for yet another oncologist's opinion. Doctors there confirmed the original prognosis: nothing could be done.

Back in Beaufort, Pat continued during lucid moments to speak of completing his novel, but as these intervals became fewer and fewer, he slept when he was lucky and drifted in a delirium of medication when his luck failed. Ketamine brought quick, trance-like relief, but afterward left him agitated and disoriented. In this state, he took a last trip to a hospital in Charleston, the family praying for a miracle, Pat befuddled by drugs.

DURING THOSE DREADFUL FEBRUARY DAYS, Linda and I were in Key West. On the nineteenth, I turned seventy-three, and if that and the specter of Pat's death weren't sufficient to sear my mortality into mind, I was due for an MRI of my prostate at Memorial Sloan Kettering in New York City.

On February 25, I wrote Lenore: "With the utmost caution and trepidation I broach a subject that's been on my mind since Pat became ill. I feel there's unfinished business between us, none of which is likely to be resolved now. But I would like him to know that I'm concerned about him and care for him and am sympathetic to his situation, especially as I set off next week to NY to have my cancerous prostate assessed . . . Could Susannah pass along my regards and tell him that I'm praying for him. If he'd like to see me or be in touch in any way, I would welcome that. On the other hand if that would cause him more trouble than it could possibly be worth, I'd understand that too."

Of course, I could have flown to his bedside, whether he wanted me to or not. But I feared I'd be turned away. His sister Carol Ann had already attempted a deathbed reunion, only to be barred from his room. Pat didn't need another terrible scene, and I didn't believe I was equal to one either.

Gripped in a cold spell as icy as a corpse's fingers, New York broke down all the defenses I had built up in Florida. At Sloan Kettering, I filled in a lengthy questionnaire, convinced that none of it applied to me. Other patients in the waiting room looked worse off. Or so I assured myself. They had cancer. I was under "active surveillance," a status that sounded purely bureaucratic. As long as my numbers held steady, as long as the lentil-size tumor didn't metastasize outside the prostate capsule, I was good to go on watching and waiting.

I wasn't dying. Pat was dying. Thinking about him helped me not to think about myself. Or maybe this was just another way of thinking about myself. His absence had long exerted a strong presence in my life—like silence in a piece of music or blank space on a page of poetry. As I was inserted into the claustrophobic confines of the MRI machine, I prayed that Pat wasn't in too much pain. (But how much was too much?) I prayed that he wasn't paralyzed by fear. (Would he rather be conscious or comatose? Which would I prefer?) After a frenzied life, he deserved a peaceful death. (But as he would have reminded me, what does deserving have to do with anything?)

As Susannah later told me, Pat experienced periods of lucidity in Charleston and summoned Jessica, Melissa, Megan, and her to his room. Although she couldn't recall his exact words, she remembered him rambling on about war and how Jessica and Melissa's father, just like his own, had been a fighter pilot. He had died in Vietnam, and Lenore's uncle had been killed in World War II. Pat urged them to honor their dead relatives as defenders of the country.

Susannah believed that Pat longed to say something that would live on after him. "Some choose children," he blurted. "I chose literature." To which one of the girls replied, "We noticed." Even at death's door the Conroys couldn't pass up a punch line.

As Pat subsided into a silence relieved only by the occasional cough or fragmented word, Susannah said he looked like an athlete "who had left it all on the field." Then remembering her father's sport had been basketball, she amended that to, "He left it all on the court."

Sandra and the girls gathered for a conference with the team of physicians, and while they asked questions, Pat lay mute and motionless. Chemotherapy, the doctors advised, was now more harmful than helpful. Liver disease, they repeated, had limited their options from the start. After four hospitalizations in six weeks, they suggested hospice care. No more aggressive interventions, no machines. One doctor asked if he wanted to go home, and Pat said, "Yes," and didn't speak again.

From then on, the conference dealt with practical details. In Beaufort, should they carry him upstairs? Or was it better to bring his bed downstairs where he'd have a view he loved?

Meanwhile, the results of my MRI indicated no change in the lentil-size tumor. Still, the oncologist recommended I undergo a biopsy. Not that it would put my mind permanently at ease, but it would tide me over until the next round of tests in spring.

Alone and at loose ends, I walked the freezing windy streets. Linda had offered to accompany me here, but I preferred to manage my anxiety on my own and share lighter moments with her by telephone. At Sloan Kettering, an attractive female Asian doctor quizzed me about my sex life.

"Erections?" she asked.

"What about them?"

"How often do you have them?"

"At my age how often am I supposed to have them?"

"Some men in their seventies never have sex," she said. "Some have it every day."

"With the same woman?" I asked. That got a laugh out of Linda but no reaction from the earnest young MD.

I knew that if Pat were here, not even cancer could have kept us from laughing. He'd probably tease me about my itty-bitty tumor, joking that it was something you'd barely notice in a salad or soup bowl. A mid-list malignancy, he'd call it—while he had the block-buster bestseller variety.

IN 1983, PAT HAD WRITTEN when he left Rome that our "life changing friendship . . . has four distinct parts like a weathervane and it all moves in harmony and we know how all the winds of the world are blowing when we're together. The full diminishment of losing you has not hit me yet and I don't think I could stand it if I faced it fully now."

The day after my MRI, March 4, 2016, I had no choice but to face his loss and confront the full diminishment of his death. The news reached me via emails and phone calls from London, Rome, Madrid, and Paris, Canada and throughout the United States. Everyone sent condolences at the passing of a man I hadn't laid eyes on in decades. It was some small consolation that they still thought of us as friends, the link between us intact.

Susannah emailed, "I was with my Dad a few days before he died and wanted to let you know that he was thinking about you and you were on his mind and in his heart. Megan also asked me to send a message from her that she thought of you often over the past month and that some of her favorite memories of Dad are when you were together.

"There is a service on Tuesday at 11 a.m. at St. Peter's Church located on Lady's Island, South Carolina. No obligation to come, but know that you are most welcome."

I couldn't make it. The funeral fell on the same day, precisely at the same hour, as my biopsy. But I thanked Susannah for letting me know I had been in Pat's heart, which I imagined as an immense chambered nautilus, huge enough to hold all his loved ones. As Pat, a true prince of tides, would have known, a nautilus possesses a counter-shaded shell, dark on top, bright on the bottom, cunningly devised to confuse predators. Everything Susannah relayed to me, everything journalists reported, reinforced this image of a deeply camouflaged and conflicted heart.

For most of his adult life Pat spurned the Catholic Church but conceded that "goosebumps spread down the keyboard of my spine" every time a priest intoned, "I will go to the altar of God, to God the joy of my youth." Such a priest presided at a requiem Mass for Pat, and out of the vast congregation a handful of his siblings and Susannah received communion.

Despite his love-hate relationship with the Citadel, he had invited the corps of cadets to attend his funeral and a number of them did, including two Summerall Guards in full regalia, with polished brass and shako hats. Among the twelve hundred mourners, some eulogized Conroy as a basketball prodigy who had once scored fifty-five points in a game. Some praised his books which had made the town proud, others his loyalty and humility for resettling in the place where he had started. Some recalled that he had excoriated the state as a refuge for racist bigots. In revenge, he had been labeled a "nigger lover," and now, as if to embrace that ugly epithet, he chose to have his mortal remains and immortal soul buried outside of Beaufort in an African American cemetery.

AFTERWORD

THE COUNTERLIFE

*ie and become the man you are.* That's what the ancient Greeks believed. With death, the lifelong process of becoming ended and the person in full emerged. But Pat Conroy remained, just as he had been in life, a protean figure who cast a large shifting shadow. Fulsome obituaries, personal tributes, and reminiscences from fellow writers poured in, and he was no sooner buried than his grave became a pilgrimage site.

In Beaufort, people proposed erecting a statue in his honor. Others, including Pat's widow, Cassandra King, thought a more fitting memorial would be a literary center, providing museum space for his memorabilia, classrooms for readers, and a magnet for visiting authors and lecturers. Hailing him in its mission statement as "one of America's best loved writers and truth-tellers, the Conroy Center continues Pat Conroy's courageous and generous-hearted legacy as a teacher, mentor, advocate and friend to storytellers of every kind."

Jean-Paul Sartre opined that most writers aren't as good as their books. But in many respects, Pat Conroy was better than what he wrote. He fought against child abuse, sexual abuse, racism, and violations of women's rights. He advocated coeducation at the Citadel and supported Shannon Faulkner when she broke the school's gender barrier in 1995. Then after Ms. Faulkner withdrew from the Citadel, citing psychological distress and death threats to her family, Pat paid for her college education elsewhere. In recognition of Pat's international stature, President Clinton invited him to fly aboard Air Force Two to the 1997 Irish peace accords.

But as our mutual friend Steve Geller observed years ago in Rome, the gods of laughter, those cosmic comedians, never rest. A week before a memorial service on the waterfront in Beaufort commemorated Pat's life, Alan Fleischer died alone in his New York apartment on May 8, 2016. His body wasn't discovered until the following day.

Fleischer had long since disappeared from public view after a series of sensational newspaper headlines charged him with sexually molesting his daughter. The University of Arizona, although under intense pressure to fire him, kept Fleischer on its medical school faculty until he fell into a depression and committed several errors during operations. After losing his license to perform surgery, he accepted a buyout from the university and moved east.

Among his personal effects, Fleischer's survivors discovered a cache of documents related to his decade-long legal battle with Pat Conroy. In addition to hundreds of pages of affidavits, sworn depositions, trial pleadings, financial statements, medical records, and newspaper clippings, there were letters from Pat that had been introduced into evidence during court proceedings. All these papers were offered to me. Did I want them?

Well, I did and I didn't. To the extent that Pat's dispute with Dr. Fleischer had played a part in our friendship, I thought I had already covered it. Still, I was curious about the contents of the file, and as the author of four books and countless pieces of investigative journalism, I felt a professional responsibility to double-check all the available information.

The documents arrived in an overstuffed FedEx box that weighed more than ten pounds. It took days to separate them according to subject matter and arrange them in chronological order. As I read and digested the legal jargon, I was reminded of *Short Circuit*, which had originated as a lyrical hymn to tennis and ended as a forensic examination of the game's underbelly. Again I had gone searching for gold and discovered uranium. How should I treat this radioactive material, much of which contradicted Pat's reputation for kindness and truth telling.

After some debate, I decided to follow Pat's invariable editorial advice: Put in everything. As he had warned Susannah and Lenore, if you do "not tell the whole truth about me . . . then my whole life will have been a lie."

To someone raised in a military milieu and steeped in myths of American sports, the U.S. legal system probably resembled an athletic contest, with rules as straight as the lines on a basketball court, and winners and losers as clear-cut as the numbers on a scoreboard. Pat never mastered its arcane protocols and ambiguities.

From the moment I first met him, he maintained that he fled Atlanta to escape Lenore's ex-husband, a wealthy brain surgeon who hounded her for custody of their kids and filed frivolous suits against Pat. In self-defense, Pat had filed countersuits and accused Alan Fleischer of attempting to bankrupt him. But the documents tell a different story. Supported by his income tax records, Fleischer presented himself to the court as a father of modest means pleading to have his alimony reduced because his ex-wife had hooked up with a rich, famous author.

This sort of domestic conflict was commonly resolved according to civil law. But somehow *Conroy v. Fleischer* mutated into a slow-growing cancer that spread and consumed everybody. It was the real-life equivalent of *Jarndyce v. Jarndyce*, the imbroglio in Charles Dickens's *Bleak House* that raged for generations and bankrupted all parties to the litigation.

Fleischer certainly played his role in this fatal folie à deux. He hired lawyers he couldn't afford and filed affidavits that cost more than he could hope to recover. But Pat did the same thing, piling up expenses far in excess of what Alan owed in child support. Worse yet, Pat refused to leave it to his handsomely compensated attorneys to cope with the case. He intruded at every turn and dispatched defamatory letters to Fleischer, Fleischer's wife, his attorneys, and his psychiatrist.

Plenty of litigants have undoubtedly been tempted to take the law into their own hands. But few ever supply a paper trail of evidence for the opposing side to exploit. On top of charging Alan with perjury, Pat characterized Fleischer's lawyers as "contemptible . . . I've never run across such stupid lawyers." Then he singled out a judge in Georgia for his ignorance, complaining that he misspelled "meretricious" in a decision.

As he did to Lenore and Susannah, Pat threatened in letters to expose everybody unless they did as he demanded. "I'm telling my full story to the *Atlanta Weekly* . . . because I'm a minor figure in Georgia, I know this information will be widely disseminated . . . a violent, drug abusing crazy man [is] operating on brains" at Emory University School of Medicine. Pat wrote the med school chairman that he personally wouldn't trust Fleischer to perform surgery on "a gerbil's anus."

Rather than intimidating the defense, these threats struck Fleischer's attorneys as a golden opportunity. They alerted their client, "Your best evidence lies in Conroy's letters which admit to a substantial effort to poison minds . . . against you."

Unwittingly Pat damaged not just his legal case, but his career and his family. Unlike his intemperate outbursts at Susannah when age and alcohol might account for his invective, the letters in this file had been written in Rome, while he was still in his thirties and supposed to be completing *The Prince of Tides*. Instead he churned out hundreds of seething pages, vilifying Fleischer, undermining his own marriage, and jeopardizing his children.

In one sworn deposition Pat was queried by Alan's attorney about his sexual relationship with Mrs. Fleischer, meaning Lenore. Pat glibly replied that he had had sexual relations with both Mrs. Fleischers, meaning he had also slept with Alan's current wife, Alice. This prompted Fleischer's lawyers to charge that because Alice had rejected him and married Alan, Conroy was motivated by revenge.

Fed up with what Fleischer described as hateful, megalomaniacal diatribes, Alan pleaded in a letter to Lenore, "It is time for relief. For the well-being of all . . . please have Pat cool it."

Lenore cautioned Pat that their hatred of her ex-husband was interfering with what was best for the children. But this fell on deaf ears. He called her a fool, easily duped by Alan.

When the Conroys returned to Rome for their second stay, Fleischer transferred to Tucson, Arizona. In court he testified that he left Atlanta for the same reasons as Pat and Lenore had. He was desperate to start over, free from family strife. He still hoped to have access to his children during vacations and summers. But the dispute soon swerved beyond questions of custody and child support and became a criminal case.

When I first learned of Emily's harrowing allegations of sexual abuse, I urged Pat to let the appropriate authorities deal with them. Instead he compiled a narrative based on interviews with his stepdaughter and stitched together a thirteen-page single-spaced *J'accuse* entitled "Emily Fleischer's Testimony of the Sexual Abuse by Her Father, Dr. Alan Fleischer." He turned this over to the police, to the press, and to Alan Fleischer. In an accompanying letter, he wrote that Emily had "had her entire childhood polluted by the satanic evil of her father . . . You kept your daughter as a sexual slave. There was bondage, violence, and you turned your home into a pornographic nightmare for your child."

He accused Fleischer's wife, Alice, of being his "facilitator," and wrote Fleischer's psychiatrist, a witness in the case. Calling the psychiatrist "a whore," and charging that he had known of Emily's abuse and covered it up, Pat threatened to sue for malpractice. As usual he vowed, "I'm going to blow this story sky-high and take my case before the public." He boasted of his contacts in the media, particularly CNN, who he said stood poised to broadcast the story. (Decades later, in his posthumous oral biography, Pat falsely claimed that the psychiatrist had been convicted of sexual abuse and imprisoned for life.)

Unless he got satisfaction in court, Pat vowed he would reveal in writing how Fleischer "took off Emily's clothes in the middle of the night and he masturbated on her." He drafted an eight-page book proposal and sent it to Fleischer, to his wife, to his psychiatrist, to Fleischer's brother Barry and Barry's wife, to his editor Nan Talese, and "to everyone I've met in the legal system." Once he finished *The Prince of Tides* he swore he would start this new project if Fleischer didn't agree to Pat's demands.

In yet another letter he wrote, "Your daughter Emily's story is now complete." In addition to penetrating her vaginally, orally, and anally, Alan had, according to Pat, tried to strangle his daughter when she resisted.

"I've thought long and hard after hearing Emily's story of flying out to Arizona and killing you myself. And I tell you this with the utter confidence that any jury in the United States would carry me out of a courtroom on their shoulders after Emily told her excruciating story."

"I want prisoners to have a chance to do to you what you've done to your daughter . . . I've told Emily that it will never happen again, Alan, and that's a promise I'll die to keep. If you ever touch your daughter again, I'll feed your genitalia to your dogs."

This was the sort of rhetoric Conroy readers would recognize from his novels, where villains are punished and victims always rescued by a hero. But in the real world of courtrooms, combative lawyers, and compromise, Pat was cutting the ground out from under his stepdaughter and himself. With his vituperative letters, he exposed himself to charges of witness tampering; of intimidating the defendant, his family, and his friends; and of bringing fraudulent charges against Fleischer to publicize his next book and land a lucrative contract. Worse yet, by offering Fleischer the opportunity to buy the rights to that book and bury it, Pat could be accused of extortion.

Pat then willy-nilly provided Alan a perfect defense by conceding, "Emily has told more lies, more outrageously, more creatively and more often than any child I've ever known. A story she tells in the morning will have gone through five variations by mid-afternoon. With Emily, we are not dealing with a young George Washington."

Although he maintained that he believed his stepdaughter in

this instance, no jury would convict a defendant, a doctor no less, on the basis of testimony by a child whose own stepfather had impugned her honesty. This may explain why prosecutors in Pima County, Arizona, never arrested or indicted Alan Fleischer, and why authorities in DeKalb County, Georgia, after handing down an indictment, never extradited him. Fleischer had voluntarily submitted to a lie-detector test, which he insisted vindicated him. He had also undergone a Psychological Report and Risk Assessment at the Center Against Adult and Adolescent Sexual Aggression. After clinical interviews with Fleischer and his wife, and a review of Pat's letters and Emily's allegations, the Center subjected Fleischer to a CAT 200 computer–assisted program to "measure penile response to target and standardized stimulus materials." In plain language, wires were attached to Dr. Fleischer's penis as he was shown erotic pictures, some of children. Then his state of arousal was measured.

In an eleven-page summary, psychologist Steven R. Gray reported: "Dr. Alan Fleischer, based on this examination, does not demonstrate any of the known physiological, emotional or psychological correlates associated with multiple events of child molest [*sic*] incest or rape. He therefore presents no risk to the community at this time."

In the end, after all the charges and counter-charges, the hyperventilating headlines and tens of thousands of dollars in legal fees, Pat's threats and insults had only prolonged the case and made it impossible to prosecute. Alan Fleischer was never cross-examined under oath. But then neither was Pat or Emily. If Emily had in fact been abused, Pat had destroyed her chances of justice. If she hadn't been abused, he had destroyed Alan's reputation and his life.

Touchingly, at the bottom of the last page of her "testimony," Emily had scrawled a note to Alan Fleischer, "Dear Dad. Just read this over. I'm sorry that it's true. But I still love you."

•

IN ANSLEY PARK, THE SOURCE of Susannah's middle name, Lenore Conroy lives in a modest, rented, two-bedroom house. She relocated to Atlanta to be near her children and her grandson, Wesley. Now in her seventies, still trim enough to wear stylish blue jeans, Lenore volunteers at a local hospital, occasionally travels to Europe to visit friends, and plays no part in the literary life of the city.

When Pat died, and journalists contacted her for a comment, Lenore declined to speak. This had always been how she handled the press. As often as her former husband belittled her in his books, she stayed silent. Partly this non-response was an attempt to spare herself and Susannah from retaliation. Partly it came from a conviction that nothing she said in self-defense would change anyone's mind. "Pat," Lenore pointed out, "was a very popular, charming guy." She recalled a court appearance in San Francisco, when Pat was appealing to pay less alimony. The judge interrupted the proceedings to announce that his mother was a Conroy fan.

I remained, in my fashion, a Conroy fan. But in fairness, and for the sake of accuracy, I felt Lenore should speak for the record. Less than a year after Pat's death, just months after Alan Fleischer's death, I visited her in Atlanta and asked how she felt these days.

"Mostly relieved," Lenore said. "The last year's been grueling. Finally I feel I can crawl out from under the past."

The past, it seemed to me, pressed in all around us. On the walls of her house hung paintings I remembered from Rome. A bookshelf contained my complete works, which, depending on the story Pat told, Lenore had stolen from him or he had abandoned when he decided I had betrayed him. In a corner loomed the life-size Venetian statue that had presided over the apartment on Piazza

Farnese. Leaning forward at the shoulders, hair swept back in a sixteenth-century version of a mullet, wooden right hand touching his wooden chest, the gentleman seemed to be listening pensively to our conversation and making up his mind.

Janet Malcolm, writing about Sylvia Plath and Ted Hughes, observed that a literary marriage never ends. It stays alive like the whiskers on a corpse as couples trade insults, acquaintances chip in their opinions, and critics debate the meaning of long-buried secrets. I described the documents that had been discovered among Alan's personal effects and asked whether Lenore was aware of how badly Pat had undermined their legal position with his irrational behavior.

She expressed shock; she knew nothing about his abusive letters to everybody involved in the case. On the other hand, she conceded they sounded like Pat. "His problem was he never understood when he stepped over the line. He had two speeds—on or off. Red hot or ice cold.

"Look how he treated Emily," Lenore added. "After all their hours together talking about her being abused, Emily felt very close to Pat. Close enough that she changed her last name to Conroy. The *New York Times* obituary listed her as his daughter. But Pat dropped her. Her story no longer interested him. Her neediness got in his way. He didn't mention her in his will."

"Was Susannah in the will?" I asked.

"Yes, and I'm grateful for that. But there are things I can't forgive."

"Apparently Pat had things he couldn't forgive either." I mentioned the money he accused her of stealing. "He claimed his brothers wanted to have you arrested."

She laughed. "Lock her up! Lock her up! I feel like Hillary Clinton. The truth is, money made Pat nervous and guilty. He depended on other people to deal with it for him. Then he complained that they screwed him.

"When he spoke at colleges, he sometimes didn't pick up his honorarium. Or else he handed it back to the host institution to spend as it liked. It never occurred to him," Lenore said, "that we had to account for that money and pay taxes. I finally got his checks mailed to our address. Then I deposited them in the bank to cover household expenses."

Expenses, she emphasized, that were always higher than Pat appreciated—when, that is, he bothered to consider them at all. On top of supporting six kids in private schools, and paying the mortgage on two houses, and compensating retinues of lawyers and therapists, Pat gave lavish gifts, covered the college tuition of absolute strangers, and extended unsecured loans to almost anyone who asked.

"When he lived for months on Fripp Island," Lenore said, "he never thought about the bills in San Francisco. His brothers and relatives used to pile in on me, and the cost of groceries alone was enormous."

She recalled the summer of '94 when Pat was having an affair on Fripp Island and she packed up Susannah and flew back to the West Coast. Three of Pat's brothers were vacationing in the house in Presidio Heights. They claimed they knew nothing about the other woman in Pat's life, and Lenore let them stay on as long as they had originally planned.

"The way I processed things back then," she said, "people get through these problems. I believed I could put them behind me and fight for my marriage. So I made plans to celebrate Pat's forty-ninth birthday in South Carolina. Then you called and said he didn't want me there. After that, I had trouble getting him to pay for anything, even Susannah's medical bills."

I pointed out that she emerged from the marriage with the house and $10,000 a month.

"Which he soon got reduced to $5,000, then to nothing at all," Lenore fired back. "He always portrayed me as a greedy pig. His father called me Lenoinks. Which was ironic since Pat said I was Santini with tits. But our settlement was based on Pat's income. The year of the divorce he made over $800,000. I know a writer's income can go up or down, but it looked like his would zoom up with the publication of *Beach Music*. I negotiated in good faith and assumed he did too. But right away he started doing what he hated Alan for doing. He claimed I was killing him financially. He filed suits so I had to hire lawyers. He was a financial bully. He blamed me when Susannah refused to see him, but he never considered how hurt she was by his hideous emails."

I couldn't defend what he had written to his daughter, but I suggested that he inherited from his father the mistaken belief that a stern ultimatum could solve any problem.

"I got so sick of hearing him brag he was the son of a warrior," Lenore protested, "and that that made his craziness okay. To write that I hate Emily and wanted to get rid of her, how did he expect her to feel? And to put in his memoirs that he married me on the rebound and that I secretly stopped using birth control and tricked him into having a baby, how was Susannah supposed to feel? The fact is, Pat and I discussed having a baby, and since I was in my mid-thirties, we decided it had to be soon. Anyway, if he loved Susannah so much, why does it matter when I got pregnant?"

This prompted her to wonder why his books hadn't been better fact-checked. "It's one thing to shade the truth and embellish his own experience. But what about the rights of other people and the truth of their lives?"

I explained that I had interviewed Pat's longtime editor, Nan

Talese, who conceded that Pat's books had never been fact-checked. "I'm not a newspaper," she said, pointing out that Pat had signed a standard publishing contract spelling out his responsibility for the content of his work.

My final and most difficult question to Lenore concerned the day of Susannah's birth, when Pat rushed from the hospital to our apartment, sobbing that he had been humiliated in front of nuns when a doctor informed him that Susannah had been delivered by cesarean section because Lenore had herpes.

Of all her possible responses—tears, fury, an abrupt end to the conversation—Lenore offered the one I least anticipated. She laughed. "He actually told you that?"

"He did, and I bring it up now only because—"

"You don't have to apologize. I'm surprised you waited this long to ask about something so bizarre. I never had herpes. Pat did."

In November 1981, Pat had flown to Atlanta, she reminded me, to consult a cardiologist about a heart problem. Because he presented with symptoms of a sexually transmitted disease, the doctor had him tested and the lab report was positive for herpes. Although Lenore showed no symptoms herself, her ob-gyn advised her to have a cesarean. This was weeks before she went into labor, and it was Pat's own doctor, not some stranger at an Italian hospital, who disclosed he had herpes.

"Why he went to your place and acted so upset baffles me," Lenore said. "Why would he tell you that? What could you do except conclude I'm a terrible person? It sounds so puritanical of him, like I was a fallen woman. Look, we met when I was thirty-five and had been divorced for years and already had two kids. I never pretended to be a virgin. We were both adults. If I had had herpes— which I didn't—we would have dealt with it and gone on with our marriage. Which was precisely what we did when Pat was diagnosed with herpes."

Lenore paused a moment before remarking, "Divorce reduces everybody to such pettiness. It killed me that when Pat came back to San Francisco to collect his stuff, he didn't just take what belonged to him. He took the Marine Corps flight jacket that Don Conroy had given Gregory. The jacket meant a lot to Gregory. It was a symbol of his acceptance into the Conroy family. Why would Pat do that to a teenage boy?"

Then she smiled and confessed that she wasn't above a bit of pettiness herself. "During our separation Pat breezed back into town for an award ceremony and needed his tuxedo. He left a message that a go-fer would come and fetch it. I was so furious I did something awful."

"What?"

"I brought the tuxedo to a tailor and had it taken in two inches at the waist and in the butt. He hated being fat, and I knew this would drive him nuts."

"I guess it could have been worse. You could have run over him with your car."

THE ERNEST F. HOLLINGS SPECIAL Collection at the University of South Carolina houses Pat Conroy's papers. When donors put up the money to purchase the archive, Tom McNally, dean of University Libraries, announced to the press that this was a rare opportunity to obtain a celebrated South Carolinian's complete work. Because Pat had never learned to type—his father dismissed typing as a chore for women—there were handwritten drafts, as well as fair copies, of all of Conroy's books, except for his first self-published effort, *The Boo*. (Pat expressed relief that that manuscript had been lost, joking that it was too dreadful to preserve.)

Everything else was said to be intact—his journals, diaries, letters from and to Pat, even letters from his lovers, his Selective Service file (which presents a much more complicated picture of his draft deferment than Pat had ever provided), photographs, birthday cards, and miscellaneous souvenirs. According to Mr. McNally, lawyers had advised Pat to keep his financial records and divorce documents confidential, but Pat insisted that they too be made available to the public. Mr. McNally told reporters, "He's written about his family himself. He's wide open, and he wants all his archives to be just the same."

Yet in February 2017 when I visited Columbia, South Carolina, the Conroy collection was not as open as Pat wished. His financial and divorce records had at some point been put off-limits. In addition, the transcripts of taped interviews that Pat gave his oral biographer had been sealed for twenty years. While selections from these interviews were published, the leftover tapes are inaccessible even to Pat's children.

Susannah in particular worried what might be on the embargoed tapes. She already felt that the published material was rife with inaccuracies and defamations, and she wrote the University of South Carolina Press to register her objections. Pat had utterly disregarded his promise to quit writing about Susannah's mother. He went so far as to declare, "If Susannah doesn't like the book—too bad—because I don't think I've lied too much."

Although I couldn't verify the terms of his divorce settlement or determine why Pat accused Lenore of stealing millions of dollars, his diaries and journals provided a great deal of other information about his daily life. He recorded many of his conversations with friends and family, and even his arguments with Lenore. "The women I love are always secret agents," he wrote—and he wasn't reluctant to confess his own failings. "I caught the disease of the time. Selfishness, lack of courage, sadness."

The journal entries for the early months of his marriage mention nothing about Lenore's secretly going off birth control. Nor do they express any displeasure about her pregnancy or suggest that he married her on the rebound. On December 7, 1981, Pat described Susannah's birth by cesarean section and his delight when a nun brought his baby daughter for him to see for the first time. There's nothing about a doctor informing him that his wife had herpes and nothing about his hurrying to our apartment and sobbing that this was the most humiliating day of his life. Instead, he wrote that he drove Lenore home to Olgiata and served her breakfast in bed.

It was cold in the library; the thermostat was set low to protect the rare books and manuscripts. I kept my Barbour coat on as I pored through Pat's papers, which were delivered in cardboard cartons, each one stuffed with labeled folders. I was allowed to take notes, but obliged to do so in pencil, not ink, and I could examine only three boxes at a time.

I requested his journals for 1994, 1995, and 1996, realizing there was every chance they might reveal that Pat had never cared for me half as much as he had professed to. In the period before and after his divorce, before and after he asked me to call Lenore, he might have regretted his dependence on me. Or perhaps he had wearied of being a famous writer with a less successful friend.

The librarian came back empty-handed; the journals for '94, '95, and '96 were missing. Like any diarist, Pat had occasionally skipped days. But to let three years slip by without a single entry—that struck me as implausible for someone of his obsessive-compulsive nature.

The librarian and I discussed the possibilities. Maybe the emotional upheaval of his divorce had left Pat in no condition to update his diary. He later wrote that he had been suicidal. Then again, maybe those journals had been misplaced and would turn up later. Although the librarian didn't mention it, there was also a chance those journals had been removed.

I requested the folder of my correspondence with Pat. It included my letters beginning in the early '80s, but none of those I had written him in '94 and '95 trying to break the impasse between us. Nor did the folder contain any of the emails we exchanged in 2000 when we attempted to reconcile, then when Pat solicited my help in reconciling with Susannah.

Yet if a lot had been lost from the archive, much remained. Some of it I remembered as if it happened this morning, and incidents that I had forgotten were restored to me by Pat's descriptive skills. Gradually I stopped fretting about what was missing and surrendered to the gift that made his novels and memoirs spellbinding.

Pulled along by his prose and the pleasure of Pat's company, I knew I couldn't stop time or change the course of events or reverse the damage that had been done. But I felt that this was my last, best chance to be close to him.

It wasn't, I confess, an unalloyed joy. In his writing, as in his emotional struggles, Pat wavered between rhapsody and rage, with language alone as a spindly bridge between the extremes. Some pages shimmered with insight, others ached with pain: "There are times when I know I'm my father's son," he had written. "The anger is explosive; I've been worn down by the long war of attrition . . . I went berserk at Lenore tonight . . . At night I want to leave Lenore;

in the daytime I do not. But I do not want to spend the rest of my life like this."

So much depended on his work. When he finished eight pages of *The Prince of Tides*, he wrote: "Lenore says I look happier . . . after I've written something, anything."

He recalled Roman dinner parties, preserving them as if in aspic. Concerning the evening with the Styrons, he noted that Bill "told stories about the writing life and listened to ours . . . I wonder if all writers talk about other writers with that same combination of humor and neurosis that we do." Later when Styron plunged into depression Pat emailed me that Bill had always been kind to him. Many writers were bastards, but Bill had been "one of the good ones." (Inexplicably, in his oral biography, Pat characterized William Styron as self-centered, aloof, churlish, and rude.)

He relished life in Italy, the good food, the wine, the company of friends. At El Toula restaurant celebrating Marya Steinberg's thirty-seventh birthday, he remembered, "Lenore had smoked goose breast that was heavenly—rich and velvety with a delicate taste which lingered long after you'd swallowed." The evening ended with Marya describing how she fell for her husband, Edward: "I believe in love at first sight because it happened to me," she said.

For a man who sometimes misremembered or conveniently forgot crucial events, Pat had keen recall for the ebb and flow of social conversation. From a lunch with the *Newsweek* bureau chief Andy Nagorski, he quoted me, "At an intimate moment a girl I dated in college said, 'I hope you don't mind that I sleep with a retainer.' I thought she slept with the houseboy or the gardener. Then she put something in her mouth which made her look like Yogi Berra with a catcher's mask."

Imitation, it is said, constitutes the sincerest form of flattery. Pat went one better and copied down stories verbatim about my in-laws, about Linda's American Gothic grandmother, about my brothers, sisters, mother, and father. He consistently overrated my tennis and delivered as touching a compliment as I've ever received. "I'll never be able to bring Mike's consummate passion to the game. Or his passion about most things."

What moved me most were the set pieces that captured the spirit of our life together. Pat recalled a freezing winter day when our two families drove into the Alban Hills, searching for snow. Gregory, Emily, and Megan seldom got to see it in Atlanta, and what started off as a short jaunt evolved into a lengthy quest. Finding no snow at lower elevations, Pat plowed on into the Apennine Mountains, leading the way in his BMW, while the Mewshaws in their rackety VW brought up the rear.

In the Gran Sasso National Park, we boarded a funicular that sported a sign warning visitors that wolves and bears, boars and bobcats roamed the area. The kids, beside themselves with excitement, stopped looking at the snow that lay all around us, and began begging to go after wild game. It took all Pat's powers of persuasion to get them to be satisfied with renting sleds and tobogganing downhill through bands of bright sunlight and dark fog.

Pat's diary brought it all back—his rambunctiousness, his insatiable appetite for fun. He was like a St. Bernard puppy that hadn't been housebroken—brimming with affection, yet always in danger of smashing furniture. Most of his faults, I decided, were ones of excess. Even his wobbles as an author were mostly the result of trying too hard to walk on a high wire. A line from one of his favorite novels, *Madame Bovary*, summed up Pat's sense that: "Human speech is a cracked kettle on which we tap out crude rhythms for bears to dance to while we long to make music that will melt the stars."

I LEFT THE LIBRARY AND set out for the South Carolina coast. My trip to the Low Country had about it the sensation of a four-hour downhill glide. Plenty of time to contemplate what Susannah had said: At the end of his life I had been in Pat's thoughts and in his heart. Again I pictured his heart as a chambered nautilus with a counter-shaded shell. From above, its dark side blended invisibly with the ocean's floor. From below, its bright side couldn't be distinguished from sunlight slanting through seawater. Pat hadn't chosen this camouflage any more than he had chosen his blue eyes. It was the natural adaptation of a battered child anxious to hide in plain sight and protect himself in all directions.

WHEN I HEARD THAT PAT had chosen to be buried in a Gullah cemetery belonging to the Brick Baptist Church on St. Helena Island, I envisioned a bosky dell overarched by palms and live oaks, and crowded with moss-covered tombs. Instead, his stone stands on parched sandy soil, tufted with coarse weeds. The surrounding chain-link fence suggests a farmer's stockyard, and across the road, dry-docked boats and stacks of railroad ties bake in the sun smelling of creosote.

The inscription on Pat's tombstone reads, "My wound is geography, but it is also my anchor, my port of call." A border of pinecones is pressed into the ground around his grave, framing mementoes from devoted fans. Coins of various currencies, a Hong Kong $10 bill, lyrical poems and earnest personal notes in clear plastic jackets, conch shells, oyster shells, carnival beads, ballpoint pens, Citadel souvenirs, a softball, a sand dollar, a small basketball, and a miniature bottle of bourbon—they looked to me like the flotsam of a lifetime tossed up in his turbulent wake.

As I paused there, a white-haired man older in appearance than his seventy-three years, I might have been reflecting on my own mortality. But I was actually fumbling to make sense of Pat's life and death. There floated to mind a few lines from Norman Mailer's eulogy for Ernest Hemingway. In a suicide that had shaken the faith of a whole generation, Papa had shoved a shotgun into his mouth and blown off the back of his head. In some critics' estimation, this violated his famous code of stoic courage. But Mailer, not known for his generosity to competitors, commented, "The truth of [Hemingway's] long odyssey is that he struggled with his cowardice and against a secret lust to suicide all his life, that his inner landscape was a nightmare, and he spent his nights wrestling with the gods. It may even be that the final judgment on his work may come to the notion that what he failed to do was tragic, but what he accomplished was heroic, for it is possible he carried a weight of anxiety within him from day to day which would have suffocated any man smaller than himself."

In my opinion, Pat Conroy carried within himself no secret lust to suicide or deeply buried cowardice. Rather, his self-destructive impulses were right on the surface, and he openly depicted the nightmare of his inner landscape. The great weight of anxiety that oppressed him was that no matter how hard he struggled, he couldn't escape his childhood. His worst fear, I believe, was that he would kill somebody else. Or almost as bad, that he would beat his children as savagely as he had been beaten. That he never did so represented, in my opinion, an achievement as significant as any in his career.

I've never managed to stay mad at Pat Conroy, no more than

I have ceased wishing he were still in my life. This despite the fact that, to borrow from Saul Bellow, his "pathologic element could be missed only by those who were laughing too hard to look." He had hurt me. But who that ever breathed air has not hurt somebody or never been hurt himself? He was my friend, and I never had a better one. But among my regrets is that I didn't get a chance to ask Pat this question: Who ever loved him more than I did?

ACKNOWLEDGMENTS

Writing is a solitary art, an act of willful isolation. Or so authors often lament. But in fact every book is a collaborative effort. I'd like to thank my agent, Michael Carlisle, and my editor, Jack Shoemaker. Then, too, I'm indebted to a list of friends who read *The Lost Prince* in its earlier incarnations. A tip of the hat to Tom Carney, Zach Leader, Jonathan Levi, Andy Karsch, Jonathan Galassi, my sons Sean and Marc, and Lucinda Hahn, who went further and suggested substantial editorial improvements. Finally I'd like to thank Lenore and Susannah Conroy for agreeing to be interviewed, and Pat Conroy's widow and literary executor, Cassandra King, for her permission to quote from his letters, emails, and diaries.

And again, as always, boundless gratitude to my wife, Linda, for her patience and cheerful support.

INDEX

MICHAEL MEWSHAW's five-decade career includes award-winning fiction, nonfiction, literary criticism, and investigative journalism. He is the author of the nonfiction works *Sympathy for the Devil: Four Decades of Friendship with Gore Vidal* and *Between Terror and Tourism*; the novel *Year of the Gun*; and the memoir *Do I Owe You Something?* He has published in *The New York Times*, *The Washington Post*, the *Los Angeles Times*, and numerous international outlets. He spends much of his time in Key West, Florida.